The Pagan Path

Janet Farrar, Stewart Farrar
& Gavin Bone

Phoenix Publishing Inc.

This edition printed 1995

PHOENIX PUBLISHING, INC.
Portal Way
P.O. Box 10
Custer, Washington USA 98240

Distributed in the U.K. by
ROBERT HALE LTD.
Clerkenwell House
45-47 Clerkenwell Green
London EC1R 0HT

Distributed in Canada by
PHOENIX PUBLISHING INC.
#276; 20465 Douglas Crescent
Langley, BC V3A 4B6

ISBN 0-919345-40-9

Cover photograph by John Threlfall

Printed in the U.S.A.

This book has been manufactured on recycled paper using vegetable based inks.

Table of Contents

Introduction

Paganism has always been a factor below the surface of the Western world ever since that world became officially Christian. Until comparatively recently the official religion of any State (in either of its two main forms, Catholic or Protestant) could be, and was, rigorously enforced. During the most ruthless centuries, that enforcement was, in millions of cases, by burning or hanging (including that of Catholics by Protestants, and vice versa).

The words 'pagan' and 'heathen' originated in the Roman Empire. Where modern soldiers call non-soldiers 'civilians'—i.e., townspeople—Roman soldiers called them *'pagani'*—i.e., country bumpkins, hicks. So when Christians started calling themselves 'soldiers of Christ', they used this same word for non-Christians.

From about the 18th century onwards, in Christian Europe, the State enforcement of an official religion gradually 'mellowed' into such establishment pressures as monopoly of education, endangered employment, social ostracism, legal discrimination, exclusion from elected parliaments, maneuvering of electoral boundaries, and so on. This mellowing has by now reached the stage of complete religious freedom, at least in legal theory.

The situation has varied, of course, from country to country—again, at least nominally. (The Jewish minorities in particular could confirm this.) The United States, for example, was founded on the constitutional right to freedom of religion, though forces still exist which are actively striving to sabotage that right. Article 44 of the Constitution of the Irish Republic guarantees the same freedom of religion to all citizens, though as late as 1972, when that Constitution was amended by referendum, it still recognized 'the special position of the Holy Catholic and Apostolic Church.' While in Britain, on the other hand, the Sovereign is still legally 'Defender of the Faith' (i.e., of Anglican Protestantism, known in America as Episcopalianism), and among religious leaders, only the Anglican heads are *ex officio* members of the House of Lords; but even in Britain, many Anglicans would now favor Disestablishment, the ending of their Church's official links with the State.

This Establishment structure produced a bizarre situation while this book was being written. The Anglican Church itself, both ministry and laity, had decided by majority vote in its Conclave to introduce the ordination of women, but the minority who were opposed to it challenged the decision through legal channels, claiming that only Parliament had the right to make it. Fortunately they failed, and the first 32 women were ordained priests in March 1994 (see p. 121).

During the past half century, the effectiveness of the pressures which religious orthodoxy could exercise has weakened considerably, partly through the tremendous expansion and immediacy of worldwide communication. To take the Irish Republic as an example, until comparatively recently Church dictatorship and censorship ruled Irish life. But as soon as most homes in the land were receiving British television as well as Irish—and Radio Telefís Éireann had to compete with its variety and its frankness—the maintaining of a spiritually watertight compartment became impossible. We ourselves have lived here since 1976, and have observed marked liberalization of expression and action even in those years.

That same half-century has seen Paganism emerge from the shadows in the Western world to become public, articulate, and, in various forms, organized. The last shreds of its illegality were disappearing. In Britain, the ancient Witchcraft Acts were repealed in 1951 (largely at the request of the police, because they were unworkable) and replaced by the Fraudulent Mediums Act—of which any sensible Pagan or occultist could only approve, since it was carefully worded to curb only the money-making confidence tricksters.

One symptomatic result of this, as far as the Wiccan path of Paganism was concerned, was that Gerald Gardner could safely publish his books *Witchcraft Today* (1954) and *The Meaning of Witchcraft* (1959)— launching pad of the modern witchcraft revival movement. Before 1951, those books would theoretically at least have laid him open to prosecution. Since Gardner, there has been a steady output by many authors on the subject, and frequent appearances by Wiccans on television and radio. The gutter press, and the wilder fringes of Fundamentalism, have stepped up their attacks now that the subject is open, but there have also been many sensible interviews and articles in responsible journals.

Magazines and newsletters which are themselves Pagan have also proliferated in many countries. So have public festivals, fairs and other gatherings, attended often by many hundreds of people.

Wicca happens to be our own particular Pagan path, our way of ritualizing and living the basic philosophy, but we share the general Pagan view that different paths have equal validity, one's choice depending on one's personal wavelength. It is the philosophy itself which matters.

The question remains: What is that philosophy? Can the essence of Paganism be defined?

We feel that it is important to try to do so, which is why we have written this book. Pagans of different paths should be able to clarify what they have in common, so that they can respect and support each other. And sensible non-Pagans should be helped to understand the true facts behind the distorted image which their more bigoted colleagues are holding up for a target and demanding they attack it as the work of Satan. All who are seeking spiritual inspiration and anchorage, whether they are Pagans or non-Pagans, should be able to coexist in mutual respect, and even to learn from each other. Religion should not be a monolith; it should be a mutually enriching spectrum. The Earth has enough problems for humankind to tackle without our species paralyzing itself with religious hatred and sectarianism.

For a comprehensive picture, we have included both an explanation of the various aspects of the philosophy of Paganism itself, and as wide a survey as could be managed of the many ways in which its followers practice it and organize themselves—particularly in Chapters 4, *The Rainbow of Paths*, and 21, *Questions and Answers*.

We would emphasize again that this book is intended both to help Pagans to clarify their own ideas, and to help non-Pagans to understand the reality of their Pagan neighbors, in contrast to the distorted image which has been, and continues to be, propagated by certain Fundamentalists. It is offered as a basis for discussion, and comments—from all sides—will be welcomed.

JANET FARRAR
STEWART FARRAR
GAVIN BONE
IRELAND, 1994

1.

The Religion of Paganism

Paganism is a religion. It is not atheism, agnosticism, or indifference to religion, as too many people believe—or would like to have us believe.

What is religion?

There are two fundamentally different beliefs about life and the evolution of the Cosmos. The materialist view is that it has all arisen from the blind interaction of random factors. The religious view is that it is the purposeful manifestation of an ultimate Creative Intelligence. These two beliefs are mutually exclusive, though their incompatibility should not (and with reasonable people does not) prevent cooperation between people who hold them on problems which affect them both, such as human welfare and the protection of the Earth and its creatures.

Religions vary widely in their deity images, symbology, and mythology. But if there is an ultimate Creative Intelligence, there can only be One; so difficult as it may be for some people to accept, all sincere religions worship the same deity, however they envisage It, and are therefore all different paths to the same truths.

On this basis, Paganism is unquestionably a religion in its own right.

Pagans are inevitably drawn to the religious view of the Cosmos because of their dedication to Nature and Mother Earth. If one walks along a country lane, and sees the myriad life-forms, both animal and plant, which inhabit the hedges, woods and fields—all different and unique, but each one of them successful—it is almost impossible not to believe in an Ultimate Intelligent 'programming.'

Chaucer, for example, obviously sensed this when, observing the habits and activities of birds, he wrote:

And smale fowles maken melodie
That slepen all the nacht with open ye,
So pricketh hem Natur in hir corages.
(And small birds make melody
That sleep all night with open eyes,
So Nature prompts them in their little hearts.)
(The Canterbury Tales)

Nature 'pricketh' every one of the Earth's multitudinous species differently, according to its environment and needs—and it works.

All too many religions have developed a dictatorial hierarchy and imposed dogma, which in practice, for the ordinary worshipper, can distort or suppress those religions' basic truths. In particular, Christianity and Islam—i.e. the monotheist religions which will not accept the use of different deity-symbols to approach different aspects of the Ultimate—include many Fundamentalists who insist that their own path is the only true one, and that all others are mistaken, or even the work of Satan. Judaism, although also monotheist, is far less infected by this monopolist attitude.

Paganism rejects rigid hierarchy, imposed dogma, and Fundamentalism, and fully-aware Pagans are therefore much more tolerant and understanding of other paths.

All movements have their fringes; and it must be admitted that handfuls of Fundamentalist Pagans do exist. One such, for example, objected in print to Stewart having quoted the Bible in a lecture, even in a relevant context; this he defined as 'Xtian shit.' He could not accept the fact that the Bible is not a book, but an anthology, spanning many centuries—a mixture which we define in detail on pp. 42–44—and in any case only the tail end of it is 'Xtian' (an offensive abbreviation).

Fortunately the great majority of sensible Pagans reject Pagan Fundamentalism along with all other expressions of religious monopoly.

Why and how do the symbologies, meaningful mythology, and deity-forms of the various religions of the world differ so widely?

We shall be going into this in more detail in later chapters, but the fact is that on our present level of existence and spiritual evolution, we cannot apprehend the Ultimate directly, except perhaps in brief flashes of intuition. To attune ourselves to It in our daily lives, we have to symbolize It in forms we can understand—which, since we are human, means in human form. (As somebody said: "If I were a horse, my God would have four legs.") To monotheist, patriarchal Christianity, God is typically envisaged as a bearded grandfather, or in his Christ form as a young man in first century Hebrew garb. In Pagan Greece, the Earth Mother Demeter was envisaged as having a vegetation daughter, Persephone, who spent half the year in the Underworld and half flourishing on the surface. In Ancient Egypt, the Mother figure Isis and the God of Wisdom, Thoth, worked as magical partners. And so on.

There is nothing wrong in any of these concepts. They are tuning-signals to the Ultimate, suiting the particular wavelengths of people living in given environments and cultures, and with particular personal experiences and characteristics. The tuning-signals differ, but the Ultimate remains the same.

An interesting contemporary example of the tuning-signal syndrome is the Elvis Presley cult. To most people, Elvis was merely an excellent performer. But there are thousands who have almost deified him—to the extent, in many cases, of believing that he is not dead, or that he will reappear at some time (even at prophesied dates). It is easy to mock at his 'worshippers'; but it is clear that for many of them (excluding the ones who simply jumped on a fashionable bandwagon) his particular charisma filled a spiritual vacuum. In a word, it resonated with their starved wavelengths, and they instinctively responded. It is the vacuum which calls for sympathy, not the response for mockery.

Elvis is not the only example, in and before history. It may well be that Jesus and Buddha, in addition to the impact of their teaching, had personal charisma which so affected their followers that it gave birth to a deification which both of them would have rejected—and to a belief in their eventual return. And as for pre-history, many scholars hold that Osiris and Isis, for example, were possibly an early pharaoh and queen of Egypt whose achievements for their country were so remarkable that they became, in the popular mind, the outstanding God and Goddess of its later culture. The same must be true of many deity forms whose original humanity is forgotten.

In a modern Western context, the most noticeable characteristic of the Pagan use of such tuning-signals is that they include the God and the Goddess, a complementary polarization at Ultimate level which Christianity, Judaism and Islam have all abandoned. (Though as we shall see in Chapter 5, *Christianity,* at least in its Catholic form, has allowed the Goddess in through the back door, in the carefully circum-scribed person of the Virgin Mary; and serious Hebrew thinking in-cludes the Shekinah, the feminine communicating aspect between God and humanity.) Pagans find this Father-God and Mother-Goddess symbology more fruitful, and there are many non-Pagans in whom it strikes a chord of sympathy.

Pagans also use a variety of God- and Goddess-forms as tuning-signals to particular aspects of the Ultimate. This does not mean they fail to recognize that the Ultimate remains One. It means that they understand that the Earth, and its creatures including humankind, have a complexity of needs and problems which call for a corresponding variety of effective tuning-signals to aspects of that One.

Catholics do the same thing in a different way—by invoking saints. Their monotheism forbids the use of different deity-forms, so they elevate historical, or sometimes legendary, humans to the position of tuning-signals for the aspects concerned. A Catholic appealing to St. Christopher, or an ancient Greek appealing to Hermes, for safety on a journey would in fact have been using the same method of attunement to an aspect of the Ultimate.

The Vatican showed its misunderstanding of the principle when it began, in recent years, removing legendary individuals from the official list of saints. Whether or not St. Christopher actually lived does not detract from the fact that centuries of travelers have built him into a powerful tuning-signal.

Fundamentalists of any religion fail to recognize this tuning-signal approach, even though unknowingly they share it. Some Christians, for example, are convinced that the Ancient Egyptians worshipped animals, because they portrayed many deities in animal form. Yet they would be outraged if any non-Christian suggested that they themselves worshipped a sheep and a pigeon (in other words, a Lamb and a Dove) because they use them to symbolize Divine aspects. Such people often condemn other religions for what they do themselves. St. Augustine, for example, attacking the Pagan concept of the Triple Goddess, asked "How can a goddess be three persons and one at the same time?"—and this from a believer in the male Trinity!

Respect for other religions involves respect for their holy places. A Pagan man will take his hat off in a church, put it on in a synagogue, and take his shoes off in a mosque, and a Pagan woman will observe the women's rules in the same places. There are unfortunately still a few Pagans who fail to understand this principle; a sad example of such failure, in Bristol in England, is given on p. 146.

2.

He and She

Men and women must be seen and treated as equal. This is a fundamental of Pagan thinking and practice.

It does not mean that male and female are regarded as identical, nor, at the other extreme, that the differences in their natures are seen as mutually exclusive. Those differences are a matter of emphasis; and each sex includes buried elements of the other—in Jungian terms, the *animus* (the hidden male aspects within a woman's psyche) and the *anima* (the hidden female aspects within a man's). The degree of emphasis, and the depth at which the animus or anima is buried, vary from individual to individual.

Understanding of this has been increased by the recent discovery of the differing functions of the left and right halves of the brain.

The male factor represents the fertilizing, energizing, intellectual, linear-logical, left-brain-function aspects; it tends to analysis, taking things to pieces to see what they are made of. The female factor represents the formative, nourishing, intuitive, cyclical, right-brain-function aspects; it tends to synthesis, putting things together to see how they relate to each other.

The two factors are equal and complementary, and Pagans believe a genuine recognition of this is necessary to creative living, both personal and communal.

They also believe that this creative polarity is the active principle of the Cosmos, and the cause of all manifestation. It applies at Divine level, too; until the Ultimate polarized itself into the two aspects, it remained as pure existence without manifestation.

In Cabalistic terms, Kether is such pure existence; the rest of the Tree only comes into being when Kether polarizes into Chokmah and Binah (see p. 10). The Cabala is an ancient Hebrew system, to a certain extent modified and developed in modern Western occult thinking. Its most important concept is the Tree of Life of ten Sephiroth or spheres, defining the aspects and process of evolution, manifestation, and interaction from the Divine Ultimate to physical being. Many Pagans find Cabalistic thinking helpful—though not all, as we shall see in Chapter 21, *Questions and Answers*.

We have explained this in terms of time, because that is an understandable way of looking at it. But the sequence itself may have been eternal—or alternatively, the recent confirmation of the Big Bang which started cosmic evolution as we know it may point to an instant in time when the nature of the Ultimate caused it to polarize. Or yet again, it can be argued that the Ultimate is itself reincarnational, cyclically creative, withdrawing into pure existence between phases of cosmic evolution—a series of Big Bangs, each more fruitful than the last because of the Ultimate's experience of those that went before. Debate on the question is interesting but academic, because it is the billions of years of *this* stage, and our particular phase of it, which demand our active attention today.

Pagan belief in Divine Polarization explains the most striking difference between Paganism and the monotheist religions of the Western world: the worship of the God and the Goddess, as the two fundamental aspects of the Ultimate to which we can and should attune ourselves.

The emphasis in today's Paganism often tends to be on the Goddess aspect, for two reasons. First, that She has been forced underground by two millennia of patriarchy, and concentration on Her is an understandable effort to revive Her and restore the balance. And second, Her manifestation as Mother Earth is under threat, to counter which the same concentration is to be expected.

But Pagans do not forget that He and She are equal and complementary, and that our continuing aim must be to restore and consolidate that balance.

We have already pointed out that extremism is to be found on the fringes of Paganism, as with any other movement; and some radical feminists tend to suppress the God as vigorously as patriarchalism has suppressed the Goddess. But the mainstream movement does not support this attitude, knowing that both suppressions are equally harmful. (See p. 147 on this.)

'As above, so below.' Humanity is a two-gender species, and we can use this fact to help us attune to the two aspects of the Ultimate. They are not mutually exclusive, at either Divine or human level; as we shall see in Chapter 10, *Reincarnation*, the immortal part of each human is, like deity, both male and female. But in any one incarnation, one is either a man with a buried anima (female aspect) or a woman with a buried animus (male aspect). It may be said that the God speaks to the man's consciousness, and the Goddess whispers to his anima, while the Goddess speaks to the woman's consciousness, and the God whispers to her animus, so no human is isolated from either Divine aspect.

In Pagan ritual and symbology, the woman is a channel for the Goddess and the man for the God, because this is their natural emphasis. But intercommunion would be greatly hampered, if not impossible, if they did not listen as well to the 'whispers' of their animus and anima.

'As above, so below' was the condensed form of the Hermetic statement: 'That which is above is as that which is below, and that which is below is as that which is above, to achieve the wonders of the One Thing.' In other words, the Ultimate and its countless forms of manifestation are of the same essential nature. This concept is symbolized by the interlocking triangles of the hexagram (Fig. 1).

Fig. 1—As above, so below.

To refer in more detail to the Cabala, the top triangle of the Cabalistic Tree of Life consists of three Sephiroth or spheres—first Kether, which is pure existence; second Chokmah, which is raw directionless energy; and third Binah, which takes that energy and gives it form. Chokmah and Binah are known as the Supernal Father and the Supernal Mother, respectively. Until Kether overflows and polarizes into Chokmah and Binah, nothing 'happens'; there is no creation, manifestation, or evolution. Further down the Tree, the essentially male and female aspects develop and become enriched: organization, disposal of the superfluous, inspiration, desire, intellect, imagination, and so on. The final, tenth, Sephira is Malkuth, 'Kingdom'—today's world, in which all these aspects are active and should be in balance. (For the complete layout of the ten Sephiroth, see p. 67.)

Another metaphor is that of the electric battery. Unless it has two terminals which are equal but complementary, no current flows.

At the human level, the polarization is into male and female. Biologically, without that polarization we would not be born. Mentally and spiritually, we would have tunnel vision (which uncontrolled patriarchy has tended to develop anyway). To say it again—the male-female differences are a matter of emphasis, not mutually exclusive, otherwise they could not communicate or feed and complement each other.

This concept is well expressed in the Chinese Yang-Yin symbol (Fig. 2). The white, masculine Yang half contains a black Yin (anima) spot, and the black, feminine Yin half a white Yang (animus) spot.

Fig. 2—The Yang-Yin symbol

In the case of homosexuals (whose rights Pagans, including the heterosexual majority, firmly insist on), the polarity principle still stands, though its balance is more subtle, and varies from individual to individual; and the degree of 'speaking' and 'whispering' involved varies accordingly. Each gay or lesbian must discover his or her own balance of these, and not make the mistake of rejecting the fundamental principle of polarization simply because in their case its operation is more complex.

Complementary equality between men and women is characteristic of Pagan activity and religious practice. In this, almost more than in anything else, Paganism differs from most other religions. Christianity and Islam are both heavily patriarchal, as is Buddhism in its pure form; so is Judaism, though at a serious level of thinking, the Jewish concept of the Shekinah modifies this. Japanese Gods and Goddesses seem to have equal standing—their supreme deity being the Sun Goddess Amaterasu, whose symbol is the national flag—yet Japanese society is strictly male-dominated. Hinduism, theologically if not yet fully socially, is better balanced.

Insistence on the equality of men and women is (like environmentalism) an issue which improves the mutual understanding between Pagans and a growing number of their non-Pagan fellow citizens. Women's liberation has, increasingly in the last century, become a public issue on simple grounds of fairness. With travel, communication, economic potential, and the availability of information all increasing by leaps and bounds, Western women are no longer satisfied to be second-class citizens, the slaves (whether pampered or exploited) of a male-run society. The battle is being won stage by stage, from the Suffragettes' achievement of the vote, to Church of England women winning (while this book was being written) the right to ordination.

More and more men, too, are realizing that the subjugation of women restricts and dehumanizes them as well. The struggle is by no means over yet; but after two millennia or more, patriarchy is on its last legs. At its height, even well-intentioned men found the nature of women difficult to understand; for example, Sir Walter Scott (1771-1832):

> O Woman! in our hours of ease,
> Uncertain, coy, and hard to please,
> And variable as the shade
> By the light quivering aspen made;
> When pain and anguish ring the brow,
> A ministering angel thou!

Bewildered as he was, he had the honesty to acknowledge her built-in Great Mother aspect. She was doubtless patiently fond of the poor confused creature!

Pagan men strive to understand the nature and problems of women, both as a whole, and of those close to them. Patriarchal attitudes have a dreadful record on this. One friend of ours was brutally raped as a teenager, with considerable vaginal and uterine damage; her father (whom she loved) never spoke to her again for the rest of his life, convincing himself that she had a miscarriage and was a whore, blinding himself to the surgical evidence. There was the Victorian case of the man whose wife had twins, and who ignored the existence of one of them because 'only common women bear twins.' And a minor but symptomatic instance: Stewart has for years kept a computer record of Janet's period dates, with the average duration of the last five, notes of D and C's, and so on. Janet finds it useful, and it can be printed up at any time to show to our doctor, who appreciates it. But on one occasion a locum was on duty, and when she showed it to him he was shocked at Stewart's 'invasion of your privacy'!

Such instances, whether traumatic for the woman or merely trivial, are all too common even today, and sensitive Pagan men work to counter them.

It must be admitted that some women contribute to these attitudes. A friend of Stewart's, a woman motoring correspondent on a London daily, wrote a very sensible piece on the effect of premenstrual tension for women drivers. She received an abusive letter from a woman reader, asking how she dared to discuss such matters in print, and saying (since she'd mentioned her son in the article) that she was 'unfit to be a mother.'

It can possibly be argued that the patriarchal period was an inevitable stage of evolution, when emphasis on the left-brain function was needed to conquer the laws of the material universe, from the practical mathematics of Ancient Egypt and the first scientific thinking of Classical Greece to the technological revolution of this century. But even if that is so, patriarchy has outlived any possible justification; further progress, even technologically and certainly socially and economically, demands a balance of left- and right-brain functions; so obsolete patriarchy, fighting to hold on to its dominance, must be conquered and supplanted.

The strength of Paganism is its recognition that male-female equality is not just a matter of democratic justice; it is in accord with the basic motive-power of the Universe.

Whatever the insistence of patriarchal dogma, grass-roots Christians have all too often been aware of what Geoffrey Ashe has called 'a Goddess-shaped vacuum.' It was this disturbing factor which prompted the official Church, at the Council of Ephesus in 431 AD, to promote Jesus's mother Mary to the status of Theotokos, Mother of God. She was the Goddess let in through the back door, and carefully controlled, entitled to *hyperdulia* or super-veneration (a step up from the *dulia* which saints were allowed), but not to the *latria* or worship accorded to the male God. Ashe (*The Virgin*, p. 4) maintains that without this promotion of Mary, Christianity 'would have dwindled to nullity for lack of what it supplied.'

One wonders what the Hebrew teenager who bore the man-child Jesus would have thought of this elevation!

Our years in Ireland have taught us that ordinary Catholics could not care less about *hyperdulia* and *latria*. To them, Mary fulfills the Goddess function. They tend to appeal to her, rather than to the austere figure on the Cross, on human and emotional issues—and she has a reputation for being able to bend the rules and dogma which have become attached to the Father and Son. Janet does many Tarot readings, and most of the people who have come to her in Ireland are good Catholic women—very often with problems they would be reluctant to take to a celibate male priest. If Janet, dealing with a Catholic woman's problem, feels an appeal to the Goddess principle is called for, she tells her to express her need while lighting a candle to the Virgin Mary—an attitude which has upset one or two Pagan critics, who fail to see that the principle is just the same.

These women Tarot customers, incidentally, have come again and sent their friends; and some of them are in very important public positions. We report this, not to boast, but to emphasize that the need is not confined to the 'woman-in-the-street.'

We shall be dealing with various aspects of the male/female balance in later chapters.

3.

God and Goddess Forms

Even those non-Pagans who understand, and possibly sympathize with, the Pagan concept of the God and Goddess are sometimes puzzled by the great variety of forms under which Pagans worship them.

All these forms, in fact, are tuning-signals to the same two aspects of the Ultimate. It is as though that Ultimate were an infinitely powerful radio transmitter/receiver with an infinity of frequencies, whereas each of us has a limited power and range of individual frequencies. But if we attempt sincerely to contact the Ultimate, it will respond to those personal-frequency signals. We use particular personal frequencies to invoke particular aspects of the God or the Goddess.

God and Goddess forms representing various aspects are developed by, and acquire their 'personalities' from, the cultures, environments, and histories of those who seek to invoke them. They also evolve along with the humans who relate to them. They are not unlike furniture, clothing or architecture, in that their form incorporates their roots and development as well as their contemporary function.

An American witch talking to Stewart was puzzled because he felt there was no existing deity to meet his needs as a computer programmer. Stewart said that as far as he was concerned, Hermes, Mercury and Thoth were all Gods of knowledge and communication, and therefore today they were also Gods of computers. If Gods and Goddesses stood still, they and we would still be living in caves.

Janet has an interesting recurrent dream, particularly when there is turbulence on the astral plane from which she instinctively seeks protection. She finds herself, breathless from her escape, in what she calls 'the exclusive club at the edge of the universe,' occupied by various Gods and Goddesses all in modern dress. Isis and Horus are seated drinking at the bar, she a beautiful mature woman in smartly casual clothing, he in jeans and sweatshirt. Hermes is in a business suit, but with a pilot's badge on his jacket, and holding a portable telephone. Frey has a billfold full of every imaginable credit card. Aphrodite is in a slinky backless dress and stiletto heels. Anubis, Heimdahl and other guardian deities are bouncers at the door, checking who comes in. Pan is wearing a miner's hat, and a man is grooming and combing the goat's-hair of his legs. (Pan has tended to be adopted recently by many gay Pagans.) One or two Aztec Gods look rather like punk rockers, with body adornment and piercing. A few patriarchal deities, including Jehovah, look somewhat the worse for wear. And so on. Janet cannot buy a drink, and when she tries to pick up Frey's glass he puts it out of her reach. Recently she asked him if she could buy one herself, to see what happened. He told her: "You wouldn't like this stuff. But if you go outside, I'll send you one out, and that'll be different." (There may be a parallel here to the tradition in Ireland and elsewhere, that one should never eat or drink as a guest in fairy territory, or one will emerge to find that centuries have passed.)

Janet is still finding extra meanings to details of this dream, though its basic message that deity forms have evolved from yesterday, but are not imprisoned in it, is obvious to her.

Gavin points to the British company, Mercury Telecommunications, as a nice example of this principle in everyday business life.

Many deities have names which simply describe their aspect-function, For example the Greek Nike ('Victory'), Helios ('Sun') and Gaia ('Earth'), the Irish Macha ('Battle'), the Nordic Hel ('Underworld'), or the Buddhist and Tibetan Bhaisajyaguru ('Supreme Physician'). We list a small selection of these at the end of the chapter.

But the leading deities of the various pantheons tend to have names which are purely titles, indicating their overall supremacy. The Near Eastern Baal and Baalat, and the Nordic Frey and Freya, simply mean 'Lord' and 'Lady.' In Ireland, the Dagda means simply 'the Good God.' Osiris and Isis (in Egyptian Wset and Aset) both mean 'throne,' which not only declares their ruling status but may also recall the possibility that they originated from a highly-honored prehistoric pharaoh and his queen; and her name may well have been the root of those of the supreme Assyro-Babylonian Mother Goddess Ishtar, the Canaanite Ashera (worshipped for centuries in the Temple at Jerusalem as the consort of Jehovah), the Phoenician Ashtart/Ashtoreth, and the Nordic Ostara/Eostra (after whom Easter is named, because she was honored at the Spring Equinox).

Baal and Baalat, via the Carthaginian Baal-Hammon and Tanit, were also the root of the Irish Balor and Danu and the Welsh Beli and Dôn, even if that ancestry has been forgotten.

Modern Pagans, in their general rituals, tend to use the title-names— either in simple modernized forms such as the Horned God and Great Mother, or in the forms of the national cultures of those Pagans' home countries (or often in America of their family heritage), such as the Nordic, Celtic, Italian or Greek.

But the aspect-names also have their uses for particular needs, such as those of the computer programmer mentioned earlier, or when healing, irrigation, safe travel, artistic skill, or some other specialized category is concerned.

It is sound and effective practice to distinguish clearly between the two. Using either the title-names or the aspect-names, according the needs of the occasion, augments the power of the 'tuning' process. And the more one studies and understands the meanings of those names, the greater their power for oneself.

We mentioned on p. 7 that monotheist Catholicism uses the same aspect-tuning principle by appealing to particular saints; and in Ireland we have come across an interesting example of this—the belief that if you want to sell your house, burying an image of St. Joseph in its grounds will quickly find you a buyer. (We are told the same belief is found in Italy.) Shops selling religious goods and artifacts can confirm the strength of this belief; when the house market is sluggish, they lay in more statuettes of St. Joseph because the demand for them rises sharply. We know at least one family who maintain that it worked for them, and who are we to question their tuning-frequencies?

But perhaps our favorite is St. Jude, the champion of hopeless cases. As *The Oxford Dictionary of Saints* explains, he acquired this reputation because the similarity of his name to that of Judas made people reluctant to call on him; so when a bit of business does come his way, he is so pleased that he gives it his special attention!

Even if those examples make us smile, the smile is friendly. We remain convinced that the aspect-tuning principle is sound, whatever form it takes.

Some Examples of Aspect-Deities

These exist in countless thousands, throughout history and round the world, so our sample here is small and random, to give some idea of the wideness of that range.

Thoth (Egyptian): He started in predynastic times as a Moon God, and typifies the fact that many early moon deities tended to be male, because until precise solar calendars were evolved, the moon was the most accurate time-measurer—a clearly left-brain function. Egypt was one of the first cultures to develop an accurate solar calendar, locked annually to the heliacal rising of the Dog Star, Sirius, on July 19—'the going-up of the Goddess Sothis.' Thereafter, he developed naturally into a god of wisdom, learning, mathematics and writing (which he was said to have invented), husband of Ma'at, Goddess of Justice, Truth, and the laws of Cosmic Order to which her husband gave practical expression. He acted time and again as Isis's magical working partner, complementing her essentially right-brain function. He remained titular ruler of the moon, in memory of his earliest function, but left it in the hands of a caretaker Goddess with the charming name of Woman-Light of the Shadows, with whom he consulted periodically; this typified the shift of lunar symbology from the male, time-measuring significance to that of the female menstrual cycle and the illumination of the darkness of the Unconscious. As God of Scribes, he has always been Stewart's patron deity—a choice happily reinforced by the fact that July 19 is Janet and Stewart's wedding anniversary (the significance of which date they were unaware of at the time of their marriage in 1975). The choice of aspect-deities is often a very personal matter.

Arianrhod (Welsh): Her name means 'Silver Wheel,' representing the circumpolar stars which never set below the horizon at any time of the year, which were known as Caer Arianrhod ('the Castle of Arianrhod'). This was the resting-place to which souls were believed to withdraw between incarnations. She is therefore a Goddess of Reincarnation. Little remains of her actual mythology, apart from the fact that she was the daughter of the Welsh supreme deities Beli and his wife Dôn, and mother by her brother Gwydion of the Young God Lleu Llaw Gyffes ('Lleu of the Skillful Hand') and the Sea God Dylan. But the power of her name in folk tradition is unmistakable. Typically, there is a point in Caernarvon Bay marked on the map as 'Caer Arianrhod—Submerged Town (Traditional).' She is clearly very ancient, and may even predate the division of the Western Celts into the Gaelic (Irish, Scottish, and Isle of Man) and Cymric (Welsh, Cornish, and Breton) cultures, a division whose common roots are underlined by the Carthaginian and Irish ancestry of her Welsh parents Beli and Dôn, which we mentioned above.

Pan (Greek): His name means 'All,' or possibly 'Pasturer.' God of Nature and the Wild. Originally from Arcadia, his worship extended to Athens, according to tradition, when he gave the Athenians victory over the Persians at Marathon in exchange for honoring him. After the victory, Athens built a temple to him on the Acropolis, and his cult spread throughout Greece. Portrayed as goat-footed and horned, he tended to merge with the ithyphallic Priapus, and was identified by the Romans with their Faunus. His loves were many, including the Moon Goddess Selene, but he was also in constant pursuit of the anonymous nymphs of his woodlands—often memories of primordial local Goddesses, and very much his wild female counterparts, quite unlike the coy damsels of Victorian art. Caves were often dedicated to Pan and a nymph. Wild as he was, he was also a music-maker, playing his Pan pipes. Plutarch's story of Thamus hearing a voice calling 'Great Pan is dead!' was much quoted by Christians anxious to banish him; but what is far more likely is that Thamus was hearing the ritual lamentation for the annually dying and resurrecting Vegetation God Tammuz (see Adoni below), known as the 'All-Great' in Greek ('Pammegas'), and mistaking it for 'Great Pan' ('Pan megas').

Sif (Nordic): Fertility and Corn Goddess, second wife of Thor and one of the Asynjor, the collective name given to the twelve Goddesses of the Norse pantheon. She had beautiful hair, which the trickster God Loki cut off while she was sleeping. Thor, furious, compelled him to have the dwarves fashion her new hair of pure gold, which took root and grew when she put it on. Loki's act may symbolize the destruction of corn-stubs by fire, and the successful sowing of a new crop. Sif also represented peace and friendship, conjugal fidelity, and family happiness. She was said to have been able to change her shape into that of a swan.

Weyland the Smith (Anglo-Saxon): Smith and Goldsmith God. Weyland the Smith has been an ineradicable part of English folklore for a millennium and a half, in spite of Church attempts to suppress him. But his origins are far older than that; his Nordic original was Volund.

Volund/Weyland fashioned the sword Mimung for the Aesir, the Gods of Asgard, and the one with which the Anglo-Saxon hero Beowulf slew his dragon. Volund's legends came with him when he became Weyland in England. The huge stones of a Neolithic long barrow, erected at least 5,000 years ago, in the Vale of the White Horse at Uffington in Berkshire (named after the famous hill-cut figure of a running horse overlooking it), has been known as Weyland's Smithy since long before the Norman Conquest. It is said that if you leave a horse there overnight, with a silver coin placed on the stones, when you return in the morning Weyland will have shod it for you. When Weyland's Smithy was excavated in 1921, two Iron Age money-bars were found there, so the tradition may be very ancient.

Kwan-Yin (Chinese): Goddess of Fertility and Healing, 'she who bears the cries of the world.' Also known as Sung-tzu Niang-niang, 'the Lady who Brings Children.' Her image is in most Chinese homes, sitting on a lotus flower, or sometimes on a lion, with a child in her arms. She is also described as a magician, a teacher of magic, an oracular Goddess, and sometimes as a prostitute. In rural China a man normally approaches her through a woman intermediary; if none is available and he has to appeal to her himself, he apologizes for the omission. She was of Buddhist origin; the Buddha's own teaching had no deities, and certainly no Goddesses, but the grass-roots religions which grew from it could not live with this theological vacuum and soon began to envisage them.

Adoni (Phoenician): The annually Dying and Resurrecting Vegetation God. Originally the Sumerian Dumuzi, he also became Tammuz to the Assyro-Babylonians, and Adonis to the Greeks. His importance in this part of the world is typified by the fact that although he is an aspect-deity rather than a supreme one, his name merely means 'Lord.' His Goddess lover was Astarte/Ashtoreth (Phoenician), Inanna (Sumerian), Ishtar (Assyro-Babylonian), or Aphrodite (Greek). In several of these versions, he was killed by a boar, and the grieving Goddess descended into the Underworld to try to get him back. During her absence, the Earth was sterile and barren. The Assyro-Babylonian version of this is typical: Ishtar had to shed part of her garments and jewelry at each of the gates of the Underworld, finally appearing naked before her sister Ereshkigal, Queen of the Underworld, to plead for his return. The Gods, alarmed at the Earth's barrenness, forced Ereshkigal to release him. Conducting him back, Ishtar regained all her adornments. When the two of them returned, the Earth became fertile again. The celebration of the death and rebirth of the God, every year after the harvest, was a very important occasion for the women of the Near East. They mourned his loss, planting little gardens of quickly-fading plants such as lettuce, and when these died after a few days, they threw them into springs, rivers or the sea. After this, sorrow was turned to rejoicing for the God's rebirth. This ritual was condemned by Hebrew patriarchy—see Isaiah xviii:9-11 and Ezekiel viii:13-14—but post-exilic Hebrew women continued the custom, covering it up by pretending they were mourning for 'the daughter of Jephthah the Gileadite' each year (Judges xi:39-40). The Greek Aphrodite and Adonis version of the legend is romantic rather than agricultural, but this was not insensitivity. It was because the Dying and Resurrecting Vegetation theme was already vividly dramatized for the Greeks by Demeter and Persephone. Incidentally, Plutarch claimed that the Hebrew ban on eating pork was because it was a boar that killed their Adoni.

Tiamat (Assyro-Babylonian): The Goddess of Salt Waters, who with her fresh-water consort Apsu begat the primitive chaotic world and ruled it. 'When above the heavens had not been formed, when the earth below had no name, Tiamat brought forth them both.' The Hebrew word for 'waters' in Genesis i:2 is 'tehom,' admitted to be a corruption of 'Tiamat.' She is 'the unconscious in its most primitive disorganized state and therefore in need of attention' (Chetwynd, *A Dictionary of Symbols*, p. 76). The younger Gods under Sky God Anu fought to bring order and fruitfulness to the chaos. In the battle, the Storm God Marduk cut Tiamat's body in two to form the Sky and the Earth. She thus remained the Great Mother Womb, the belly of the Unconscious which so disturbs patriarchy. Her son/lover was Kingu, the male generative principle which the Primordial Mother produces from within herself.

4.

The Rainbow of Paths

Some Pagans feel no need to engage in ritual practice, either alone or in a group, but merely live their lives with a Pagan outlook and by Pagan standards, though they may attend Pagan festivals. Most Pagans, however, do feel that need, and work either in groups or solo, in a variety of patterns known as 'paths.' It is typical of the cheerful untidiness of the movement that this variety is continuously growing. In this chapter we shall try to define some of them.

Several of these are, strictly speaking, organizations rather than paths, while others can be called both; and some are paths within paths. But we have included them for a more complete picture.

Wicca: This is the generally accepted term for the witchcraft movement, which itself consists of many paths. It derives from the Old English *wiccecraeft* (witchcraft), *wicca* (male witch), *wicce* (female witch), which in turn stem from the Old Teutonic root *wike-* (to bend). Incidentally, the word 'warlock' is no longer used for a male witch; it derives from the Old English *waerloga,* meaning 'traitor, enemy, devil,' and was much used in Scotland in this derogatory sense.

When Gerald Gardner's books triggered off the witchcraft revival in Britain in the 1950s (see the next entry) it met a growing need, and all those who took advantage of it tended to call themselves witches as a result. Now that the movement has grown substantially, and spread to other countries, it has become clearer that the need was for the liberation of the Pagan attitude as a whole, so Wicca has become one form of practice, or family of practices, among many others.

Gardnerian: This Wiccan movement, which virtually launched the modern witchcraft revival, is named after Gerald Gardner (1884-1964).

He was a customs officer and rubber planter in Malaya, and writer on Malay weapons, who retired to the New Forest in the south of England just before World War II. There he came in contact with a coven of witches who initiated him. He revealed some of their practices, disguised as fiction, in his novel *High Magic's Aid* published in 1949. In 1951, Britain's long-standing Witchcraft Laws were repealed (see p. 2). It was no longer a criminal offense to be a witch, so Gardner wrote two non-fiction books, *Witchcraft Today* (1954) and *The Meaning of Witchcraft* (1959), which revealed considerably more detail. He was much criticized by some of the Craft for making public what they felt should remain secret, but he had started an irreversible process, at a time when thousands of people were consciously or unconsciously seeking a pattern of activity to express their Pagan attitude.

By now he was running his own coven, and his Book of Shadows—the secret handwritten book of rituals which had to be copied down by each new initiate—was a mixture of what he had learned from his parent coven, elements which interested him such as some of Aleister Crowley's work and details of Freemasonry, and ideas of his own. He was constantly amending it, and for the final and definitive version he had the help of his High Priestess at the time, Doreen Valiente, a gifted poetess and ritualist who frankly improved it a great deal, herself writing some of its memorable passages and weeding out (for example) much of the wilder Crowleyana.

(We have seen some of his various Books of Shadows in Doreen's possession, which reveal how haphazardly he tended to work on them. Some of the pages had shopping lists on the back!)

The Gardnerian Book of Shadows did not remain secret for very long, as it came into an increasing number of initiates' hands. It was stolen, quoted and misquoted, misrepresented and distorted by several writers, until as one speaker said at a public Esoteric Conference in London in 1971, 'it is now in the public domain.' It finally became important, and only fair to Gardner's memory, to put the distortions straight; so with Doreen's agreement and help, Janet and Stewart published the full text as part of their book *The Witches' Way* in 1984 (also known in one American edition as *The Witches' Bible*, Part 2).

Some Gardnerians tend to regard his Book of Shadows as Holy Writ, to be observed exactly as it stands, but Gardner's real contribution was that at the very time when it was needed, he provided a sound and workable system which could be adapted, amended, or expanded to suit the needs and ideas of individual covens, and to meet changing local and world conditions.

For example, Janet and Stewart did this in their book *Eight Sabbats for Witches* (1981). Feeling that Gardner's Sabbat rituals were too sketchy, they suggested more substantial ones—in Celtic terms, as they were living in Ireland—and adding rituals for Wiccaning, Handfasting and Requiem, none of which were covered in Gardner's Book of Shadows. Many other writers and groups have done the same, which is a healthy building on Gardner's foundations, whatever the Holy Writters think.

Alexandrian: An adaptation of Gardnerianism founded by Alex and Maxine Sanders in the 1960s. Its Book of Shadows was copied by Alex presumably from that of his initiator, and was somewhat incomplete and scattered with errors (doubtless from careless copying along the way) compared with Gardner's own. He also frequently practiced Ritual Magic, and some of his followers did the same. Alex (who died in 1988) was a genuinely gifted magical worker, but also a born showman (he even managed to die on May Eve), very public in his activities, and he and Maxine initiated people on a production-line basis. (In Wiccan practice, a man is initiated by a woman, and a woman by a man.) Rather like the Parable of the Sower, some of these fell by the wayside, but many went on fruitfully to found their own covens and run them their own way. Janet and Stewart were initiated by Alex and Maxine in the Spring of 1970, and founded their own coven at Yule of that year. Like many Alexandrian initiates, we no longer label ourselves as such, but prefer simply to call ourselves Wiccan; and if pressed for a more precise definition, to say that our own practice follows 'the general Gardnerian/Alexandrian tradition.' Visiting the United States confirmed for us that this attitude was realistic; we were shown many Books of Shadows, of many differently-named paths, and to be honest ninety percent of them were basically Gardnerian.

Maxine—now Maxine Worsley—runs her own groups quietly and sensibly in London, no longer conscripted into melodrama as she was when she partnered Alex.

In 1972 a tradition combining both Alexandrian and Gardnerian was founded in the United States. It was called Algard by its founder, Mary Nesnick. In 1976 the tradition claimed over fifty covens in the USA. Today there is little evidence to show that any of them survived, under that path name at least.

Traditional: A term used after the Gardnerian breakthrough by already-existing British covens who wished to make it clear that their traditions derived from their own sources, and not from Gardnerianism. They are not, however, necessarily hostile to it. In America, Traditional tends to mean adhering consistently to a particular tradition, very often because of racial roots (e.g. Welsh Traditional, Celtic Traditional), instead of being Eclectic.

Hereditary: A term used by covens and witches who claim to have learned witchcraft from a continuing family tradition. Often this claim is genuine, but there are some who are exaggerating things in their own minds because Grandma read tea-leaves—and whose Grandma didn't? Alex Sanders claimed to have been initiated by his grandmother, but all the evidence points to this having been a fantasy.

Eclectic: Groups who devise their own system of practice by choosing elements from various others and combining them. This can work well if it is carefully done, otherwise it can have its dangers—see p. 149. The Georgian Tradition founded by the late George Patterson in Bakersfield, California, is Eclectic in nature.

Dianic: Women's groups which concentrate on women's mysteries and the Goddess aspect. The term was originally adopted from Margaret Murray, who described witchcraft as a 'the Dianic cult.' Several feminist Craft traditions now exist under this label, headed by such names as Starhawk, Z Budapest, and Morgan McFarland. The healthy ones do not belittle the God aspect, or treat men with contempt or hostility; they will cooperate with men on appropriate occasions, and attend Pagan festivals as equals. There is, however, an aberrant fringe using the Dianic label, which exhibits these negative attitudes; on these, see p. 9.

Fairy, Faerie: In Europe this term is used to define those involved specifically with Nature spirits, for example in Ireland with the Tuatha Dé Danann and the persistent fairy folklore, and with the pre-Celtic tradition. In the United States this is the name given to the tradition formed by Victor Anderson and the late Gwydion Pendderwen, which although embracing much of the European tradition also includes material from the Alexandrian Book of Shadows. It is also important not to confuse the two traditions mentioned above with the Radical Faeries, a men's mystery and homosexual spirituality group existing in the United States. This tradition was formed due to the belief, among many homosexuals, that the current American gay movement was too patriarchal in nature and therefore lacked spirituality.

Classical Mystery: This term we have used to define those individuals or groups studying the Greek, Roman or Egyptian Mystery Religions which first came into being between five and three thousand years ago. Many of the original passage rites have been accurately reconstructed from historical research, by those involved in these traditions, with the intention of gaining wisdom and the spiritual insight possessed by the priesthood of these early civilizations. Groups practicing these traditions may or may not define themselves as Wiccan or Ritual Magic in nature.

Ritual Magic: This is distinct from Wicca, though there are people who practice both on different occasions. Ritual magic is complex and formal, with precise robes, tools, temple decorations, and verbal formulae. Much of it is based on Golden Dawn practice, on material gathered from medieval grimoires (such as *The Key of Solomon*—see Bibliography under Mathers), or on Aleister Crowley's writings.

Most ritual magicians seem to be male; perhaps because it is essentially a left-brain type of activity. They tend to practice solo, though there is also a tradition for including a woman assistant.

Golden Dawn: The Hermetic Order of the Golden Dawn was the first major, and publicly known, occult organization in Britain—thoroughly Ritual Magic in nature. It was founded in 1887 by members of the Societas Rosicruciana in Anglia (see Rosicrucians below), and involved elements of Freemasonry. It acquired many distinguished members, including the poet and Nobel prizewinner W.B. Yeats, the actress Florence Farr, the gifted but uncontrollable Aleister Crowley, and S.L. MacGregor Mathers, translator of the grimoire *The Key of Solomon*. Clashes of personalities eventually split the Order into various offspring. The Order itself has long ceased to exist, but many groups still use its complex rituals, most completely revealed by Israel Regardie in his four-volume book *The Golden Dawn*. The American organization the New Reformed Orthodox Order of the Golden Dawn (NROOGD.) has nothing to do with the Golden Dawn tradition and practices, but adopted the name originally as a joke; it is in fact a serious coalition of Wiccan groups.

Thelemic: This term is applied specifically to those following Aleister Crowley's system of Ritual Magic. It is named after Crowley's Abbey of Thelema founded in Cefalu, Sicily in 1920. Those practicing Thelemic Magic follow much of his written work for guidance and many of the rites of the Ordo Templi Orientis (OTO), the Order of which he was made international head in 1925. They generally regard him as a magical genius (which there is no doubt he was, however bewildering some of his teachings), and his activities and philosophy as being widely misunderstood.

Druidism: The revival of Druidism predates that of witchcraft by over fifty years; the first Druidic groups being established during the period of Celtic romanticism, which existed in Britain during the late 1800s. Since this period they have been regularly seen at Stonehenge every Summer Solstice. This has resulted in them becoming one of the most well-known of the Pagan paths, and the most widely accepted by the general British public; and there are groups in America practicing Druidism. Druids, like other Pagans, are polytheistic, and most groups consider themselves as attempting to revive the best aspects of Paleopagan faiths within a modern scientific, artistic, and holistic approach. Most are involved with ecological projects, which have included reforestation and the protection (by direct action in some cases) of sacred sites. The actual rituals which modern Druids practice have had to be devised by inference from tradition and folklore, since the Druids themselves left no written records, training their successors entirely by word of mouth and example. The modern rituals can only be judged by the standard Pagan test: are they self-consistent, and do they work?

In Wales, the National Eisteddfod—an important annual contest of music and poetry—has long been conducted entirely in Druidic symbology, the judges (from the 'Chief Druid' downwards) being appropriately robed and addressed.

Bardic: This exists within the wider Celtic and Druidic traditions as a form of mystical storytelling, and is often an aspect of other paths rather than a path in itself. The original Bards had great power within their societies, and normally traveled from place to place relaying news and passing on the magical myths and legends of their peoples. In recent years this tradition has been revived in today's Paganism, and it is now not uncommon to find this form of storytelling at Pagan moots, festivals and coven meetings.

Earth Magic: An Earth Magician studies and uses the power of the Earth as a holistic organism. They are generally involved with dowsing, ley lines, stone circles, and sacred sites (e.g. Glastonbury) and correcting any imbalances in the energy present. It is generally believed that these imbalances may be caused by badly planned buildings and roads which disrupt the energy flow. The result may be the repolarization of a positive ley line into a 'black stream' which may cause illness, accidents and poltergeist activity. In China and Hong Kong this problem has been taken seriously for thousands of years and still is. The art of Feng-shui is still practiced, and it is the normal custom for a 'Feng-shui man' to be called in during the planning stage of a building by the contractors. An Earth Magician may also tap this energy for the purpose of healing rites on individuals and for the planet as a whole.

Voodoo, Santeria, Orisha: A practice which developed among African slaves (particularly Nigerians of the Yoruba people) imported to South and Central American countries. Fundamentally it embraces their native African beliefs and practices, but during slavery it adopted the names of many Christian saints, and of the Virgin Mary, as disguises for their deities, to allay the slaveowners' suspicion. After the abolition of slavery, many of the original African deities emerged more openly; the fervent worship of the sea, river and lake Goddess Yemaja, for example, is widespread in Brazil. Voodoo is particularly strong in Haiti (where it is called Voudon, pronounced in the French manner). The term Santeria is more used on the South American mainland, and by Pagans in the United States who follow this path. Some of the latter prefer to call it Orisha, which simply means 'Deities.'

Santeria is also very strong in Puerto Rico, the United States' semi-colony which may become its 51st State (a matter on which its 3½ million population is divided—the last vote, in 1976, being heavily in favor of remaining a 'commonwealth'). U.S. laws on religious freedom apply here, and Santerian ritual animal sacrifice has been declared legal. The Puerto Rican Catholic Church is strongly hostile to Santeria—largely because a big proportion of the people who go to the Santerians for help or advice are Catholics.

Shamanism: The current revival of 'Shamanistic' practices within Paganism occurred much later than that of witchcraft, and while some shamanistic groups regard themselves as Wiccan, others do not. Whereas the revival of witchcraft is firmly planted in the early 1950s and in Britain, the interest in shamanism, and the return of its practice, did not begin until at least a decade later, in the early to mid-1960s in the United States. Two names stand out as the cause of this revival:

Mircea Eliade, French anthropologist and writer, whose book *Shamanism: Archaic Techniques of Ecstasy* is still considered one of the finest anthropological works on the subject; and Michael Harner, Ph.D., who can be considered to be the 'Father of Neo-Shamanism,' just as Gerald Gardner can be considered to be the 'Father of Modern Witchcraft.' Michael Harner, who has been a practicing shaman for over a quarter of a century, has written several books on the subject, including one of the first practical books on techniques. Harner is head of the Foundation of Shamanic Studies, and former Professor and Chairman of the Department of Anthropology of the New School for Social Research in New York. He has taught at the University of California, Berkeley, and at Yale and Columbia on the subject.

During the early 1960s Harner did much field work on shamanism, including research in Mexico, Lapland, North America, the Canadian Arctic and most important of all, the Upper Amazon basin. It was during his visit to the Amazon that he met a Jivaro shaman and partook of the *ayahuasca*, an hallucinogenic plant, which enabled Harner to 'travel to the underworld' and 'discover his power animal.' It was after this experience that he began his work, on what he has coined 'the shamanic state of consciousness' or SSC for short. The Swinging Sixties were ripe for Harner's work on this subject; Timothy Leary was advocating the use of hallucinogens as a spiritual experience ('Turn On, Tune In and Drop Out'), the permissive society was at its height, and there was a yearning for new experiences. Many felt a need to return to ethnic culture and smaller 'tribal' groupings, because of the failure of society at the time to cater for their spiritual needs; and finally, there was a definite need, by many, 'to get back to Nature' and a more naturalistic form of living. The writings of Carlos Castenada, and his fictional 'Don Juan,' have also spawned much in the 1970s, but it must be remembered that his books were fiction. Many of the rites and experiences Castenada put to paper were correct, but out of context with the tribe they were supposed to have originated from. Regardless of this criticism, his books are still the first works many Pagans have read on the subject.

Shamanism is not only the oldest of the Pagan paths, but also the ancestor of all the main magical traditions. Both witchcraft and Ritual Magic have their roots in these practices, but unlike them it is generally, by its very nature, a form of solo magical work, although a group of practitioners may work together on the same project. The shaman (feminine shamanka, although this is of recent etymology) normally enters in to a trance state (Harner's SSC), to perform a number of tasks.

These can include healing work or divination, but always involve entering into dialogue with 'the spirit world.' There are three main ways the practitioner can enter into trance: by rhythmic drumming, rattling, or chanting; by 'path working' (a form of meditative practice used by all the magical traditions); and finally by the use of a hallucinogenic preparation. This third method is the most controversial of all, and there has been much debate within the Pagan movement about its acceptability, morally and legally. There is no doubt that the use of such preparations should be done with great care, and with the assistance of an experienced shaman of many years' standing. We would only condone it with this proviso, and would emphasize that breaking the law invites the prosecution which all too many authorities are eager to find excuses for.

During the process the shaman will call upon his 'Power Animal,' a form of spirit guide to protect and assist him as he enters the 'Underworld.' While in the Underworld he will, if healing, battle the offending spirit; and if divining, ask assistance of the spirits present.

Since the 1960s neo-shamanic practice has continued to develop. Interest in Native American Indian 'medicine' has grown. This has mainly been spurred onwards by some (but by no means all) native medicine men, who have felt that the time is ripe for their traditions to be carried on by their white brothers. Sun Bear, Wabun, and Brooke Medicine-Eagle, are but a few, but they have been condemned for it by more traditional medicine men. Interestingly enough, both the New Age movement and the Neo-Pagan movement have adopted ritual practices from many of the Native American tribal groupings. It is not unusual to see 'medicine wheels' (a form of healing circle), and sweat lodges (a ritual purification and a form of vision questing) at gatherings of both movements. It is very likely in the near future that shamanism, if it is not already doing so, will act as a bridge between the two movements. Obviously, Native Amerindian practice has been much more accessible to the American Pagan public than to the European. In Britain the adoption of their practices has been predominantly by the New Age movement, although it can be found, as in America, within feminist and Dianic groups. This has been mainly due to such Wiccan writers as Starhawk, who have successfully combined witchcraft, feminism and some practices of Native American origin. (On the dangers of adopting Native American practices too freely, see p. 150.)

In both Europe and the United States, many Pagans are beginning to examine their own traditions for their shamanic origins. Pagans practicing Celtic, Norse and Anglo-Saxon shamanism are generally on the increase. These are usually reconstructed from historical material, as no continuing tradition has survived (except very locally), apart from those which evolved into witchcraft. The main reason that many have felt urged to reconstruct a tradition, rather than to adopt a similar, 'living' tradition, such as Native American medicine, is the need (as in the 1960s) again to search for their own ethnic roots.

Shamanic practice predates the pantheonizing of deities or spirits, and in many cases (such as the Norse) its practices were frowned upon or outlawed on pain of death; for example, the homosexual practices which existed within Norse shamanism or Siedr. Homosexual practice within shamanism can still be found in contemporary native cultures in some parts of the world. In one case, this takes the form of the shaman's apprentice dressing and acting as a woman during his period of training, and acting as the shaman's 'wife' during this time. This is regarded as necessary, so that the student can contact his female guardian or other self (his anima). As the anthropological evidence for homosexuality in some shamanic practices is unquestionable, homosexuals within the Pagan community have also widely adopted shamanism.

With the need to return to ethnic roots, many Wiccans have adopted shamanism as part of their practice, and in many cases, it has replaced Ritual Magic as the main *modus operandi* for some working groups. The use of drumming, chanting and dancing has become the common form of ritual to raise energy for magical work. Shamanism has several advantages over Ritual Magic, one being its open, unstructured approach, which allows free expression during rites and a free flow of magical energy. Unfortunately, because shamanism is relatively unstructured, it has also been used as an excuse to ignore basic occult laws, with the result that the energy raised may, in inexperienced hands, become uncontrollable.

Rosicrucians: A movement which originated in Germany as the Fratres Roseae Crucis ('Brothers of the Rosy Cross'), said to have been founded by Christian Rosenkreutz in 1398 AD, a possibly mythical character. In the early 17th century, people claiming to be members of this Society published four pamphlets with alleged accounts of Rosenkreutz's activities. These aroused much interest among would-be students, whose eager inquiries met with no answer, so the Rosicrucian story fell into disrepute; it was not till the middle of the 18th century that groups claiming to be Rosicrucian began to appear and be active.

In the 19th century, European political conditions required the strictest
secrecy by such people, but the atmosphere in England was far freer,
so the semi-public Societas Rosicruciana in Anglia was founded. It was
leading members of this who founded the Hermetic Order of the Golden
Dawn, which quickly overshadowed it in importance and influence.
Today's Rosicrucian Society, based in America, is a different kind of
organization, issuing correspondence courses to fee-paying students.

Chaos Magick: This appeared in the early 1980s 'post punk' era,
initially as a rebellion against the more dogmatic traditions which had
remained unchanged since the late 1960s. Since then it has become
firmly established as a form of practice within the wider Pagan community. It would be wrong to label it as a system, as its eclectic nature
enables the Chaos magician to adopt from any era of human activity
including the existing magical and occult traditions, art, literature,
quantum physics and more recently from computer technology—the
dawn of the Cyber Pagan is upon us! It places its emphasis on the
individual developing their own beliefs, creativity and experience
rather than being taught them by a teacher or 'Guru' figure. 'Nothing
is true, everything is permitted' is the only rule that seems to apply to
the Chaos Magician. This has resulted in Chaos Magick being branded
as anarchic and unethical in nature. Although the first can be seen to be
true, and in fact is seen as one of its strengths by its practitioners, the
latter is certainly untrue. It certainly rejects the need for an enforced
moral code, but it does encourage personal morality and the necessity
to uphold ones own values. It therefore places final responsibility for
his/her actions on the individual themselves. It is beginning to play an
important role in shaping modern Pagan thinking by encouraging the
individual Pagan to think for themselves rather than accept established
dogmas without question.

Strega: Italian for 'witch,' and used by many American Wiccans of
Italian tradition as a name for their path. Some of them use red chili
peppers on their stalks as ritual wand-symbols, the pepper being decorated with either a male or a female crown, according to the particular
group's emphasis. (Strega on the whole is strongly matriarchal.) Each
witch in one group we know of must make a tiny bronze sickle for
gathering herbs (herbal knowledge is important to Strega). We have
been given much information on this by a brother and sister of an
American-Italian family who were taught herbalism by their mother
and grandmother. Interestingly, the word Strega is best known to the

general public as the brand name of an Italian liqueur; it is made in Tuscany, in Benevento (a strong center of witchcraft tradition) to a secret witches' recipe.

The Northern Tradition: This is a term which has really only recently come into usage. It refers to *all* the traditions of the northern European peoples, which include: the Norse, Icelandic, Germanic and Teutonic, Anglo-Saxon and Frisian, and can also be said to include the growing interest in Latvian, Lithuanian and Estonian Pagan roots. Some writers also include Celtic elements of pre-Roman influence.

Asatru: A word of Scandinavian origin meaning 'belief in the Gods.' It generally refers to those practicing the Pagan beliefs of the Norse, German, and Icelandic peoples. The term 'Odinism' has until quite recent years been used, but this, unfairly, excludes the other deities of these traditions: the main male deities of Asatru being Frey, Odin, Thor and Tir; and the main female deities being Frigg, Freya, and the Norns (Fates). Unfortunately, the Asatru has in the past gained, unjustly, the reputation for being right-wing in political orientation. This came about due to ignorant people misunderstanding its magical symbolism and relating it to the Neo-Nazi movement; the sick fringe became attracted to the latter in its recent revival. Careful examination of Asatru philosophy shows it to be anything but racist; the main misunderstanding arising from its belief in racial consciousness. Its philosophy does not see one race as being superior to another; rather it sees the necessity of accepting differences in race on an equal basis. Asatru followers therefore see Hitler and Nazism as perverting their traditions and thus reaping the vengeance of their Gods.

Two root pantheons, at first in conflict but later merging, have affected the development of Asatru—the aboriginal, agricultural Vanir, and the invading warrior Aesir.

Odinism: This can be considered to be one cult within Asatru. It revolves around an individual taking Odin as his personal deity, and then emulating his sacrifice for knowledge (the Shamanic initiation). This practice is based on passages 138 to 142 of *The Poetic Edda*. It reads as follows:

> I hung from that windswept tree, hung there for nine long nights;
> I was pierced with a spear;
> I was an offering to Odin, myself to myself.
> No one will ever know the roots of that ancient tree.

No one came to comfort me with bread, no one revived me with drink
from a horn.
I peered at the worlds below;
I seized the runes, shrieking I seized them;
Then I fell back.

From Bolthor's famous son, Bestla's father, I learned nine powerful
songs.
I was able to drain the precious mead from the cauldron Odrorir.
Then I began to thrive, my wisdom grew; I prospered and was fruitful.
One word gained me many words; one deed gained me many deeds.

Within Odinism there is a strong code of conduct and honor based
on the *Havamal*; the sayings of Odin as law-maker. One criticism of
Odinism is that it is patriarchal in nature. This is a misunderstanding;
careful examination of the myths around Odin show how he is at the
will of the Norns, the Norse Fates.

Skaldic: Norse equivalent to Bardic.

Seidr: A word of Scandinavian origin (Anglo-Saxon equivalent Seith,
root of the word 'Soothsayer'). Generally considered to be the oldest
of the northern traditions. A heavily Shamanic form of practice, which
consists of a Volva or Vala (Prophetess) being conducted into a trance
state by the other participants singing a traditional song. The Volva
would then prophesy for those who would ask questions of her. The
principal deities of this tradition are those of the Vanir; Frey and Freya.
There was originally a form of sexual magic involved in its practice,
probably related to fertility rites. Interest in this tradition is growing
among both Asatru and Wiccans, and we know of at least one well-established practicing group.

Seax-Wicca: A relatively new tradition within Wicca, founded by
Raymond Buckland in 1974, and based purely on his book *The Tree:
The Complete Book of Saxon Witchcraft.* When the tradition first came
into being there was much debate by the older traditions as to its
legitimacy. For many it has become their first experience of Wicca, due
mainly to its simple rituals and rite of self-dedication. It is open and
democratic in nature. The main reason for Buckland's reconstruction
of the tradition was that he had become dissatisfied with Gardnerianism
and dismayed at the 'power trips' and 'egotism' which had occurred
within it. It is often said that it took one weekend for him to put it

together; whether this is true or not is debatable and irrelevant, as since 1974 it has, without doubt, proved itself as a bona fide tradition.

Jewitch: The name chosen by an increasing number of groups who are investigating the pre-patriarchal roots of their Hebrew ancestry as a basis for their Wiccan practice.

Society of the Inner Light: A British order founded by the late Dion Fortune, called by her the Fraternity of the Inner Light, and thoroughly Pagan/occult in her lifetime. It was at first very similar to the Golden Dawn, but gradually developed its own nature. After her death in 1946 it renamed itself the Society of the Inner Light, and departed steadily from her teachings. It makes a point of insisting that Dion Fortune was not a witch and not associated with any coven, and that the Society itself has no connection with witchcraft. It is still active, and teaching students a mixture of elements such as the Alexander technique, dianetics, and scientology. It owns the copyright of her books, and is thus in the slightly ironic position of profiting substantially from the continuing sale of her Pagan writings.

Discordianism: Whereas the polarity of most working magical groups consists of the accepted ones of male/female, positive/negative, creation/destruction etc., Discordianism works on the polarities of humor/seriousness and chaos/order. It was founded (or rediscovered) in the late 1960s by two young Californians, Kerry Thornley and Gregory Hill, who claimed that the Goddess Eris (Greek deity of Chaos) had enlightened them in a bowling alley and sprinkled them with fairy dust! The result of this experience was the *Principia Discordia: How I Found Goddess And What I Did To Her When I Found Her* ('Wherein is contained absolutely everything worth knowing about absolutely anything'), which they published as a book (see Bibliography under Malaclypse the Younger). This is without doubt a religion of paradox; what started as a joke in the 1950s snowballed within the Pagan community of the United States, and by the 1970s had spread to Europe. What they did not realize was that they had hit upon a serious mystical truth. It has been used by most Pagans as a check against egotism, pomposity, and generally taking themselves and their beliefs too seriously. As such it has become an important part of some groups' practices. Since the publication of the *Principia* several other forms have developed, including the Ancient and Honorable Order of Bill the Cat (see p. 156), who is Lord of all that is obnoxious and nasty (Janet has been made a High Priestess of this Order), and Bob, a send-up of television evangelism and its associated money-making campaigns. To be a serious follower of Eris is a contradiction in terms, but as it is a tradition of paradox it is therefore possible for it to be serious!

Hinduism: Without doubt the largest of the Pagan faiths in existence within the world today. The practice of Hinduism has spread to almost every continent (except Antarctica), but is deeply rooted in the culture of the Indian subcontinent and the East Indies. Both Hinduism and European Paganism have their roots in the Indo-European religions which existed before the great migration period. Both have Triple Goddess aspects (in Hinduism that of the Durga, Kali, Lakshmi, Saras-vati and others) and similar God archetypes. The interest in the West in Hinduism began during the 1960s, and many teenagers of the period rejected Christianity for this easily-accepted Pagan faith. This can be attributed to the opening up of sexual attitudes and the realization that sexuality has an accepted place in spirituality, which Hinduism obvi-ously recognizes and Christianity, on the whole, rejects. In the United States there have been growing ties between the Pagan and Hindu communities. (During our 1993 tour we were lucky to witness this interaction, and were invited with the rest of the community we were staying with, to take part in the Festival of Durga at the local Hindu Temple.) Such ties should be encouraged.

Shinto: The official religion of Japan, Shinto means 'The Way of the Gods.' This term did not come into being until the arrival of Buddhism and the need to differentiate between the two. Even so, they became intermingled, and modern Shinto is a fusion of both religions. It still shows evidence of its early Pagan roots with the survival of the phallic fertility cult, purification rites and the more well-known ancestor wor-ship. It has a complex mythology, including a creation myth. This myth centers around Izanagi and his sister deity Izanami, who separated the primal chaos with their celestial spear. This resulted in the formation of the Onogor, the central pillar of the Earth. There are also myths relating to the birth and death of the Sun Goddess, Amaterasu. The concept of divinity in Shinto is animistic, and anything that is unusual in nature, e.g. an oddly-shaped tree or rock formation, is considered to be divine or 'Kami,' and is thus worshipped. Many of its sanctuaries or Miya are found next to such objects of veneration. Shinto practice and mythology has many similarities with modern Asatru.

5.

Paganism and Christianity

The Pagan movement in the Western World (as we have defined it) exists in a predominantly Christian environment. The millions of its fellow citizens range from friendly and reasonable neighbors at one extreme to bigoted Fundamentalists at the other. It is important, therefore, for Pagans to be clear-minded about their attitude to both, and to the differences between the healthy foundations of Christianity and the dogma and hierarchy (some of it crippling) which have been built upon them.

Christianity includes a wide range of actuality, both historically and today. Most Pagans will accept that Jesus himself was a great teacher and spiritual healer; and millions of his grass-roots followers do attempt to practice in their daily lives what can be discerned of his teaching of 'love thy neighbor as thyself' and 'blessed are the peacemakers,' after centuries of political editing and distortion. Some of them even follow his promise that any of them can practice spiritual healing—'the works that I do shall he do also; and greater works than these shall he do.'

The distortion of Jesus's teaching started with St. Paul, who virtually launched his deification (which Jesus himself, in his time and culture, would have found blasphemous). The total Divinity of Jesus was declared at the First Ecumenical Council of Nicaea in 325 AD, in opposition to the troublesome Arian sect; and that of the Holy Ghost was upheld by the Second Ecumenical Council at Constantinople in 381 AD to counter the equally troublesome Macedonians, thus establishing the Holy Trinity as dogma. (The powerful symbolism of Three-in-One at Divine level is also found throughout ancient and modern Paganism, in the concept of the Triple Goddess—see p. 131.)

Paul was also pathological on the subject of sex and women; some of his statements on the 'God-ordained' status of women must even embarrass many modern Fundamentalists. For example:

> But I would have you know, that the head of every man is Christ; and the head of the woman is the man.... For a man ought not indeed to cover his head, forasmuch as he is the image and glory of God; but the woman is the glory of the man. For the man is not of the woman; but the woman is of the man. Neither was the man created for the woman; but the woman for the man.
>
> (St. Paul, 1 Corinthians xi:3 and 7-9.)

Thirteen centuries later, the official Church reached about its lowest ebb in this matter—for example in the notorious *Malleus Maleficarum* ('Hammer of the Witches'—the word for witches here being a feminine noun) which became, with Papal approval, the handbook of the witch persecution:

> What else is woman but a foe to friendship, an inescapable punishment, a necessary evil, a natural temptation, a desirable calamity, a domestic danger, a delectable detriment, an evil of nature, painted with fair colors!
>
> (Jakob Sprenger & Heinrich Kramer,
> *Malleus Maleficarum.*)

Jesus, on the other hand, clearly treated women as equals, even within the social limitations of the time—as indeed do his decent grass-roots followers today.

The Gospels were written decades after Jesus's death, and the legend of the Virgin Birth (not mentioned in the earliest, Mark, written probably in the AD 60s) was an obvious addition to appeal to Gentiles, who by then were being proselytized—the notion of great men conceived by divine impregnation of their mothers being a long-established tradition in Pagan mythology, attributed for example to the Pharaohs, to Alexander the Great, and even in some popular belief to Moses. The same tradition is widespread in Oriental cultures. In no case, until the Christian version, was it suggested the mother was a virgin wife to her husband.

The Bishop of Durham, the Right Reverend David Jenkins, in his 1991 book *Free to Believe* (see Bibliography), declared: "I do not consider a belief in the literal Virgin Birth necessary to the doctrine of the Incarnation nor to Christianity." He explained:

> If we are honest with ourselves we must face the fact that there are important and disturbing implications in a rigid insistence on a literal Virgin Birth. Obsession with virginity carries some pretty dangerous baggage. It is an emphasis which developed as the Church moved out into the Greek world. It does not fit into the Hebrew-based world of the Bible with its strong affirmation of family life and normal sexuality. False obsessions lead us into dangers of distortion and confusion. For example, Mary is supposed to be the mother figure and yet she is represented as a virgin. No wonder Christians have been known to get into a terrible muddle over sex and the place and role of women. We need to consider the possibility that this is yet another area where we have misinterpreted the Word of God. A misinterpretation which, I believe, comes from a literal approach which is not appropriate to the way people originally wrote and used the texts.

The Moderator of the Church of Scotland, the Very Reverend James J. Weatherhead, recently expressed a similar view about the Virgin Birth.

The quotation from the Old Testament which is officially held to foretell the birth of Christ—'Behold, a virgin shall conceive, and bear a son, and shall call his name Immanuel' (Isaiah vii.14)—in fact expressed the Hebrew dream of a Messiah who would occupy the Throne of David and secure the Kingdom of Judah for eternity. (And by the way, the word translated as 'virgin' here, in Hebrew merely means 'young woman.') This monarchic dream persisted, and was shared by John the Baptist and his followers; when it began to become clear that Jesus regarded his mission as spiritual, not monarchic, John was worried, and sent the message: "Art thou he that should come? or look we for another?"

On this subject, an interesting suggestion about the Three Wise Men was first made in 1603 by the astronomer Johannes Kepler, and is today accepted by many scholars. The actual year of the birth of Jesus was not officially fixed until 525 AD, and in fact it is generally worked out by today's experts that he would have been born somewhere between 8 and 1 BC. In 7 BC an event occurred which only happens once every 139 years—the 'Triple Conjunction' when the Earth, Jupiter and Saturn are in a straight line. In 7 BC this conjunction occurred in the constellation Pisces, which only happens once every 900 years.

The Three were not Kings, whatever the popular carol says; the Bible merely refers to them as 'wise men.' In their period, this would doubtless have meant they were also astrologers, and they would have been well aware of the Triple Conjunction—and of the facts that Pisces was associated with the Hebrews, that Saturn protected them and would aid the consolidation of the Throne of David, and that Jupiter was associated with royalty and with good fortune. So the 'Star of Bethlehem,' which brought them to the city where they were told it had been prophesied that the King of the Jews would be born, was more than likely this rare Triple Conjunction—whose significance would be lost on ordinary people ignorant of astrology, whereas a 'bright star' hovering over the town would have been seen by everybody. Moreover, the Three had 'seen' (i.e., been aware of) the 'star' many weeks earlier, when it prompted them to begin their journey; this is believable of a known conjunction, but hardly of a hovering localized phenomenon.

Kepler's interpretation would also explain the acute interest of Herod (who would have had astrological advisers) in the Three's mission—and their prudence in not reporting back to him.

There is much evidence that Jesus, if not Essene-trained, was at least strongly Essene-influenced. (The Essenes were an unorthodox Hebrew cult with a settlement on the shores of the Dead Sea, who wrote the Dead Sea Scrolls.) This would explain one statement of his—'I and the Father are one'—which is much quoted to assert that he claimed personal divinity. In fact the Essenes used a Friday-night ritual declaration 'I and the Heavenly Father are one'—but their Saturday-morning declaration was 'I and the Earthly Mother are one.' The Essenes believed that humankind stood midway between the Heavenly Father and his angels, and the Earthly Mother and her angels, and must be in harmony with both—a belief symbolically expressing a principle with which today's Pagans strongly agree. If, as seems likely, it was the Essene statement which Jesus was quoting, he was declaring harmony, not identity (and one cannot help wondering if he ever quoted the Earthly Mother statement as well).

Jesus specifically warned his hearers not to regard himself as the Source: "He that believeth on me, believeth not on me, but on him that sent me" (John xii:44). He called himself the Son of Man, which in Hebrew terminology of the time meant a human channel for God. And if he also admitted to being Son of God—did he not say we all were such Sons or Daughters? Otherwise why did he tell his followers to pray to 'Our Father, which art in Heaven'?

The worst thing that happened to official Christianity, after St. Paul, was when from Constantine onwards it became an integral and important part of the Imperial Civil Service. Hierarchical discipline was imposed, and reincarnation (which, as we shall see in Chapter 10, was taught in the early Church) was declared anathema and replaced by the once-only reward or punishment of Heaven or Hell. Do as the bishop commands, or you will burn in hellfire for eternity....

Until the end of the 4th century, there were many Gospels circulating, and the New Testament as we know it had not been officially defined. Then the hierarchy decided on the four which they regarded as acceptable (and almost certainly edited even those), while the many other Gospels which did not suit the official picture were suppressed and where possible destroyed.

As we have said, many ordinary Christians strive to follow Jesus's positive teachings—his emphasis on 'Blessed is he who' rather than on 'Thou shalt not.' But all too often, particularly among Fundamentalists, Christianity has become a mere union ticket; one acknowledges Jesus's name, and that ensures one's salvation. We are tempted to quote him again: "Not every one that saith unto me, Lord, Lord, shall enter into the kingdom of heaven."

Also, we feel, too much emphasis is laid on his death rather than on his life. If we were Christians, we would like to build a church which had behind the altar, not a man being tortured to death on a cross, but Jesus with his arm round a little girl, and Mary carrying the boy child. In such an atmosphere, it would be easier to attune oneself to the principles of life, love and healing which he actually taught. (Would any Christians like to try it?)

There are, unfortunately, on the fringe of the Pagan movement elements of Pagan Fundamentalism, too. They tie one universal label round everything from the Vatican to their ordinary Christian neighbors, regarding the whole spectrum as enemies. We shall consider this dangerous aberration in Chapter 17.

All such Fundamentalists, whether Christian or Pagan, should consider the real meaning of the Parable of the Good Samaritan. Its moral was not merely kindness to the unfortunate (which was part of Hebrew teaching anyway). Jesus had said "Love thy neighbor as thyself," and one of his audience asked "Who is my neighbor?" Jesus told the parable in reply. The shock to his audience, in that time and place, would have been that the neighbor who showed love, and must be loved, was a Samaritan, a heretic, a religious untouchable. The impact would have been the same as if, talking to Fundamentalists today, he had made his Samaritan a Witch.

In our experience, many Pagans know the Bible better, and more understandingly, than most Fundamentalists, many of whom merely know a selection of quotations from it (often out of context or in questionable translations) which they misinterpret to suit their own prejudices.

Strangely enough, Catholics have in the past not been encouraged to read the Bible themselves, but have been confined to what bits the priest fed to them; and something of this still persists. Janet once debated with a distinguished Dublin Catholic priest on radio, and a listener phoned in with a rather stupid question. During the next commercial break, the priest said to Janet: "Doesn't know his Bible, that man, does he? Must be a Catholic." (Incidentally, the priest was later rebuked by his bishop for referring to Janet on the air as 'this priestess,' but declined the rebuke.)

To regard every word in the Bible as literally true, and the Word of God, is self-evident nonsense. One can only believe that by rejecting all that has been learned about cosmic, Terran, and human (not to mention animal) origins and evolution, confirmed by fossils and by carbon dating; about the astronomy of the Universe, in which Earth is only one of countless billions of planets where life is possible and unquestionably must exist; about proven history; about the nature and meaning of symbology and mythology; and a host of other authenticated factors—not to mention that some passages in the Bible contradict others. And can one really believe (for example) that every species in the world, including presumably kangaroos and so on from unreachable lands not then known to exist, could be packed into a family-made wooden Ark?

The 'literal truth' of the Bible is sidestepped where convenient. For example, the references to Jesus meeting 'his mother and his brethren' (Matthew xii:46, Mark iii:31, Luke viii:19) would appear to demolish once and for all the dogma of Mary's perpetual virginity; but Fundamentalists claim that in this case 'brethren' merely means 'cousins, relatives.' The word 'cousin' or 'cousins' appears in a couple of other places in Luke (in i:36 Elizabeth is referred to as Mary's cousin, for example) so why should he, Matthew and Mark not use it here, if that was what was meant?

The Bible is not a book, it is an anthology, written by various authors over a millennium at least. It is a mixture of tribal legends (mostly locally revised versions of other Middle Eastern legends), poetry, heavy patriarchalization by Levite revisers during the Babylonian exile, self-righteous records of genocidal treatment of conquered tribes, passages of genuine spiritual insight, complex laws appropriate to a tribal society in a particular environment but almost entirely inappropriate to today, and folk proverbs. It also includes two books which are totally Pagan, neither of them mentioning the Hebrew God at all—the erotically beautiful Song of Solomon, and Esther, the story of the *hieros gamos* or Sacred Marriage of a priestess of the Goddess Ishtar (of whose name 'Esther' is the Aramaic form) to the enthroned king, to validate his right to rule; Ishtar was also a Goddess of Sovereignty, and the *hieros gamos* to a priestess representing the appropriate Goddess was strictly observed in many countries—pre-Christian Ireland, for example; the legendary Queen Medhbh of Connacht (origin of the fairytale Queen Mab) was such a priestess: 'Until Medhbh had slept with the lad, he was not King.' (Incidentally, her name is pronounced 'Mave,' to rhyme with 'cave.')

Those who believe in the literal truth of the Garden of Eden story fail to notice that Genesis opens with two quite independent Creation legends. In the first (Genesis i.1-ii.3) God—named as Elohim, a word etymologically plural and a strange combination of masculine and feminine—creates man and woman in 'his' (their) own image. In the second (Genesis ii.4 onwards) man is created from the dust of the earth, and woman from man's rib. The two legends are incompatible; and the first clearly derives from pre-patriarchal thinking.

To take just one example where a Biblical story revises an older Middle Eastern legend—that of Noah's Ark. The Assyro-Babylonian Goddess Ishtar had herself inherited it from an earlier Moon Goddess named Nueh, whose name, masculinized, is the obvious root of the name Noah. Ishtar herself was very much associated with water, and when the Earth was flooded—a disaster which she had prophesied—according to one version (and the Nueh original) it was she who sailed the Ark which the Water God Ea had advised the human Utpanishtim to build; and it was she who sent out first a dove, then a swallow, both of which returned, and finally a raven, which did not. Later versions attributed these actions to Utpanishtim, and the biblical Noah inherited his role. After the Flood had subsided, Ishtar lifted up her necklace of the jewels of Heaven and rejoiced—clearly the origin of the Biblical rainbow.

Anyone who doubts this and other examples of the Biblical revision of existing mythology is deliberately closing his eyes to proven historical fact.

The New Testament is quite different from the Old; as we saw above, it is founded on reasonably genuine history, politically edited, and followed by Pauline propaganda and the visionary book of Revelation. This final book has been in many places misinterpreted as a diatribe against Satan, in passages which are in fact heavily metaphorical attacks on the Emperor of Rome.

Similar misunderstandings abound of passages in the Old Testament; for example, the much-quoted statement 'How art thou fallen from heaven, O Lucifer, son of the morning! how art thou cut down to the ground, which didst weaken the nations!' (Isaiah xiv:12), the only use of the name Lucifer in the Bible, refers not to the Devil, but to the King of Babylon, at that time the occupier of Palestine; it is part of a song, in the traditional Hebrew lamentation rhythm. Lucifer ('light-bearer') is the Morning Star, the planet Venus, and is a satirical metaphor for the tyrant King—one of whose royal titles was 'Day Star, Son of the Morning.' But through ignorant reading, Satan has become stuck with the name.

Mistranslations, too; 'Thou shalt not suffer a witch to live' (Exodus xxii:18) is in Hebrew 'Thou shalt not suffer a poisoner to live'—understandable in a land dependent for drinkable water on widely-scattered wells and few rivers.

In case anyone thinks these comments are prejudiced Pagan propaganda, *Peake's Commentary on the Bible* (see Bibliography) is recommended reading. Written by genuine (and Christian) scholars, it explains the actual meaning and context of every passage in the Bible, book by book and mostly chapter by chapter. An interesting example: of Revelation it says 'In addition to elements drawn from Old Testament and Jewish tradition there are a number of traits (especially astrological and mythological) that are of pagan origin.'

The Reformation freed part of Christianity from Vatican dictatorship, and allowed more freedom of choice in Christian paths, ranging from Quakerism to High Church Protestantism. But it also had the negative outcome that Protestantism discarded the Goddess-aspect tuning-signal (however circumscribed) provided by the Virgin Mary, and the aspect tuning-signals (equally circumscribed) provided by the saints.

An example from our own experience: as a Christian Protestant teenager, Janet was somewhat reluctantly persuaded to act as a Sunday

School teacher. One Sunday she decided to talk about St. Francis and his devotion to animals. The children loved it—but Janet was reprimanded afterwards for what she had done, because 'St. Francis is Catholic.' Surely a waste of a unique and memorable tuning-signal? (We wonder if there are Protestant Fundamentalists who want San Francisco renamed!)

We once had a long talk with a young Irish nun with a fine record in practical community work, who believed in the ordination of women; that priestly celibacy should be a personal choice; that Pope John Paul I was murdered; and so on. Later that day we met an elderly colleague of hers who had similar views. They would have made the Vatican's hair stand on end—and they are far from untypical.

Grass-roots Catholic objections to Vatican domination are not confined to women, or even to the laity. Father Pat Buckley, a practicing priest of County Antrim in Northern Ireland, wrote an article published in *Gay Community News* in September 1992 condemning the Vatican rulings on homosexuality, birth control, etc., its silence on the Holocaust, and its record on the Inquisition and the Crusades. "Do not be disturbed by the strange flat-earth noises emanating from Rome," he wrote. "These people are not the Church. We are."

While this book was going to press, Father Buckley appeared on Irish television's top-of-the-ratings *Late Late Show*. He now runs from Larne what he calls 'a parish without frontiers,' continuing to press for the changes in attitude he believes necessary. Many other priests send people to him for help, while asking him not to make the fact public. Interestingly, the television audience (certainly mostly Catholic) loudly applauded two of his statements: that he believed in the ordination of women, and that if he met someone he wanted to marry, he would do so openly, without leaving the priesthood. He has written a book titled *A Thorn in the Side* (see Bibliography).

To which may be added the Catholic priest who, deeply impressed and moved (as we were) by the astonishing American experiments in language communication with chimpanzees, confessed that he simply could no longer accept the Vatican ruling that animals have no souls. And the American nun who succinctly told Pope John Paul II: "You can't push the toothpaste back into the tube."

Perhaps the outstanding American Catholic ecumenist today is Father Matthew Fox, with his Institute for Culture and Creative Spirituality, whose teachers include Catholic scholars, Rabbis, a Voodoo and a Wiccan Priestess, quantum physicists, Shamans, and many others.

Father Fox insists that his work is not alien to original Christianity, but only to the sin-centered mainstream churches. "There is no way," he said in one of his talks, "that the historical Jesus would have worshipped in a church staring into the back of someone in front of him! He would have been out there dancing on the Earth giving thanks." He sees the body as divine and sacramental, and accepts the Hindu Chakra system. His movement celebrates the Eight Sabbats, and he points out that early Christianity did the same.

Not surprisingly, Fundamentalist Christians picket his talks in America, and the Vatican has officially silenced him for a year. He is about to be expelled from the Dominican order, and he is constantly investigated for heresy—so far without success. He is determined to remain a priest if he can, maintaining that nothing has changed from without, only from within.

Such positive Christian attitudes are unfortunately matched by heightened Fundamentalist militancy—for example, in American political elections. Typical of this is Virginia, where over a quarter of the electorate describe themselves as 'evangelical conservatives.' While this book was being written, burning questions there, in everything from the Governorship election (which the Republican, Fundamentalist George Allen won) to the local school board ones, have been: Should pictures of witches be allowed on classroom walls during Hallowe'en festivals? Should children be taught to be 'global citizens'? Should classes hold mock political elections? According to the Fundamentalist candidates, the answer to all these is a firm 'No'; pictures of witches will encourage children to dabble in Paganism, talk of global responsibilities undermines patriotism, and mock elections undermine parental authority. And lawyer Michael Ferris, Allen's running-mate for the Lieutenant-Governorship, fought in the courts in 1992 for parents' right to forbid their children to read *The Wizard of Oz* when it was on the school curriculum, because it portrays some witches as good. During the campaign, Allen and Ferris described public education as a 'godless monstrosity.'

The current trend by Fundamentalist Christians of accusing Pagans of 'Satanic ritual abuse' started in 1980 with the publication of the book *Michelle Remembers*. This trend culminated in the United States with the McMartin child abuse case, which cost the State of California $30,000,000. It resulted in no convictions, and the only positive thing to come out of it was a discrediting, to a certain degree, of the Fundamentalists claims.

Prior to *Michelle Remembers* there had been several books published by supposed witches turned Christian, but none of these had mentioned child abuse. The Fundamentalist and 'moral majority' faction, before the claims of ritual abuse, had been similarly unsuccessful in their attacks on homosexual parents. There appears to have been a pattern in whom they attacked on the issue of children, and when faced with legal opposition on the grounds of civil rights, as they were over the homosexual community, their resolution on the issue crumpled and they attacked the next easiest minority, the Pagan community.

In Britain the same pattern emerged, with Fundamentalists finally attacking the Pagans. The best known Fundamentalist launching these accusations was Maureen Davies of the Beacon Trust; she was originally part of a similar organization called the Reachout Trust, but was 'asked to leave' because they found her activities too extreme. Both these groups set themselves up as 'authorities' on the occult and ritual child abuse. Maureen Davies held lectures for social workers and police officers before she was finally discredited by a team of investigative journalists on television; she was unable to produce any proof of ritual abuse, claiming, "I just know it takes place."

To date, although there have been attempts, there have been no successful prosecutions on the grounds of ritual abuse in Britain; but this has not prevented damage being done to other individuals. One example was the Orkney Island ritual abuse case, where the children were taken away at the dead of night by armed police to the mainland. The parents accused were not Pagan, but Quakers, and although they were never prosecuted, it took them several months to get their traumatized children returned to them.

Obviously the child abuse issue is the most extreme reaction by Fundamentalists against Pagans. Pagans sometimes find their festivals picketed by Christian groups, or even their venue canceled (see p. 169). In some areas of the United States it is unsafe even to wear a Pentagram openly for fear of being harassed (see pp. 166–170). On both sides of the Atlantic, Pagan communities have felt it necessary to protect themselves against Fundamentalist slander. In North America several groups, including the Massachusetts-based Witches' Anti-Defamation League and the Canadian-based Wiccan Information Network were formed. Much of their work is educational, and they have good communication with law enforcement agencies and local government—particularly the Wiccan Information Network, which produces information for police officers involved in possible occult-related crimes.

In Britain several Pagan pressure and community support groups have been formed. These act under the umbrellas of both the Paganlink network and the Pagan Federation (see pp.167–169); one of the first of these was the Pagan Anti-Defamation League (PADL) set up by members of the Federation in the early 1970s. Its role was very much to protect the rights of the Pagan community by monitoring the media's coverage of Paganism and witchcraft, particularly if adverse, by coordinating protest action and by increasing public awareness of the religion.

The Pagan Anti-Defamation League was later joined by the Sorcerer's Apprentice Fighting Fund (SAFF) which registered itself as a non-profit-making charity. (The Sorcerer's Apprentice is an occult shop in Leeds which was firebombed by a Fundamentalist fringe group in the mid-1980s.) It is involved in protecting not only the rights of the Pagan community, but also those of other alternative religions. It is now well-established nationally, and has over a thousand members. It has financed several legal actions protecting the rights of Pagans; from the legality of carrying an athame to anti-defamation action against a major British newspaper. It was instrumental in bringing to light an attempt to pass an anti-witchcraft Bill in Parliament by Geoffrey Dickens, MP, and uncovering the truth about the ritual abuse myth which was used against Pagan families by Fundamentalist Christians. It was responsible for several communications with the British Home Office regarding child abuse allegations, and succeeded in obtaining a statement from them refuting the MP's claims:

> First of all, as you point out, according to press reports, Mr. Geoffrey Dickens MP has sent the Home Secretary a dossier of child abuse cases allegedly connected with witchcraft. However this has not been received and the Home Office has no other evidence that there is a problem of the kind that Mr. Dickens describes.

In 1989 SAFF launched The Occult Census, the first serious attempt to record the activities of practicing occultists in Britain, demographically and sociologically. When published this covered population, occult involvement, age and sex, education and occupation, general interests, politics etc. It estimated that there were over 250,000 witches/Pagans throughout Britain. The reasons the SAFF gave for the census was that factual evidence was needed to dispel the Fundamentalist myth that all occultism was dangerous and anti-social. The Occult

Census was to reveal by serious analysis that occultists were 'intelligent, *responsible, aware*, and informed members of (our) society.'

The antipathy from Christians is normally from the Fundamentalist fringe, and generally grass-roots Christians and Pagans get on well. Cooperation between the two is increasing, with Pagans being invited to attend Inter-faith councils, both in Europe and in North America. In 1993 one of the biggest steps forwards for Pagan/Christian relations was made with the invitation of members of the Covenant of the Goddess, Pagan Spirit Alliance, and the Fellowship of Isis to attend the World Council of Churches (see p. 161).

We ourselves have witnessed this cooperation, having attended a memorial service organized by the Free Spirit Alliance in Maryland. A commemorative ritual for the 200th anniversary of the Salem Witch Trials was held in a church hall, with the local Christian Minister and some of his parishioners in attendance. We attended a similar commemoration in Salem itself. As non-Christians, it would be inappropriate for us to appear to be taking sides between the two main Christian paths. But the evidence compels us to admit that bigoted and militant Fundamentalism, on the ground, seems to be basically a Protestant phenomenon, while the focus of Catholic reactionary attitudes is clearly the Vatican itself, striving to discipline grass-roots Catholic feeling. Can this perhaps be linked to Protestantism's complete rejection of the Goddess principle, compared with Catholicism's veiled acceptance of it?

Christian Fundamentalists do not only persecute other religions. For example, the minority Evangelical movement in the Church of England uses various tactics, including financial ones, to pressurize the majority.

The Rev. Philip Hacking is Chairman of Reform, a pressure group of about 350 Evangelical churches around the country. On BBC television, in February 1994, he explained that his own and several other member churches had decided to withhold a part of the contributions which they normally pay to the local diocese, because they object to their funds being used to 'subsidize people who have liberal views.'

The BBC commentary said that: "The rise of the Evangelicals has provoked another wider concern. Even those who would describe themselves not as liberal, but as solid middle-of-the-road Anglican, fear that Evangelicals could force a change in the character of the Church." As one woman member of St. Peter's Church in South Weald, in Essex, put it: "I think perhaps Evangelicals are more intolerant. They tend to think that only they are right, and that nobody else's way of worship can be tolerated." The Rev. Colin Travers of the same church also admitted to being worried, and said: "There are many roads to God, not just one particular doctrinal road."

The BBC program concluded that this dispute, between the Evangelicals and the rest, is likely to replace that between those for and against women's ordination, as the major confrontation within the Anglican Church.

Within Christianity itself, current trends seem to be polarizing increasingly into positive and negative. We are quite certain which side Jesus himself would have taken. Christianity in its present state is an adolescent child, still bearing the acned scars of Paul and Constantine. Thanks to Christians like Matthew Fox, she will regain her latent Sophia, Wisdom, and emerge from puberty as a beautiful bride of the Cosmic Christ, ready to take her true place among the religions of the world.

We have gone into the Christian question in some depth because, as we pointed out at the beginning of this chapter, today's Western Pagans live in a predominantly Christian environment. A constructively selective attitude to the fact is therefore, for Pagans, of real importance.

But a similar analysis could be made of Judaism (at least in its ancient patriarchal form) and Islam; though in our experience, most modern Jews, and grass-roots Moslems uncaptivated by Fundamentalism, are far more tolerant and understanding of other faiths. The Egyptian government, for example, is doing all it can to halt the activities of Islamic Fundamentalists in that country.

Finally, an interesting example of the clash between Pagan ecumenism and Christian monotheism: early Christian missionaries to India talked to Hindus about Jesus, and many Hindus accepted that Jesus was obviously a holy figure. So they put his picture in their temples alongside those of their own deities—and could not understand when the missionaries were shocked!

6.

No Place for Satan

The favorite, and crudest, Fundamentalist accusation against Pagans (and against witches in particular) is that they worship Satan. It is quite simply not true, and it is astonishing how widely and unthinkingly this blatant lie has been believed.

Worship of the Devil would be totally incompatible with the principles we have outlined so far. Pagans regard evil as an imbalance to be corrected, not as an independent force or entity.

Satan is a creation of Judaeo-Christian Dualism, which has replaced the concept of creative polarity with that of Good and Evil as two independently existing forces at war with each other, instead of regarding evil as a state of imbalance requiring healing action. Dualism has also tended to identify 'Good' with the masculine and with spirit, and 'Evil' with the feminine and with matter. (The Christian Scientists' *Scientific Statement of Being*, for example, actually declares: "There is no life, truth, intelligence or substance in matter... Spirit is the real and eternal; matter is the unreal and temporal.")

We have already looked at Paganism's view of the masculine/feminine polarity; here it should be added that Paganism also regards all levels of reality, from spirit to matter, as mutually complementary and necessary to each other. As the Cabala puts it: 'All the Sephiroth are equally holy.' We shall have more to say on this in Chapter 7, *Magic and Divination*, and Chapter 10, *Reincarnation*.

Jung made a substantial contribution to clear thinking on the levels of the psyche with his definitions of the Conscious Ego and the Personal and Collective Unconscious, which should be in healthy interaction with each other. Official Christianity, with its fear of the feminine aspect, has always distorted this interaction into a Dualist confrontation between 'good' and 'evil.' Paganism accepts the Jungian view—and is grateful to him for providing definitions which make the healthy interaction easier to understand and describe.

Pagans, as we have seen, worship the same Ultimate as anyone else, however they may symbolize It. Monotheists, paradoxically, believe in *two* Ultimates, existing independently and at constant war with each other.

Satanism as a cult is alien to Paganism, which totally rejects it, whatever Fundamentalists and the gutter press claim. It is a negative image of Christianity, and its followers are often merely rejecting their upbringing by a wholesale inversion of parental beliefs, saying 'up yours!' to Mum and Dad. The notorious Black Mass is not a Pagan ritual; it is a Christian heretical blasphemy, a calculated mockery of the Mass by renegade Christians. Most Satanist groups are merely foolish; others are seeking publicity (and its attendant profits) by deliberately shocking; but some of them are secretly and calculatedly dangerous.

We do know of at least one group in Britain which calls itself Satanist, doubtless for initially rebellious reasons, but whose actual practices are above reproach; it will not allow anyone to be harmed, and we find its choice of name unfortunate and misleading. There are also groups which investigate the dark side, with the firm intention of getting natural light and dark in balance, and the names some of them choose may result in their being mistakenly regarded as Satanist.

The Christian image of Satan is a post-Biblical invention. In the Old Testament, Satan is a servant of God; his task is to test people's genuineness and ability to resist temptation (the book of Job gives a vivid account of this), and to report back to God accordingly. Not an endearing function, perhaps, but certainly not an 'evil' one. Nor was Satan made into a 'fallen angel' rebelling against his master, until much later.

Horns, throughout the Old Testament, are not a devilish symbol, but a sign of God-given power. This symbol is recalled by the well-known Michelangelo statue of Moses in the Vatican, which is equipped with horns.

But during the medieval persecution centuries, the image changed. The Church inquisitors knew that Pagans and witches worshipped a Horned God of Nature, which prompted them to equip Satan with horns so that they could say: 'Witches worship the Devil—look, he has the horns to prove it!' In Christian imagery, Satan is horned to this day, and most people believe mistakenly that he always has been.

Dualism's tendency to equate good with masculine and with spirit, and evil with feminine and with matter, is a symptom of patriarchal thinking. Patriarchy likes things tidy and controllable, so spiritual matters have to be tied up in hierarchical dogma, and intuitive Woman fits very uneasily into this pattern. Jesus himself treated women as equals; it was Paul who was psychotically anti-sex, and laid down rules which the patriarchal Church, once it became official, embraced eagerly. Islam and Judaism may be patriarchal, and Dualist in their own ways, but neither of them is anti-sex. This is a specifically official-Christian aspect of Dualism. The Vatican ban on contraception, for example (enforced at a time when the population explosion was already creating serious global problems), really expresses the hierarchy's nervous belief that sex is not something to be enjoyed, merely an unfortunate necessity for reproduction.

Presumably God equipped us, reluctantly, with the sex drive for that purpose; which raises an interesting question. Christian tradition has it that on the Last Day we shall all be resurrected in our human bodies, to face Judgment. Will God then have removed the sex drive from those bodies? That will make Heaven rather boring. We are inclined to prefer the Islamic Heaven, in which sex flourishes and orgasms last for an hour.

Seriously though, Pagans do not believe that Satan exists. How, then, can they worship him?

As with Paganism, there are many different forms of Satanism. It is generally accepted that it is divided into two separate types, Traditional Satanism and Modern Satanism. In their *Occult Source Book*, Nevill Drury and Gregory Tillet divide it even further into five distinct types.

The first of these is the traditional anti-Christian Satanist, so loved by Hollywood horror film producers. It is the antithesis of Christianity; holding the notorious Black Mass, profaning all the Christian rites, defiling purity and reading the Lord's Prayer in reverse. Traditional Satanism was originally a fantasy created by the Church to instill fear into the population; later some elements of society adopted it as a rebellion against the Church's harsh laws. Unfortunately in recent times, because of press reports linking child abuse and Satanism, the trappings of this form of practice have been adopted by a sick fringe involved in pedophilia as a new kink; Fundamentalism and sections of the press are therefore guilty of creating a self-fulfilling prophecy. If genuine traditional Satanists do exist, they are very secretive and remain rare.

Drury and Tillet's second type, which they describe as 'secular humanistic' Satanism, is probably the commonest; the most well-known organization of this category being Anton La Vey's Church of Satan. They do not believe in a personal Devil nor in a personal God, but are egocentric in attitude. Their philosophy is devoted to opposing the restrictions and inhibitions forced upon man by the Christian Church. They hold the Seven Deadly Sins to be virtues rather than vices, and this is echoed in La Vey's Nine Satanic Statements:

1. Satan represents indulgence, instead of abstinence!
2. Satan represents vital existence, instead of spiritual pipe dreams!
3. Satan represents undefiled wisdom, instead of hypocritical self-deceit!
4. Satan represents kindness to those who deserve it, instead of Love wasted on ingrates!
5. Satan represents vengeance, instead of turning the other cheek!
6. Satan represents responsibility to the responsible, instead of concern for psychic vampires!
7. Satan represents man as just another animal, sometimes better, more often worse than those who walk on all-fours, who, because of his 'divine spiritual and intellectual development,' has become the most vicious animal of all!
8. Satan represents all of the so-called sins, as they all lead to physical, mental, or emotional gratification!
9. Satan has been the best friend the church has ever had, as he has kept it in business all these years!

We can agree with the ninth statement only; the other eight, apart from being cynical, are all philosophically and theologically flawed. This form of Satanism remains a rebellion against the Church, and only attracts those who are dissatisfied with it. It therefore cannot be considered a true spiritual path.

Recently, Satanic groups like the Church of Satan have been making overtures towards the Pagan movement to support them against Fundamentalist opposition, arguing that 'the enemy of my enemy is my friend.' We are glad to say that the Pagan movement has rejected this call for an alliance; first of all Satanism, whether it likes it or not, has the same theology as Christianity and is not Pagan. It also has a philosophy which is totally alien to Pagan principles, disobeying the Wiccan ethic of 'an it harm none.'

The argument has been confused even further by Michael Aquino's Temple of Set. Drury and Tillet would classify this type as 'Paganistic

Satanism,' the worship of the 'forces of darkness' as found in the Roman, Greek, and in this case, the Egyptian mythologies. The Temple of Set uses Egyptian symbolism, but still adheres to the Satanic principle (Michael Aquino set up the Temple after leaving La Vey's Church of Satan) and can still be considered Satanic rather than Pagan.

Two other forms of Satanism are mentioned by Drury and Tillet. One is 'Satanic Witchcraft' (itself a contradiction in terms) which makes use of modern Wiccan symbolism in malign ritual. The second, 'Hedonistic Satanism,' is based on total free license: using anything and everything to gratify the senses, including ritual, drugs, and sex. They have no philosophical outlook, and are only concerned with the pursuit of personal pleasure. Sometimes these groups may be used to front blackmail rings. Such a group existed in the south of England during the 1970s, calling itself the 'Friends of Hekate.' This group would lure the financially well-off, and professionals in responsible positions, into hedonistic rituals, normally involving a fake sacrificial rite and sex. They would secretly photograph them, and in due course extort money and 'favors' from them. Again such groups are rare, but it does highlight yet another danger of becoming involved with Satanic practices.

7.

Magic and Divination

The working of magic is not a superstition; it is a practical fact. It depends on understanding the interaction between the various levels of reality, and making constructive use of that interaction.

These levels, which we shall discuss further in Chapter 10, are usually defined in Pagan and occult thinking as the spiritual, mental, astral, etheric, and physical levels. Each level has its own laws, but the laws of different levels do not conflict with each other. (As, for example, the laws of mathematics, chemistry and biology are different, but do not conflict with each other.) Pagans believe that by understanding these laws and their interaction, one can achieve results generally regarded as magical.

Television is an interesting parallel; though it operates of course entirely on the physical level, it depends on manipulating the interaction between that plane's sub-levels. An event occurs materially in the studio, visible and audible there on the light-wave and sound-wave levels. Camera and microphone transform these phenomena into waves on the electro-magnetic circuit level, and the transmitter's equipment transforms these into vibrations on a chosen frequency of the radio-wave level, which is independent of matter as such and moves at the speed of light even in empty space.

Our home television aerial picks up these waves, and the television set selects a particular frequency from the chaos. It transforms the signals on this frequency into electro-magnetic vibrations within its circuits, and the screen and speaker transform these into light-wave and sound-wave vibrations—which reproduce exactly for our eyes and ears the event in the studio.

All this depends on an understanding of the laws of the various sub-levels and their interaction, and putting that understanding to constructive use.

And yet a 17th-century person, however intelligent and well-educated, who could transport to our time and watch television, would doubtless regard it as magical—because two of the sub-levels involved (the electro-magnetic and the radio-wave) were not then even known to exist.

'Magic' is simply a word for the operation of laws which are not yet understood. Sensible Pagans are in the forefront of working to understand and apply those laws, where all too many followers of other religions treat them as God's mysteries beyond human understanding. If we may say so, we believe God intends us to find them out—having equipped us with brains which can advance consciously instead of blindly.

It is interesting that today many advanced scientists—in particular those concerned with subatomic physics—are more aware and acceptant of multi-level reality than are most Fundamentalists.

Magical Realms and Cosmologies

All the Pagan traditions, ancient or modern, believe in the existence of Magical Realms, Worlds and other planes. All the world's mythologies talk of such realms, and it is common practice for Pagans to study these, and their interaction with our own world, for insight into how magic works. It is not essential to have knowledge of how these realms function to practice simple forms of magic; you don't have to understand how an engine works to drive a car—but it is useful if you break down.

In early hunter-gatherer cultures, the first cosmology to appear was that of three worlds: an upper world, the abode of the Gods; a middle world, the home of man; and a chthonic underworld, home of the spirits. This belief can still be found in tribal cultures around the world, and is used by modern shamans. Magical cosmologies are microcosmic/macrocosmic, reflecting the nature of man as well as the universe.

Hence, many Pagans adhere to Jungian psychology, in which these realms are seen to represent aspects of the individual psyche: the upper world, the Consciousness; the middle world, the Personal Unconscious; and the underworld, the Collective Unconscious.

(The 'Personal Unconscious' is the Jungian term, corresponding to the Freudian Subconscious; Freud did not recognize the Collective Unconscious. Jung's terminology is becoming more generally used by occultists and Pagans, as it is far more in tune with their outlook.)

In ancient Greek mythology these three worlds are referred to as Olympus, Earth and Hades. Greek myths are complex 'psycho-dramas,' stories outlining the nature of the human mind. Modern psychology names many mental conditions after characters from these myths— Oedipus complex, Electra complex, etc.

Christianity perverted the concept of the underworld, turning it into Hell, a place of retribution and terror.

In the Brythonic Celtic and Druidic tradition these three worlds are joined by one other, visualized as four concentric circles (see Fig. 3). The center is Annwn, the underworld.

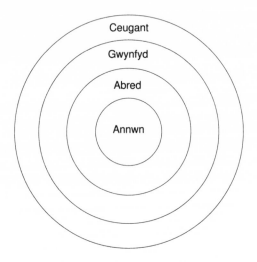

Fig. 3—The Celtic/Druidic Worlds.

In his poem *Preiddeu Annwn*, Taliesen talks about having to cross the sea to reach Annwn. The belief in having to cross water to reach the underworld is common in many myths, Water being seen to represent the unconscious mind. (In Greek myth this is the River Styx.) The next realm from the center is Abred, the middle world of struggle and evolution. It is in the upper world that the Celtic/Druidic cosmology differs, splitting it into two distinct realms: Gwynfyd, the realm of purity and attainment, and Ceugant, which in Bardic tradition is the abode of

God. This division is very similar to one that occurred in Norse mythology, their upper realm being Asaheimr (the equivalent of Gwynfyd) with the addition of Odin's throne, Hlindskjalf (of Ceugant). In Jungian psychology this is referred to as the Superconscious. .

To the three worlds were added a further four elemental realms, Earth (or in Norse, Ice), Air, Fire and Water, associated with the four cardinal points, normally from very practical reasoning. In northern Europe the south is associated with Fire because of the position of the Sun at midday, but in the southern hemisphere it would be seen as in the north. Water was associated in Europe with the West because of the Atlantic Ocean. Similar reasoning is applied to the other two elements; the East with Air because of the eastern winds, and the North with Earth because its fertility is nourished by the facing Sun.

The elements are seen to interact with the other three worlds—in the middle world by the physical manifestation of the elements, in the underworld by the creation of elemental spirits, while in the upper world they make up the element of Spirit and allow it to manifest in the middle world.

In Irish Celtic culture, these four elemental realms where referred to as the cities of Falias (North), Gorias (East), Finias (West), and Murias (South). Since the arrival of Christianity in Ireland, the upper world has became associated with Heaven and the underworld is commonly referred to as 'the otherworld,' the original Celtic names being lost.

The most complete example of all these magical realms combined is the Norse Yggdrasil, the World Tree—see Fig. 4.

Yggdrasil consists of the seven worlds we have already mentioned, plus a further two making nine (these two realms probably belonging to the original pre-Indo-European 'fairy' culture). The central axis consists of the uppermost realm, Asgardhr, the abode of the Gods and consciousness; Ljossalfheimr, the realms of the Light Elves and the intellect; Midgardhr; the abode of man; Svartalfheimr, the realm of the Dwarves and emotion; and finally Helheimr, the underworld, the abode of the Goddess Hel and the Unconscious. These five worlds are considered to make up the axis of consciousness. Midgardhr is visualized as having the four elemental worlds revolving around it, making up the physical realms. These are Nifilheimr, Ice and matter; Jotunheimr, Air and motion; Vanaheimr, Water and balance; and Muspellheimr, Fire and energy. For further reading on this we would recommend Edred Thorsson's *Runelore*.

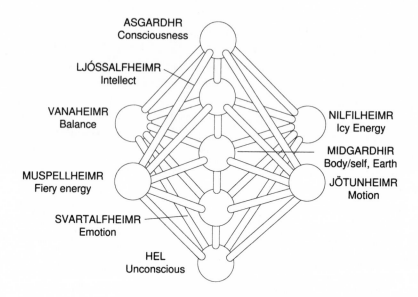

Fig. 4—Yggdrasil, the World Tree.

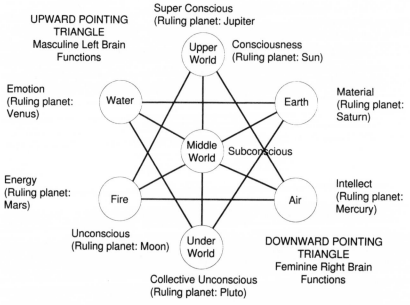

Fig. 5—the Seven-World Cosmology.

This model is used by many who follow the Asatru path, and is a complex evolved system on a par with the Cabala. (We have omitted the Cabala from this section, since it is more of a philosophical model than a true magical cosmology. The Cabala we know today developed from a fusion of Christian, Islamic and Judaic philosophy in recent times; see p. 67 for more on the Cabala.).

Fig. 5 illustrates the seven-world cosmology. We have included planetary correspondences so that it can be easily applied to any magical workings.

How Magic Works

Magic can be seen as working because of the interaction of these worlds; Shamans descend from the middle world (the Personal Unconscious) into the underworld (the Collective Unconscious). In the Wiccan rite of Drawing Down the Moon, the Goddess descends from the upper world (the Superconscious) into the middle world, the body of the Priestess, via the Collective Unconscious, which is where deity-forms (in Jungian terms, 'numinous archetypes') are contacted.

Symbology is the key to any form of magical working; it is the language of communication between the levels. Human speech-language itself derives from the representation of concepts and ideas by the use of sounds as symbols. In dreams our Unconscious communicates with us directly through symbology, and a lot can be learned about oneself from interpretation of them. Divination is based on this principle; interpreting symbols which emerge from our Unconscious by the use of Tarot, Runes or other systems.

In magic, symbols are used to access and communicate directly with the various levels. Most magical traditions have developed complex systems of correspondences, which link human-evolved concepts with aspects of the material world. Colors, sounds, plants, animals, types of wood, symbols of particular cultures (e.g. Runes or the Hebrew alphabet), and magical tools are all to be found on correspondence tables. They are not powerful in their own right; it is their effect on the mind (Conscious or Unconscious) which is.

The elements themselves are used as symbols to represent psychological aspects: Earth is equated with the material world, Air with the mind and the intellect, Fire with energy, and Water with emotions. In traditional European forms of magic the combination of these four elements was believed to produce Spirit; this is represented by the

equal-armed cross used by the Celts and the Norse, the center representing Spirit being formed by the elements which were the four arms.
In both cultures, the cross is bound together within a circle to emphasize
its strength and coherence—see Fig. 6.

Correspondences related to all the four elements are sometimes
mixed in magical practice to produce an elemental thought form. This
can be seen as the fusion of the four elements in the underworld
(Collective Unconscious) to produce Spirit on the middle world (the
Material Plane).

Fig. 6—Celtic and Norse equal-armed cross.

In case you find this variety of concepts of worlds and realms and
cosmologies, and systems of symbology, bewildering, you should
remember that in essence they all express the simple principle we stated
at the opening of this chapter: that magic depends on multi-level reality,
and on understanding and using the laws of interaction between those
levels. How those levels are symbolized depends on the history, traditions, and environment of the culture or 'path' concerned, but the
principle is the same. Whichever system suits you is a matter of personal
harmony.

Spells

A 'spell' is the commonly accepted name for a magical action
performed for the achievement of a specific result. It is simply one form
of the science of magic as defined above. It is the manipulation of
symbology to access the Unconscious (in personal workings to change
oneself) and the Collective Unconscious (the 'library' of archetypes) to

change the material situation. The realms worked in are therefore the Middle World and the Underworld. Spells have always been associated with witches, and it is still one of the major forms of magic practiced in Wicca.

Symbology in spellcraft differs according to paths. Talismans and charms can be considered types of spells. In the Northern tradition and Asatru, the terms Taufr and Galdr are used. Taufr is the employment of Runes to produce talismans. This is sometimes done by combining several Runes to produce a Bindrune. Galdr is the use of verbal incantations; again Runes may be used to reinforce them.

The morality of spell-working is simple: no one must be harmed. A warning to those who are tempted otherwise—a psychic attack which comes up against a stronger defense is liable to recoil on the attacker, in what is known as 'the Boomerang Effect'; and this is true not only when the intended victim is experienced in psychic self-defense. Many people with no psychic knowledge or training at all have naturally protective 'psychic skins,' just as some people are more resistant to germs and viruses than others. Such intended victims are liable to throw back an attack without even knowing that it has been made.

The practical rules for successful spell-working are as follows:

1. Before you start, define the effect you want to achieve very exactly, in as foolproof a way as you would in drawing up a legal document; have that definition clear in your own mind, and maintain it there determinedly during your working.

2. Devise appropriate symbology, whether mental or physical or both, for your ritual. This will link the power of the Unconscious to your action. Physical objects—such as a photograph of someone you are working to help, or an open umbrella when you are working to end a drought, or a computer keyboard when you are working for a corresponding job—have no power in themselves; their power is in the vividness of purpose they can arouse and maintain in your mind.

3. If you are working in a group, make absolutely sure that every member of it is clear about the purpose and the symbology, so that there are no weak links.

4. When all this is ready, work in a secure and uninterrupted environment; if it is your custom, work within a Magic Circle.

5. Make yourself calm, and declare the exact purpose out loud (whether you are alone or leading a group). Always include a phrase like 'provided it harms nobody'—and *mean* it.

6. Finally, raise all the power you can. Dancing or drumming often helps here—either solo, or if you are a group, by ring-dancing hand in hand.

7. When you feel the power is at its peak, launch it (if in a group, by the leader crying '*Now!*') and then immediately relax, telling yourself confidently that the object has been achieved.

Libations

These can be considered a form of supercharged prayer; as such they have always been associated with religious, rather than magical, practice. Libations can be found in all European Pagan cultures. This is attested by the number of shrines or offering-places which have been Christianized, with the God or Goddess being replaced by a saint. It is still commonly practiced in other parts of the world, particularly in Hinduism and Shinto.

A libation consists of making an offering to an aspect deity and asking for help. The practitioner is attempting to contact the deity (who is resident in the upper world) directly from his own Unconscious (the middle world). For example, someone whose path is Egyptian might make an offering to Thoth (a God of Wisdom and Learning) for help with an exam—say by burning a piece of parchment asking for this in a magical script. Concentrating the mind on writing out a magical script such as Theban or Runes helps the message to be absorbed by the Personal Unconscious. The petitioner would then leave an offering of fruit or wine.

It can be considered one of the most ethically safe forms of magical practice, the aspect deity deciding whether to grant the request. Your wish is based on subjectivity; the deity will normally give you what you need, rather than necessarily what you ask for.

In America, libations should not consist of pouring alcohol on to the Earth, for the reasons given on p. 150.

Raising Energy

A Wiccan form of this (also used by some shamanic paths) is referred to as 'raising the Cone of Power.' It consists of using the auric body (see p. 80) to throw energy at a desired goal.

Normally this involves a group rather than an individual, and consists of dancing, circling and/or drumming quite rapidly. It has the effect of opening the Chakras (see p. 78) and expanding the group's auras to the limits of the Magic Circle, which has been cast to prevent the energy from dissipating into the environment, rather than just for protection.

All these principles, plus many contemporary and historical examples, are dealt with in depth in Janet and Stewart's book *Spells and How They Work* (see Bibliography).

Divination

Most Pagans practice divination in one form or another; and most other people regard this as 'magic.' In a sense they are right, because divination is one of the phenomena which depend on the interaction between levels of reality.

Divination can be divided into various categories, and individuals may be naturally gifted, or capable of being trained, in one or more of them. For example, *precognition* is the gift of foretelling likely future events or developments. We say 'likely,' because in general Pagan thinking, the future is probability rather than fatalistic certainty, and precognition can help one to modify it.

Psychometry is the ability to handle material objects and discern their history and the psychic 'charges' they have accumulated.

Telekinesis is the ability (whether deliberate or involuntary) to move physical objects by psychic energy alone, without touching them. When it is involuntary, it can be a nuisance requiring control. For example, we have known more than one person whose very presence in a room tends to cause interference on a television set, or the burning-out of light bulbs. Children at puberty are particularly prone to cause such phenomena, and are the commonest cause of what is generally called *poltergeist* activity. Telekinesis is one field which intelligent scientists have been investigating—a classic example being the Soviet scientists' rigorous investigation and confirmation of the remarkable abilities of the Leningrad housewife Nelya Mikhailova. Nelya succeeded, for example, in separating the yolk and white of an egg by mental concentration, while she was two meters away strapped into monitor apparatus.

Clairaudience is the ability which some people have to hear psychic phenomena manifesting as sounds or words. *Clairsentience* is the tendency to be aware of such phenomena as physical pressures or touching. *Clairvoyance* is usually taken to mean general psychic awareness, but it can be used more specifically to mean the tendency to see psychic phenomena manifesting in visual form.

Divination, in the narrower sense, is taken to mean what many people call 'fortune-telling.' Pagans on the whole dislike this description, because it tends to be associated with people seeking assurance of the imminent arrival of the 'tall, dark, handsome stranger,' etc., etc. Genuine divinators sense the direction in which a person is moving, and give encouragement or warnings as may be necessary. This sensing can often include remarkably detailed flashes of precognition, such as the possibility of a car accident in vividly identifiable circumstances which the person can be warned to avoid or be on the alert for—flashes which time and again prove to be accurate, enabling the person to handle the emergency when it arises.

Practitioners of divination often use what may be called 'tools' to aid them, much as Grandma used to use tea leaves. This is not superstition, but a method of triggering communication between the intuitive Unconscious and the conscious mind—and it works. In a way, it is similar to the diagnostic use by psychologists of Rorschach ink-blot pictures for such triggering.

There are many such tools, but the most widely used ones are the crystal ball or black mirror, the Tarot, the I Ching, and the Runes.

The Crystal Ball or Black Mirror

Both of these are means of disconnecting and defocusing normal vision so that unconscious and intuitional awareness can manifest in visual form—'clairvoyance' in the strictly literal sense. Like all means of divination, they call for complete relaxation in quiet surroundings to be fully successful. Truly gifted divinators become skilled at interpreting the visual images which appear to them.

The black mirror is usually a slightly concave one, easily made by obtaining as large a clock-glass as possible (clockmakers sell them) and spraying it with matte black paint on the *convex* side.

Both the ball and the mirror are normally held in a widely-spread black velvet cloth, to cut out peripheral vision.

The Tarot

The Tarot is a deck of 78 cards, from which the ordinary playing cards have evolved. It consists, like the ordinary deck, of four suits, though with an extra court card: Ace to Ten, Page, Knight, Queen and King. The suits correspond to the four elements, and are variously named, but most usually as Pentacles (corresponding to Clubs) for

Earth, Cups (Hearts) for Water, Wands (Diamonds) for Air, and Swords (Spades) for Fire—though in some traditions the allocations of Air and Fire are reversed. These suits are known as the Minor Arcana.

The other 22 cards, which have disappeared from the ordinary deck, are known as the Major Arcana. The most general names for them, numbered from 0 to 21, are the Fool, Magician, High Priestess, Empress, Emperor, Hierophant, Lovers, Chariot, Strength, Hermit, Justice, Wheel of Fortune, Hanged Man, Death, Temperance, Devil, Tower, Star, Moon, Sun, Judgment, and World. They represent basic concepts, or what Jung called *numinous archetypes*. The only one which has survived on the sidelines, so to speak, of the ordinary deck is the Fool, who is doubtless the origin of the Joker.

After shuffling and cutting, a given number of cards are laid out face upwards in any one of various patterns—a typical one being that of the ten Sephiroth (Spheres) of the Cabalistic Tree of Life (Fig. 7).

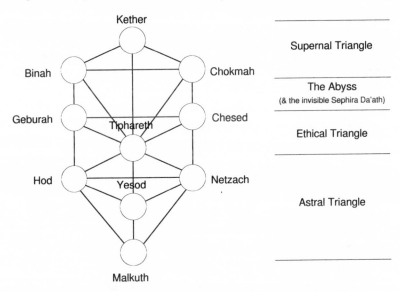

Fig. 7—The Cabalistic Tree of Life, with its 32 Paths.

The 22 traditional connections (themselves allotted to the Major Arcana of the Tarot), plus the 10 Sephiroth (ignoring the invisible Da'ath) make up the 32 'Paths.' Each of the Sephiroth represents a particular aspect or concept, to which the card which appears in it can be related. If a card appears upside down, this is taken to mean either the opposite of its traditional meaning, or a potential still unrealized; the context will usually suggest which.

Interpretations of the 78 Tarot cards vary somewhat, but a clearly written book on their generally-accepted meanings—plus a selection of layouts—is Eden Gray's *A Complete Guide to the Tarot* (see Bibliography).

It should be added that experienced Tarot readers find themselves developing personal interpretations of individual cards. These may differ from another expert's, but both may be perfectly valid. The mysterious principle of synchronicity seems to attune the 'random' dealing of cards to the concepts developed by the person using them. In the same way, the visual symbolism of the many Tarot decks available may differ from the 'standard,' some of them considerably so; but the particular deck with which a consistent reader feels at home becomes valid for him or her.

The I Ching

The I Ching (pronounced '*Ee Ching*,' not '*Eye Ching*'), or Book of Changes, is a Chinese system of divination dating at least from the century before Confucius, which has become increasingly used in the West. It is based on the complementary interaction between the Yang (masculine) and Yin (feminine) principles, and consists of 64 'hexagrams' of six lines each. The Yang lines are unbroken, and the Yin lines have a gap in them. To take an example at random, this is Hexagram 21, called Shih Ho (Biting Through):

```
 ————————
 ————  ————
 ————————
 ————  ————
 ————  ————
 ————————
```

The lines are numbered from the bottom up, and there are traditional interpretations both for the hexagram as a whole, and for each line—in this case Yang in the first place, Yin in the second place, and so on.

The hexagram is selected in various ways; the oldest traditional Chinese way is a system of casting of yarrow stalks for each line in turn, but a more general one in modern times is the tossing of three coins, with heads counting as 2 and tails as 3—so the total can be 6, 7, 8 or 9. A score of 7 gives a Yang line, and 8 a Yin line, while 6 gives a 'moving' Yin line and 9 a 'moving' Yang line. The purpose of this is to give a second hexagram, in which the 'moving' lines have been changed Yin for Yang, or Yang for Yin. The first hexagram gives the present situation, while the second indicates its potential development.

It sounds complicated, but it is straightforward in practice.

Unlike the Tarot, there is no variation of interpretations; they are expressed in ancient Chinese metaphor. To take Hexagram 21 again as an example, these are:

THE JUDGMENT
Biting Through has success.
It is favorable to let justice be administered.

THE IMAGE
Thunder and lightning:
The image of Biting Through.
Thus the kings of former times made firm the laws
Through clearly defined penalties.

Each line is then interpreted; the Yang in the first line, for example:

His feet are fastened in the stocks,
So that his toes disappear.
No blame.

The standard, and by far the best, book explaining these historic metaphors in modern terms is the Richard Wilhelm translation, I Ching, or Book of Changes (see Bibliography). The above translations of the Hexagram 21 meanings are taken from it. It has a Foreword by Carl Jung, which is most enlightening on the question of synchronicity, and the principles by which the apparently random selection of I Ching hexagrams (or Tarot cards) produces results which are relevant to the question asked—a process with which all experienced divinators are familiar, but which continues to puzzle cynics.

A typical example of this process occurred when Stewart devised a computer random-function program to produce I Ching hexagrams and the second hexagrams to which they moved. He wondered if this method was valid—so he used it to ask the I Ching. The answer which came up clearly meant 'It is valid for you because you are in tune with it, but it is not necessarily valid for everybody,' which seemed fair enough.

The Runes

The Runes were the ancient alphabet of the northern European peoples, varying slightly from area to area; for example, the Anglo-Saxon alphabet was not quite the same as the Norse. Fig. 8 shows the Elder Futhark Runic alphabet, one of the commonest found.

Each letter or Rune had a particular symbolic significance, so the Runes are still used today for divination. Marked on separate small pieces of stone or wood, they are cast randomly, and experience shows that the pattern of meanings which emerges follows the same principle of synchronicity as applies to the Tarot or the I Ching.

A set of Runes can vary from 16 to 34 'staves,' depending on the tradition and the time period they originate from. Each Rune consists of the stave (the symbol for that Rune), the meaning (the simple linguistic interpretation; e.g. The Rune 'Feoh' means 'Cattle'), and the more complex concept (Cattle were used by northern peoples as an expression of wealth, money and good material fortune).

Traditionally the Runes were thrown and then interpreted according to the position they fell in (this was sometimes based on the Northern tradition's magical cosmology, Yggdrasil). In recent times many users of Runes now have them picked out of their bag and positioned in a similar fashion to the Tarot.

Other methods

It should be clear by now that all these systems of divination depend on triggering the intuition and the unconscious knowledge of the practitioner, and that they invoke the mysterious but undeniable principle of synchronicity. The choice of system depends on the individual nature of the practitioner's psyche.

The validity of choice extends to whatever method suits that psyche—including such apparently simple practices as reading tea leaves. Alex Sanders, for example, used to read the froth left on a person's empty beer-glass, and Janet and Stewart have seen him do it with remarkable accuracy.

It is the natural gifts and experience of the divinator that matter, not the method.

FEOH (F): "Cattle"
Wealth, prosperity, success

UR (U): "Aurocha"
Strength, persistence, initiation

THORN (TH): "Thorn"
(Originally Thor?)
Protection from folly

ANSUR (A): "Mouth"
Communication from the Gods,
inspiration

RAD (R): "Cartwheel"
Travel

KEN (K): "Torah"
Casting light on a situation

GEOFU (Hard G): "A Gift"
Exchange of energy, of love, etc.

WYNN (W): "Joy"
Happiness

HAGALL (H): "Hail"
Realism: Adaptation to
unchangeable facts of life

NEID (N): "Necessity"
Patience: Do the right things,
and hold on

IS (I): "Ice"
Delay; cooling off, fading
relationship; disloyalty

JARA (J): "Year, Harvest"
Legal matters: professional
judgment; fruition or its delay

YR (IR or E): "Yew Tree"
Defense against danger;
improving situation

PEORTH (P): "Dice Cup"
Divination; unknown coming to light
(usually beneficial)

EOLH (Long E): "Elk"
Hunting; willing sacrifice;
protection; Freye's necklace

SIGEL (S): "Sun"
Victory over evil; advises against
tension and worry

TIR (T): "The God Tir"
Motivation, strength of will;
reformer, activist, enthusiasm

BEORC (B): "Birch Tree"
Birth, mother & child, project in
early stages

EOH (Short E): "Horse"
Journey; sound tackling of a
problem, often with help

MANN (M): "Mankind"
Interdependence; also balancing
within oneself

LAGU (L): "Water"
Psychism, the Unconscious; art,
music, imaginative writing

ING (NG): "The God Ing"
(Anglo-Saxon form of Frey)
Fertility, birth, new ideas

DAEG (D): "Day"
Growth, increase; discovering a
new philosophy

OTHELL (O): "A Possession"
Wealth; work; single-minded
person (good or bad sense)

Fig. 8—The Elder Futhark Runic alphabet.

Astrology

Interest in astrology, among Pagans and non-Pagans alike, is more widespread than ever. Daily newspapers, magazines, and various television programs have their resident astrologers.

Thoughtful Pagan opinions on it vary. Some accept it absolutely; others, including ourselves, are satisfied that there is 'something there' (for example, Janet and Stewart are both first decan Cancer, Janet with Scorpio rising and Stewart with Libra, and Gavin is Capricorn with Pisces rising; and we have to admit that our personalities thoroughly match the traditional interpretations thereof), but wonder if some of the small print of the 'science' has not been overstretched.

One thing we would say confidently, however: Gifted astrologers are basically divinators; they take the charts of their subjects as a trigger for their intuitional judgment, and often produce very appropriate results.

The use of computers to work out the initial mathematics is thoroughly justified, as it is 100 percent accurate and takes a tiny fraction of the time that human calculation requires. Computer interpretation of the results is another matter, because it rules out the intuitional factor altogether.

And almost everybody must agree that the newspaper and television predictions—which say what is about to happen to one-twelfth of the human race in each sign—are best regarded as mere entertainment.

Numerology

This is a favorite, if somewhat indiscriminate, New Age obsession which is shared by many Pagans. But it has its serious and its dubious sides.

On the serious side, certain single-digit numbers, and the number 13 for example, do have real symbolic significance: the unity of 1, the complementarity of 2, the thesis-antithesis-synthesis nature of 3 (as well as its Triple Goddess associations), the frequent development of 3 into $3 \times 3 = 9$ (as with the Muses), the four-element significance of 4, the four-element-plus-Spirit significance of 5, and so on.

Archetypal groups of spiritual or magical significance are time and again traditionally 13 in number—Jesus and his disciples, King Arthur and his knights, Robin Hood and his men, for instance—almost always with an associated woman figure (the Virgin Mary, Guinevere, Maid Marian, etc.). This may symbolize the completeness of the Zodiacal year ruled by the Sun and complemented by the Moon. Strangely, although the woman figure (as in those three cases) has deep significance and importance, it is the number 13 and not 14 which is always quoted, as though she were not a single element so much as the womb embracing the whole.

When it comes to the numerological significance of the letters in a person's name, this certainly has meaning in the case of the Hebrew and Runic alphabets, in which each letter has its own precise symbology, and names could be deliberate formulae built from them; in Hebrew this was a frequent practice.

The letters of the Roman alphabet, however, have no individual symbolic significance at all (with the possible exception of X for the Unknown and A-to-Z for completeness). Roman alphabet numerology is based on this table:

1	2	3	4	5	6	7	8	9
A	B	C	D	E	F	G	H	I
J	K	L	M	N	O	P	Q	R
S	T	U	V	W	X	Y	Z	

The numbers of the letters in the name which a person habitually uses are added up, and if the total is more than 9 the digits are again added up—e.g. 32 becomes 5, 46 becomes 10 which becomes 1, and so on. This gives nine different supposed meanings to the name.

On this basis, Janet Farrar gives 4, Stewart Farrar gives 6, and Gavin Bone gives 8.

Frankly, we feel that this system is meaningless. It is entirely random, based on nothing more than the accepted sequence of the Roman alphabet, unrelated to any symbology—and its rigid result for any one name leaves no room for the operation of synchronicity.

Furthermore, for example, Janet's maiden name was Janet Owen, which gives 8. During her first brief marriage, she was Janet Ewer, which gives 2. Did her nature entirely change on marriage, from 8 to 2 and finally to 4? Stewart (and, we are sure, our good friend Victor Ewer) can happily confirm that it did not.

We suggest that numerology should be confined to those areas where it has genuine symbolical meaning.

8.

Healing

Psychic healing, widely practiced among Pagans, is based on the same acceptance of multi-level reality which we discussed in the last chapter—with reference to the particular nature of the human (and sometimes the farm or pet animal) biological phenomena.

Most Pagans are also interested in fringe medicine (herbalism, for example, has always been a witch specialty), but sensible ones do not reject conventional medical science. Pagans and witches have always taken advantage of the technology of the time—otherwise this book would not be being written on a computer. Gavin is a Registered General Nurse, and combines his technical experience with what his spiritual training has taught him—and in Janet and Stewart's 23 years of coven history, he is not the only one.

When a psychic healer is asked for work, the first question should always be: "What does your doctor say?"—and the work should support that, not sabotage it. All too often, people ask for psychic healing as a short cut, or because they are afraid of what the doctor might tell them.

Psychic healers, like doctors, are well aware of what is called 'the Placebo Effect.' For example, a friend may ask for healing work—the group may agree, and schedule it for their next Circle in a few days' time—and before the Circle is even held, the patient rings up full of gratitude for the improvement achieved. Wise healers will appreciate the effect of the patient's increased confidence, but will not take lazy advantage of it; they will go ahead with the work to justify and confirm it.

The practicing of the various branches of fringe medicine, from herbalism to aromatherapy, must always be thoroughly well-informed. Unfortunately, in many countries recognized qualifications for most of these branches do not yet exist or are in their infancy, so they can often be practiced without the patient having any way of checking whether the practitioner is truly expert. This places great responsibility on would-be practitioners; they must conscientiously study the particular field in depth before making use of it. Mere enthusiastic dabbling can be dangerous and unethical.

Every healing profession has a strong ethical code, which puts the patient's needs before anything else. The first ethic of healing for Pagans must be the same as for any magical work: 'An it harm none, do what thou wilt.' In other words, don't do anything unless you are competent and confident enough to do it, and are sure it will have no harmful effect. A good example of this is shown in *Egil's Saga*, an Icelandic manuscript written in the early middle ages. Egil, a Rune Master, is called to the bed of a sick girl. There he finds a rune stave (a form of spell) hidden under her bed. It had been carved by a boy with little experience in the runes, and it was obvious to Egil that these were making the girl's illness worse, so he immediately destroyed the charm:

> A man should not carve runes unless he knows how to read; it befalls many a man who is led astray by a dark stave. I saw on the whalebone ten secret staves carved, that have given the slender girl her grinding pain so long.

Ethics in psychic healing are by no means a modern invention. The ancient Greek Hippocratic Oath is still accepted as a model.

Secondly, never perform any type of psychic healing without first taking precautions to protect yourself. You put your own health in danger if you try to heal someone when you are, or have recently been, ill or run down. It is just as unethical to put yourself in danger; you have a responsibility to maintain your own health.

Thirdly, never heal someone without his or her permission. This may seem a strange ethic at first, but by doing so you are denying the free will of that person. You may also not know 'the full case history' as a nurse or doctor would say. Every medical practitioner takes a full case history of a patient for diagnostic reasons. This includes a social history which is vital for correct diagnosis. The psychic healer and the alternative therapist should do the same.

A good example of this happened to Gavin. He was asked to do specific healing work in Circle for a frail old lady who was becoming increasingly ill. Gavin asked about her social situation, only to find out that her husband (whom she had loved deeply) had recently died. The old lady was in fact pining for her husband and wished to join him; she did not actually want to be cured. To work to cure her would have been cruel; Gavin and his Priestess therefore worked to free her of pain, rather than directly to prolong her life. She passed away peacefully.

The moral is simple; there are times when it is ethically wrong to cure someone. It is important to realize that psychically speaking, curing and healing are not necessarily the same thing. Curing may actually remove an ailment which is part of the healing process. A good example of this is giving patients a drug to reduce their temperature. In the past doctors would prescribe such drugs immediately. Now they are more careful, having realized that raised temperature is in many cases part of the healing process. Quite simply, curing is only about physically dealing with an ailment, while healing is about a holistic approach, taking into account the whole person's needs.

The holistic approach is now commonly taught to nurses, and becoming more widely accepted even by conservative elements of the medical profession. You are now more likely to find complementary therapies being practiced in hospitals and medical institutions. When Gavin worked as a nurse, they regularly used lavender essential oil in aromatherapy burners rather than expensive, potentially addictive, sedatives—with good effect.

For the Pagan, holistic practice is simply based around the Four Elements.

Earth represents the physical body. The healer must therefore aim for a good understanding of the systems of the body—the nervous, the cardiovascular, the gastro-intestinal, the endocrine, and finally the genito-urinary and reproductive systems. It is worrying how many Pagans do not have a grasp of how the human body works. We are not saying that every Pagan doing healing should spend hours studying anatomy and physiology, but a basic knowledge is essential. For example, masseurs must have a good understanding of the musco-skeletal system if they are to avoid doing further muscle damage.

Air represents the mental processes. Most Pagans who work magic have a basic understanding of psychology. The works of Carl Gustav Jung should be considered essential reading for those working in this element. The commonest type of healing in Air that Pagans perform is counseling. This normally takes the form of divination, particularly Tarot. Counseling is probably the most important aspect of divination. It is a skill, and has to be learnt and practiced. It is not just giving advice, but it is about making people aware of their options and allowing them to make their own decisions. In its simplest form it is answering a question with a question. It is certainly not telling someone what you think is best for them. An understanding of basic psychology and human nature is essential.

The emotions are governed by the element of Water. Again, knowing psychology and how to counsel is important. Sympathy is not always a good approach when dealing with the emotionally disturbed. Empathy is essential; knowing what that person is feeling. Holistic massage is based on empathy, and is often a good form of treatment, along with aromatherapy.

Fire represents people's drive, ambitions and goals. It also governs their social situation and, to a certain degree, how they interact with others in society. Social situation is considered to be an important factor by the medical profession in maintaining good health and diagnosing illness. For the healer, an understanding of sociology—how social relations work—is required, and an understanding of the basic needs of people. In psychology, a model exists which represents an individual's needs: Maslow's Triangle. It consists of a triangle divided horizontally into four compartments. The base compartment represents essential needs; food, warmth and shelter. The second compartment up, emotional security. The third, self-esteem. Finally, the apex compartment, goals and ambitions, which of course a healthy person never reaches, as new ambitions are continually being created. Any imbalance results in the triangle collapsing—in other words, ill health.

The final element (or balance of elements) is Spirit. Spirit represents the soul, and also the totality of all the other elements. It is the element that psychic healers are concerned with—unfortunately sometimes excluding the importance of the element of Earth, just as conventional Western medicine excludes the element of Spirit. The holistic system is based on the importance of all of the elements in combination; no element is more important than another. For example, as we have already mentioned, massage (the manipulation of the physical body, the element of Earth) can be used to soothe the emotions (the element of Water). Study of the element of the Spirit is probably the most fascinating, including the study of the aura and the Chakra system.

The Psychic Body

Most Pagan paths agree that the human body has a psychic aspect, consisting of power centers and the aura. How these are seen varies according to the tradition. Some paths see the psychic body as a microcosm of their magical cosmology; in Ritual Magic the first power center at the base of the spine is considered to be Malkuth, and the final center above the head to be Kether; both of these being Sephiroth (spheres) on the Cabalistic Tree of Life. In some modern Asatru teachings a similar process is applied to Yggdrasil, their magical model of the Universe. But the commonest accepted form used by Pagans is the Hindu Chakra system (which unlike the other systems does not relate to the macrocosm/microcosm philosophy). There is a common saying among occultists that you should not mix traditions, particularly the Western and Eastern mystery traditions. We would like to point out to people who feel that this system does not belong in Western Pagan practice, that if they look closely they will find that most of our traditions are of common Indo-European heritage.

The Chakra System

The Chakra system consists of seven psychic centers which start at the base of the spine and finish at the top of the head. See Fig. 9. The word 'Chakra' is Sanskrit for 'Wheel.'

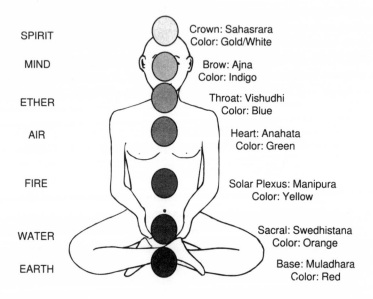

Fig. 9—The Chakra System.

To a psychic sensitive, the Chakras can be perceived as pulsating, spinning circles of light of various colors. Changes in color, particularly dulling and breaks in the continuity, indicate illness. Normally healers try to return the Chakra to its original luminescence, by visualizing and bathing the center in its proper color to heal any breaks. If the Chakra's color is violently bright, this usually indicates mental problems, and a calming color is used to rebalance. Diagnosis depends on the position of the center:

1. *The Muladhara.* This is at the base of the spine and is also known as the Root Chakra. It is the seat of the mystical Kundalini, the serpent fire, which the Eastern yogis attempt (though only with full understanding and control) to raise through the other Chakras to bring about psychic enlightenment. It is sometimes referred to as a Goddess. This Chakra is normally seen as rosy-red, and is governed by the element of Earth. If it becomes dull, it will normally be because the individual is run down by depression, fatigue and anemia. Over-coloration with violent reds and oranges will indicate violent emotions, such as rage and anger, and the inability to ground them. This center is then best balanced with soothing colors like turquoise.

2. *The Svadhistana.* This is the sacral center, and is positioned in the genital area. The color is orange and the element is Water. It has obvious associations with sexual love, and spiritual cleansing of those aspects which are no longer needed. Changes in its color and activity may indicate problems with the person's digestive, urinary and reproductive systems, and with vitality. Using green/blue light helps to soothe fears and inhibitions.

3. *The Manipura.* Placed in the solar plexus. The color is normally yellow. Because of its association with Fire, it is seen to be responsible for expansion and self preservation. It can indicate physical disorders such as infections, particularly colds and influenza, as well as circulatory problems. Over-brightness and activity can reveal the potential for mental exhaustion; soothing with violets and indigos should aid relaxation.

4. *The Anahata.* This is the heart Chakra. The color is green and the element is Air. This center relates to emotion. It can indicate circulatory problems, heart disorders, high blood pressure, or stomach ulcers. Negative emotions such as jealousy, envy, and greed can be resolved by the use of gold during visualization.

5. *The Vishuddhi.* This is positioned at the throat. The color is blue. It is related to the concept of Ether, and to communication. Dullness in color can indicate respiratory problems, including throat infections. Withdrawal and over-passivity can be healed by using clear blues.

6. *The Ajna.* This is the mystical third eye positioned on the brow. It rules the mind, and is well known for being the center associated with psychic experience. The color is violet. Like the throat center, it can be useful in the diagnosis of respiratory problems, particularly of the upper respiratory tract, mouth and sinuses. It also indicates problems with mental stress and proneness to headaches. Ego problems (particularly arrogance and conceit) can be grounded using gold and brown.

7. *The Sahasrara.* The final center, known as the Crown Chakra because of its position at the top of the head. It is the ultimate link with the person's astral body; it is therefore governed by Spirit. Its color is said to vary depending on the individual's spiritual development. It is visualized as white, which is made up of all the colors of the spectrum. In a spiritually developed person it becomes quite large, producing the classical halo effect. Breaks and discoloration can indicate lowered resistance to disease and problems with sleeping. Violent colors, such as scarlet, can be a result of over-excitement; duller colors, such as browns, of depression. Violets and purples are generally used for both, using a lighter color in the case of over-excitement and a darker, brighter color in the case of depression.

Opening and Closing the Chakras

Opening the Chakras is essential before any form of psychic healing involving direct contact. Many Pagans who work magic in a Circle, particularly raising the Cone of Power, find this quite easy, because activity such as dancing within the Magic Circle has the effect of opening them naturally. Shamans may use herbal preparations as well as dancing and drumming, but this can be potentially dangerous unless you know what you are doing.

The first stage is to find somewhere quiet and comfortable to sit. The best position to sit in is the well-known Lotus position, used in Eastern yoga, because it has the effect of bringing the Muladhara, or Root Center, into line with the other Chakras. If you are not supple enough to use this position, sitting cross-legged or kneeling will have the same effect; the important thing is to stay comfortable for a reasonable period.

The next stage is to breathe regularly. There are various breathing patterns used, but we have found that breathing out for seven seconds, holding for two seconds, breathing in for seven seconds and finally again holding for two seconds, is the most effective. It is important when breathing in to breathe from the base of the lungs, by expanding the stomach first, and then the ribs. It will take a while to get used to this, so give yourself time to master it. The next stage is to visualize that you are breathing in light. Initially this should be white light, before going on to the next stage.

Energizing the Chakras, one by one, is the third stage. Continue the breathing pattern that you began with; by now it should be natural and rhythmic. Visualize the Root Center at the base of the spine as a red, glowing, spinning ball. As you breathe in, visualize the color of that breath as the same, in this case red. This should have the effect, after several minutes, of making the Chakra expand while spinning faster and brighter.

Finally, imagine the energy from the center you have just energized moving up to the next Chakra (in this case the Sacral Center), but changing the color of the light you are breathing in, to that of the new Chakra (in this case yellow). Again it should take several minutes to energize the Chakra, which should behave in the same way as the first Center. You then simply repeat the process until you reach and energize the Third Eye or Brow Center. Then visualize all the colors from each of the energized Chakras to move swiftly up to the Crown Center at the top of the head. Allow the energy to leave the top of the head like a fountain and bathe your aura.

It takes about 20 to 30 minutes to use this exercise. We would recommend having somebody present, the first couple of times you do it, who is sensitive and able to see the Chakras; your helper can confirm when the Centers are open. With practice it takes less and less time to open your Centers, and you will eventually find you can discard this exercise completely and open them by willpower alone.

It is important to close your Chakras immediately when you have finished healing. Leaving them open can result in a loss of vitality, higher risk of disease, and mental stress. The easiest way to close them down is to eat. Most Pagans have a good 'Cakes and Wine' session after having their Chakras open in Circle, which closes them in minutes.

Another way, for people who are first learning to open their Centers, is an equally simple visualization technique. You visualize the energy draining back down from one Chakra to another. Once you have drained the energy from each Chakra to the one below it, you visualize a shutter closing it from vision. You repeat this Center by Center. When you reach the Root Center, remember that it is the only one you leave open all the time, because it acts as the body's grounding point and helps to prevent mental and psychic overload.

We have tried to provide a brief outline of the use of the Chakras and a simple user's guide. Basic visualizing techniques are easy to master, and safe for most to use. But the Hindu Chakra system is a complicated subject, and the ability to use its more subtle aspects may take years of study. Misuse of it, particularly the 'raising of the Kundalini,' is potentially dangerous.

The Aura

The aura surrounds the body and acts as a psychic shield, an interface and form of communication with other organisms. It can indicate the emotional and mental state of individuals, as well how spiritually developed they are. Every living organism has an aura, and with practice it is quite possible to see it. The easiest aura to see is that of a tree at dawn or twilight. It normally manifests as a misty gray field around the topmost branches. In human beings the part of the aura closest to the body is the easiest to see; again a gray misty area, about one to three inches wide, over the surface of the body.

In humans, the aura is generated by the action of the Chakra Centers spinning. The result is that three distinct areas exist within the individual's aura. The gray misty area closest to the body is generally referred to as the Etheric body. It is generated by the first four Chakra Centers, these being related to the elements of Earth, Air, Fire and Water. The action of these four Centers in conjunction with the fifth, Etheric, Chakra results in the formation of this part of the aura. It is therefore related to the physical condition of the body. Breaks in it may indicate recent physical injury, and these are easily detected by someone who is practiced at 'feeling' auras.

The second part is the Mental or Emotional body. It is generated by the sixth Chakra; the Brow Center or Third Eye. It is normally ovoid in shape, and how far it projects depends on the immediate mental and emotional state of the individual; in someone who enters a room full of strangers the aura will withdraw closer to the body. When that person feels more comfortable with the people around it will begin to return to its normal size. In an extrovert person it can project out as far as several feet, but in an introvert may remain always close to the body. A trained psychic sees this part of the aura as made up of a variety of colors. These, like the size of the aura, indicate the mental, emotional and occasionally the physical state of its owner.

The last, and the least easy for even a sensitive to see, is the Astral body. This connects with the last of the Chakras, the Crown. In a spiritually developed person it can extend from the body for some distance; it is said that the Astral body of the Buddha Gautama, in his last incarnation, could be seen for six miles. This part of the aura exists on the Astral plane, and is the individual's connection with the world of Spirit. It is in this, combined with the Mental/Emotional body, that the individual's consciousness moves during Astral travel in the higher planes; but during out-of-body experiences on the physical, material plane, it is only the Mental/Emotional section of the aura which detaches from the physical body. Because of the Etheric body's responsibility for continuing the life functions, it remains attached to the body until the moment of death.

Colors within the Astral and Mental/Emotional bodies can be useful in diagnosing illness and disease on a physical, mental, emotional and spiritual level. These colors are generated by the appropriate Chakras; hence the appearance of a violent red in the Root Chakra will be also seen in the aura. If this color is positioned over another Chakra, for example the Heart Center, it will therefore indicate aggressive emotions; if it is lower, over the Sacral Center for instance, it would indicate sexual aggression.

Below we have listed the colors that appear most in the aura, and outlined their use in visual healing techniques:

Red: Associated with strength, energy, and passion. Bright scarlet can indicate pride, greed and selfishness; if it is flashing, anger; positioned in the aura around the Root Center, nervous disorders. Intense red shows that the individual has been bending the rules magically, while rose-pink indicates somebody seriously smitten!

Orange: Relates to self-control, intellectual development and consideration for others. It can also indicate pride and ambition. Dirty orange can mean selfish motives. Physically, a healthy shade can show that the person is fit and full of vitality. A good color to use if an individual is physically run down.

Yellow: Like orange, related to intellect, but ability rather than development. A fresh yellow can show optimism and emotional well-being. A strong yellow can mean self-sufficiency, but a pale shade can mean the opposite, as well as weak will. In the spiritually well-developed, it can appear as gold, particularly around the head. Yellow in healing helps to invigorate the patient physically, emotionally and mentally.

Green: A sign of good health when around the lower Chakras; vibrant pale greens around the Brow and Crown Centers show that a person has natural healing abilities. Emerald shows versatility and easy adaptation to new situations, but gray and browny greens can show deceit and cunning. In healing, luminous blue/green is probably one of the most widely used colors because of its broad range of healing abilities.

Blue: Dark and clear blue indicates a high-minded and religious person; in the spiritually devoted it appears as a cobalt blue. Pale blue can show that the individual has not yet reached full potential spiritually. Blue combined with black appears in the aura of the religious fanatic, whereas combined with violet it shows affection and devotion. An excellent color to use in healing depression.

Violet: Relates to the individual's spirituality and psychic abilities, and normally shows wisdom. Ultra-violet appears when someone is highly developed psychically and spiritually.

Black, Brown and Gray: Generally these are all negative, and can appear combined with other colors. Black suggests hate and malice; and combined with scarlet, anger. With any of the other colors it can indicate negativity in the meaning. Brown is associated with avarice, but appearing with green it can mean that the person is in love; if scarlet is also present it can indicate jealous love. Gray is normally predominant in those with depression; with green present, it shows deceit.

Healing Techniques

Forms of healing using color visualization on the Chakric Centers and aura are generally referred to as 'the laying on of hands.' Here we give directions for two techniques: Chakric balancing and auric cleansing. These are the commonest forms in use by Pagans and spiritual healers.

The first stage in any form of healing is diagnosis. People seeking healing may of course be well aware of their infirmity, but many individuals may come forward because they feel 'run down' or 'low.' In both cases we would recommend that you refer to our sections on the Chakric Center and the aura; these will give you guidance as to which Centers to work on and which colors to use.

By the time you have reached this stage you should have mastered opening up your own Chakras. You will also need to be aware of which is your primary healing hand—the one which gives positive healing energy, while the other removes any negative diseased energy. One easy way to find out which is which is to clasp your hands together and then to see which thumb is on top. Normally this is the primary healing hand. Some healers find that if they repeat this exercise several times the thumb changes; this is not unusual, and means they can use either hand.

It is important to remember in both techniques to enter the patient's aura slowly, for your own protection. If you enter it too fast, you will not give your own aura time to prevent discharge of energy from your open Chakric centers.

Before beginning healing it is important to prepare properly. The first requirement is a warm, quiet room where neither you nor the patient will be disturbed. Many healers like to play appropriate music, which helps to relax both the participants, and to block out the noise of everyday life. The patient can either sit in a comfortable chair, or lie down. Many Pagans like to perform healing in Circle, perhaps with incense; this is not essential, but does give a feeling of security to aid the healer in his work.

Chakric Balancing

This form of healing consists of visualizing the appropriate colored energy and transferring it to the appropriate Chakra. You start by deciding which Center needs to be worked on, and which color you need to use; for example, if an individual comes to you complaining of problems with indigestion, the appropriate Chakra to work on will be the Sacral Center. The normal color of this Chakra is orange, but with digestive problems it will have faded or become dirty in appearance.

The first objective, in this case, will be to clear the center of its dirty appearance, by placing both hands over the Chakra and then visualizing clear light coming from the Crown Center down through your Heart Center, along your arm to your primary healing hand and into the patient's Sacral Center. At the same time you should visualize that you are removing the dirty energy with your other hand, and sending it down your body to be grounded in your own Root Chakra. Continue this until you can visualize the Center being a clear color.

The second stage is to restore the Chakra to its normal healthy color. Visualize vibrant orange coming up from your own Sacral Center, and as before, bring it down your primary healing hand into the patient's Sacral Center. Continue this until you can visualize it as a healthy orange.

It is advisable after any Chakric balancing to check and balance the patient's other Centers.

Auric Cleansing

This consists of removing from the aura any dirty energy which has collected in it (normally manifesting as black, browns or grays) and can be combined with Chakric balancing. It is particularly suitable for healing individuals under mental or emotional stress. The best Chakra to use is the Heart Center, visualizing green/blue light coming from it and down your primary healing hand.

Very slowly, move your hands into the patient's aura around the head, keeping your hands within the field of the Etheric Body, but without actually touching the patient. Start the flow of visualized light from your Heart Center into your primary healing hand, while at the same time removing any negative energy you feel with your other hand and grounding it through your Root Center. After a while you may actually wish to touch the patient, particularly if you can sense any deep-rooted negative energy; this is specially beneficial around an individual's forehead, helping to remove stress. Continue this, moving slowly down and using the same technique as for the head, until you reach the patient's feet. Covering the whole area of the body, you feel for breaks in the aura and heal them with the green/blue light that you were visualizing.

You may wish to concentrate on a particular area; for example, if a person has a headache, spend most of the time healing the area of the head. It is not unusual during healing to develop some of the patient's symptoms yourself; this indicates that your are not grounding the energy correctly. Remember to ground any negative energy that you pick up through your Root Chakra. Some healers also ground the energy by holding their hands under flowing water, or shaking the energy off during the healing process.

Herbalism

The use of herbs is common to all Pagan traditions, and is one of the oldest forms of healing known to man. Many of the drugs commonly prescribed by doctors originated as herbal preparations: Aspirin was discovered by the Druids, who scraped willow bark for its pain-killing salicylic acid; both foxglove and belladonna were prescribed by the village witch for heart complaints. Foxglove's Latin name is *digitalis*, and it is still prescribed by doctors as Digoxin, which slows and strengthens the organ's pumping action. Belladonna is prescribed in a similar fashion to the drug Atropine. (Both belladonna and foxglove should only be given in very small doses by someone who knows the exact amount—see other dangers on p. 89.)

In traditional herbalism, each plant was associated with a planet and a sign of the Zodiac. Many examples of this can be found in *Culpeper's Complete Herbal*, which for a long time was considered one of the best books on the subject, though now it should be used selectively. In many cases a herb's association with a planet or sign was based on its physical appearance—for example the orange-colored marigold was associated with the Sun. Many herbs are named after the parts of the body they were considered capable of curing; Liverwort for example, which because it had liver-shaped leaves was considered a remedy for illness of that organ. This belief, that plants which appear like a part of the body will heal that part, is not unusual in older forms of herbalism. Another belief was that the 'cure could be found near the cause.' Herbs which grew near water, for example, were used as diuretics to remove water from the lungs.

Very few modern Pagans practice these traditional forms of herbalism, although they may still pick healing herbs according to the Moon's phase or position of the planets. Herbalism has developed considerably in the past few decades, and can now be considered a medical science.

When picking herbs in the wild, many leave offerings—a typical practice of shamans, asking for the help of that herb's spirit. This offering may consist of anything from tobacco and colored stones, to a small amount of the picker's blood left on a leaf as an exchange of life energy. Nowadays it is not actually necessary to leave the city to obtain herbs; the commonest are readily available in health food shops. Growing herbs in your own yard is considered the easiest way of obtaining them, and of having a constant supply when you need it.

Herbal remedies can be prepared in several different ways: boiling and steeping the herb produces a tea-like infusion if it needs to be ingested; mixing the herb with beeswax and lanolin produces an emollient suitable to be applied externally to skin disorders; and immersing the appropriate herb in a bowl of boiling water produces an inhalant for chest disorders. The way herbs are prepared and administered depends on the herb itself and the illness concerned. Cough drops, gargles, throat syrups, liniments, lotions, pastes, tonics, and baths—the list is endless.

Here are some easy-to-follow examples taken from the *American Reader's Digest Magic and Medicine of Plants:*

Dandelion Leaf Tonic

This helps to stimulate appetite and cleanse the blood. It is traditionally given in the spring. You will need:

1–2 teaspoons dried dandelion leaves
1 cup boiling water

If you use fresh dandelion leaves, double or triple the amount (chop the leaves before measuring), rinse them thoroughly, and then pat them dry with a paper towel. Put the dandelion leaves in a teapot and pour the water over them. Let them steep for five minutes; then strain the tea into a cup. Let it cool until it is lukewarm. It is then ready to serve.

Marshmallow Root Cough Syrup

This preparation helps to ease a sore throat which accompanies a cold. You will need:

$1\frac{1}{2}$–$2\frac{1}{2}$ teaspoons chopped dried marshmallow root
2 cups water
2 cup of refined sugar
$\frac{1}{4}$ cup of orange juice

The orange juice helps to add flavor and prevents the syrup from crystallizing. Stir the marshmallow root into the water and bring it to the boil. Lower the heat and simmer for 20 minutes. Strain the decoction into another saucepan; you should have about a cup. Over the lower heat, gradually stir in the sugar until a thick syrup forms. Make sure the grains are fully dissolved. Add a little water if the mixture becomes too thick. Let the mixture cool slightly; then gradually mix in the orange juice. Pour the syrup into a sealable container and cover it when cool.

Peppermint Lotion

This externally applied lotion helps to relieve itching caused by insect bites, prickly heat and similar mild skin problems. You will need:

½ cup of water
½ cup of rubbing alcohol
3–4 drops of peppermint oil

Put the water and the alcohol in to a bottle you can cap tightly. Add the oil and shake well. Apply with cotton wool or clean sheeting.

In studying herbalism, one should distinguish carefully between British and American sources—whether books or friendly advisers. It is unsafe to assume that the same name means the same plant in Britain and America (or even in different parts of America). The safe thing to do is to learn the Latin names, which can be relied upon as international. For example, Pilewort in Britain and Ireland is a name for the Lesser Celandine, *Ranunculus ficaria*, an infusion of which is a very effective treatment for piles (hemorrhoids). What America calls Pilewort is Fireweed (known in Britain as Rose Bay), *Epilobium angustifolium*. Moreover, America has only one Celandine, *Chelidonium majus L.*, which is Britain's Greater Celandine—and to use it as a cure for piles would be disastrous. So international misunderstanding on herbs can be dangerous, and the facts should be carefully tracked down.

Many well-known herbs (e.g., belladonna and foxglove) are potentially dangerous if taken in large amounts; some are also known to contain cancer-causing agents. It is therefore important that you know the medical properties of a herb thoroughly before using it for the first time. One example is the use of sage grass for smudging (waving smoldering sage for ritual cleansing), which has become popular in Pagan practice over the last few years. It should not be used near a pregnant woman, as it has been known to induce a miscarriage.

For such reasons, some countries have felt it necessary to make it illegal to practice herbalism without a license.

Shamanistic forms of Healing

Shamanism is one of the few Pagan paths which have their own unique forms of healing. The main reason for this is that most Shamanistic philosophy sees illness as being caused by the presence of evil spirits or entities; their healing practices therefore center around the removal of this malign presence. Typical of this is Shamanic 'journeying,' in which the Shaman goes into trance to enter the Spirit or Underworld, where he 'does battle' with the evil Spirit which is manifesting in his client's body. We have found very few modern Shamans who actually use this technique, although it is still in common use in hunter-gatherer cultures around the world. Two of the commonest forms used involve the cleansing of the Etheric body.

Sucking out

Before beginning this procedure, a Shaman normally goes into trance to obtain the aid of a friendly plant spirit. After coming out of trance, he would then try to collect a sample of the plant that he saw. This is placed in his mouth before commencing the sucking.

Sucking out consists of lowering your mouth over the part of the body that has become 'inhabited' or ill, and sucking the 'intruder' or illness out into the Shaman's mouth (without inhaling it into his lungs). Sometimes a tube, decorated with power symbols and invocations, is used to make the job easier. The Shaman then blows the 'intruder' into a pot or a jar, which is afterwards disposed of.

From an auric point of view, what the Shaman is actually doing is sucking any negative energy (the 'evil spirit') out of the patient's Etheric body and into his own mouth, while trying to avoid absorbing it into his own Etheric body. Gavin has used this technique with some success, but has found that if you do not remove the negative energy from your own Etheric body, you end up with the same symptoms as the patient (on one occasion he ended up with period pains!). If you intend to carry out this technique we would therefore recommend that you ground yourself through your Root Chakra, as you would for any other form of auric healing. This also applies to our second example of Shamanic healing.

Etheric surgery

This is very similar to sucking-out except that you visualize your Etheric body around your hand entering your patient and removing the negative energy. There have been some very famous psychic surgeons over the years, including Arigo, who was known affectionately as 'the surgeon with the rusty knife.' A South American, he was famous for his ability to 'remove' diseased organs with his rusty penknife. During his operations blood would appear as well as the organ, but after he had finished there would be no wound. It is very likely that the appearance of blood and flesh were showman's tricks, but their is little doubt that his healing technique worked. Others are *not* recommended to try it.

If you are going to use Etheric surgery, it is important to visualize the cause of the illness strongly, and obey the rules we have given about entering the aura slowly. Once you have done this you should touch the patient over the site of illness and visualize your hand entering his or her Etheric body (this takes a lot of practice). You should then visualize that you are clasping your hand around the cause, and slowly removing it from the person's body. You should next go through the actions of disposing of the negative energy, such as rinsing your hands under running water, or ritually burying the energy in the soil.

You may also combine this technique with other forms of healing. You can visualize that you are soothing and massaging an area, while imagining you are bathing it in blue/green light. One illness this is useful on is asthma, when the breathing passages are inflamed and swollen, both of which it should ease.

We have given examples of healing which are normally associated with Paganism and Witchcraft. We have omitted the use of spells and magic in healing, otherwise we would have repeated much of the previous chapter. Many Pagans use other techniques, adopted from the Far East or the New Age, such as Shiatsu, Acupuncture, Holistic massage, Aromatherapy, Crystal healing etc. The Pagan philosophy behind any adoption is simple: if it works, use it!

9.

The Earth Our Mother

Paganism is the most environmentally conscious and active religion in the Western World. This is not to say that individual members and groups of other religions are not equally conscious and active on Mother Earth's behalf; but environmentalism is not a declared part of any other Western religion. In particular, the general monotheist dogma of a single life on Earth followed by the once-only reward or punishment of Heaven or Hell (or the pending-tray of Limbo) hardly encourages dedication to the Earth where that single life is supposed to be lived.

Modern Paganism's dedication to Earth is a direct inheritance from ancient Paganism. Virtually every pre-monotheist religion included an Earth Goddess in its pantheon, from the Greek Gaia to the Finnish Akka and from the Chaldaean Ningal to the Aztec Coatlicue. She even survived in the unorthodox Hebrew sect of the Essenes (see p. 40). She also appears in the Pagan religions still found in today's world, from the Hindu Privthi to the Chinese K'un and from the Tantric Ida to the Cherokee Elihino.

She is inseparable from the Pagan outlook. She is Isis Veiled, the Goddess robed in the multi-colored garment of Nature. She gives birth to us, nourishes us, and receives us back on death.

The Pagan concept of the Earth as a purposeful being received unexpected scientific support in 1975, when two distinguished British scientists, Dr. James Lovelock, FRS, and Dr. Sydney Epton, published the outlines of their Gaia Hypothesis, which was expanded into a book *Gaia: A New Look at Life on Earth* by Dr. Lovelock in 1979. It was based on two propositions:

1. Life exists only because material conditions on Earth happen to be just right for its existence.

2. Life defines the material conditions needed for its survival and makes sure that they stay there.

They produced a mass of evidence in support of the revolutionary Proposition 2. For example, Earth receives between 1.4 and 3.3 times as much solar energy as it did when life first started. Yet the heat-retaining atmospheric blanket has altered its composition at just the right rate to keep the Earth's surface temperature within the extremely narrow range, between about 15ºC and 30ºC, needed to sustain life. Not only the blanket's heat-retaining aspect: 'Almost everything about its composition seems to violate the laws of chemistry,' yet that composition has remained consistently life-supporting.

The Hypothesis cites a great deal of other factors—the salinity of the ocean, for example—which have remained within extremely narrow life-supporting limits contrary to all calculable probability.

From all this, Lovelock and Epton were forced to conclude that the Earth and its biosphere "seemed to exhibit the behavior of a single organism, even a living creature." It was this which inspired them to call their theory the Gaia Hypothesis, after the Greek Earth Goddess. They also concluded that in *homo sapiens* Gaia had developed the equivalent of a central nervous system and an awareness of herself and the rest of the Universe. "Through man, she has a rudimentary capacity, capable of development, to anticipate and guard against threats to her existence."

This could not be more in accord with the Pagan concept of the Earth Mother, and of human responsibility, as part of a two-way feedback for her health and survival.

Pagans emphasize this feedback ritually by celebrating the seasons and becoming one with other living creatures. They synchronize intimately with the planet, and liberate their personalities and enhance their perceptions and talents, in the interests of themselves, their groups and communities, and humankind as a whole. But active attunement with Nature is not merely a matter of personal development, ritual attunement, or an idealist fringe cult. At this point in the planet's history, it is vital to human survival—for two overlapping reasons.

First, humankind has become aware that industrial and technological development, plus the population explosion, have produced pollution on an unprecedented scale. Damage to the ozone layer, changes in the greenhouse effect, the decimation of the rain forests (the Earth's lungs), and the poisoning of the atmosphere, the land, and the rivers and oceans, are already having disastrous effects. Global warming, a steady rise in the sea level, and other factors are creating problems which will become catastrophic if they are not urgently and drastically dealt with. Human activity is straining the safe limits which Gaia has maintained for countless millennia.

Scientifically confirmed awareness of this has become a public issue worldwide. The politicians are alarmed by it—some responsibly, but even the most cynical of them realizing its growing electoral impact. Industrialists are aware of it—their advertising falling over itself to reassure the public that their products are environment-friendly.

The second reason is that great-power war has become, for the first time in history since great powers developed, unthinkable. Politicians and public alike know that it would be mutually suicidal, and would make much or all of the world's surface uninhabitable. It would wipe off the slate any hope of averting ecological disaster. Even localized non-nuclear wars, such as the recent pointless mutual slaughter between Iran and Iraq (which lasted eight years, cost a million lives, and left both sides exactly where they started), are regarded nervously by the rest of the world, who strive to contain them, or even to mediate to end them.

War today has become almost entirely a phenomenon of inter-communal strife—witness the tragic conflicts in dismantled Yugoslavia, or in several of the former Soviet Republics. These conflicts, all too often, have a religious basis—which makes it all the more vital to educate people away from the belief that a given dogma is 'right' and all others 'wrong,' and away from such barbaric concepts as 'ethnic cleansing.' (A sickening example in 1993 was when Magdalena Babicka at the Miss Czech-Slovak beauty contest, asked to state her ambitions, said she wanted to become a public prosecutor so that she could cleanse her city of all its brown-skinned inhabitants.)

Rejection of war as a solution to anything has, like the urge to oneness with Nature, ceased to be an idealistic dream; it has become a hard political necessity.

So has the Global Village. Economic and technological (not to mention communal) cooperation is the only possible future, and every sane politician, whether capitalist, communist, or whatever else, knows it.

Paganism has much to offer in this crisis, because two things are central to its philosophy: intelligent and intuitive harmony with Mother Earth, and mutual respect and feedback between the many differing cultures which inhabit her.

Oneness with Nature does *not* imply a naive 'back-to-Nature' attitude, throwing technological achievement and development out of the window. It implies using technology sanely, as a tool. It is modern technology, for example, which has greatly improved human health and life expectancy. It has made daily life in the advanced countries infinitely more comfortable and less dominated by drudgery. It has made travel fast and convenient. It has made intercommunication between the peoples of the world instantaneous and vastly better informed; a dramatic example was the showdown in September 1993 between Russian President Boris Yeltsin and the hard-liners of Parliament, which the world watched hour by hour as it was happening. All this for the Western world at least, and there is increasing pressure to make it all equally available to the peoples of the Third World.

And after all, it is modern technology which has made it possible for us to detect and understand such phenomena as the damage to the ozone layer—and can make it possible to find ways of halting and even correcting them.

This does not, of course, negate constructive 'back-to-Naturism,' in the sense of relating our daily lives more and more to the natural world around us—and technology can help even here, for example by using modern communication to deurbanize much human activity, and greatly to reduce daily commuting to overcrowded cities for meaningless routine jobs which can be better handled by computer, freeing humans for genuinely human creativity. Even for meaningful jobs, personal computers and modems make it possible for many workers in various fields to work efficiently from home, instead of joining in such commuting.

Reorganizing economic, educational, and employment frameworks to meet the needs of this new situation calls for public awareness and pressure on governments for new attitudes. Pagans tend to be more aware than most people of the need for these new attitudes, and to be more active in encouraging them.

Mother Earth, then, is not a temporary stopping-place, but our home, of which we are a living part, and for the health and protection of which we bear a constant responsibility.

At the ritual level, this attitude is particularly reflected, as we saw above, in the emphasis on seasonal celebrations, which are specifically designed to put us in tune with the reality of the living Earth's annual cycle, rather than (as in Christianity, Judaism and Islam) based on the commemoration of real or believed events in the religion's history.

Their nature therefore varies considerably according to one's geographical environment; one does not, for example, greet the rebirth of the Sun in Australia at the end of December (see p. 181 on this). Pagans worship Gaia—the Goddess in her Earth-Mother aspect—as She is where they are. Christianity, for example, loses much by imposing identical seasonal festivals on Eskimos and Zulus; and Judaism and Islam's annual festivals are tied to an out-of-date calendar, so that they shift in actual date from year to year and have completely lost touch with the cycle of Nature which was their original foundation.

The actual dates of Pagan seasonal celebrations have been generally accepted from the Wiccan tradition. In Wicca, they are known as Sabbats (ordinary working Circles apart from these are called Esbats). They are divided into the Greater Sabbats (Imbolg, Beltane, Lughnasadh and Samhain) and the Lesser Sabbats (the Solstices and Equinoxes). The calendar (in the northern hemisphere) is as follows:

Imbolg (February 2). This is a Gaelic word meaning 'in the belly'— the first stirrings of life in the womb of Mother Earth—and it should be pronounced 'im-OLL'g.' It coincides with the Christian Candlemas, and is sometime so called by Pagans.

Spring Equinox (March 21). Essentially, the moment of balance—of the changeover from Winter rest to Summer activity.

Beltane (April 30). Also known as May Eve. Celebration of the beginning of Summer; it was also the beginning of Summer in the Celtic two-season year, when cattle were taken up to the Summer pastures. Beltane derives from the Gaelic word for May (Bealtaine, pronounced 'b'YOLL-tinnuh,' meaning 'the fire of the God Bel'), but it has been an English word for centuries, and the English form is the generally accepted one.

Midsummer (June 22). A festival rich in Pagan folklore survives in many countries. In Ireland, for example, it is celebrated on St. John's Eve, June 24, because that is the night when, in the country, bonfires can be seen from horizon to horizon; often cattle are driven over them, or between two such fires, to protect their health for the coming year. (The same tradition is often also practiced at Beltane.)

Lughnasadh (July 31). Means 'the Festival of Lugh,' the Celtic Young God of Many Arts, and pronounced 'LOO-na-sa.' Lugh is a Celtic God (the county where we lived for some years, County Louth, is named after him) but not confined to Ireland; Lyon in France, Leyden in Holland, and Legnica in Poland were all named after him, as was Roman Carlisle (Luguvalium). At this harvest season, he represents the sacrificed-and-reborn Corn God—a concept with folk custom survivals all over the world.

Autumn Equinox (September 21). Again, the moment of balance— but this time of the changeover from Summer activity to Winter rest.

Samhain or Hallowe'en (October 31). The eve of November 1, the old Celtic New Year; Samhain (pronounced 'SOW-en'—'sow' to rhyme with 'cow') is the Gaelic name for November. At this time the cattle were brought down to the Winter pastures, which could not support all of them, so many were slaughtered and salted to preserve them as Winter food. A time for feasting, and for inviting the spirits of dead friends to be present. Folk traditions for this festival were so powerful that the Church had to Christianize it as All Saints; but the traditions survived, even if only in a 'trick or treat' form. Pagans still observe it in the old terms.

Yule (December 22). Throughout the northern hemisphere, the Winter Solstice has been celebrated as the rebirth of the Sun—a tradition so naturally entrenched that the Church in 273 AD named it as the birthday of Jesus, undated in the Gospels. Pagan Yule rituals enact the Sun's rebirth, though as Christmas has become for most people a family celebration and an occasion for exchange of presents, with many surviving Pagan elements (such as the Christmas tree, which is pure ritual magic, decorating an evergreen tree with symbolic flowers and fruit), most Pagans tend to join in that as well—and why not?

The above cycle, of course, belongs to the northern hemisphere. In Australia and elsewhere south of the Equator, Pagans have been working out their own cycle, on the principle of relating to Gaia 'as She is where you are' (see p. 181).

Also, many Pagan religions and paths have special cycle-of-the-year festivals of their own. For example, the Odinic cycle is based on the Moon, shifting from year to year; for 1994 it included:

Snowmoon (January). 17th—Charming of the Plow; Festival of Labor.

Horning (February). 14th—Vali; Festival of the Family.

Lenting (March). 20th—Eve of Summer Finding; Festival of Law, Justice and Mercy.

Ostara (April). 23rd—Sigurd; Festival of the Homeland. 30th—Walpurgis; May Eve.

Merrymoon (May). 1st—May Day. 22nd—Ragnar Lodbrok; commemoration of the Vikings. 29th—Oak Apple Day.

Fallow (June). 20th—Eve of Midsummer; Festival of Balder.

Haymoon (July). 26th—Sleipnir; Festival of Life.

Harvest (August). 29th—Harvest Monday.

Shedding (September). 20th—Eve of Winter Finding; Festival of Harvest End.

Hunting (October). 12th—Hengest; Festival of Settlement.

Fogmoon (November). 1st—Heimdal. 11th—Einheriar; Heroes' Day. 23rd—Wayland Smith; Festival of Metal Craftsmen.

Wolfmoon (December). 20th—Modranecht; The Mother Night, Eve of Midwinter; The Twelve Nights of Yule. 31st—The Twelfth Night.

(This list was taken from *Rimstock 1994*, a British annual Odinist calendar.)

Pagans are dedicated environmentalists, in their daily lives and in their public campaigning.

On this basis, many Pagans are vegetarians; but there are differing views on this subject. Some Pagans maintain that humans are omnivores, and as such part of the balance of Nature; but even they insist on decent treatment of creatures destined for the pot, humane killing, and the banning of such unnatural methods as imprisoning calves for life in crates to produce veal, or hormone feeding which can distort animals' natures, often to the point of suffering.

There is much Pagan dispute about those religions, such as Santeria, which practice ritual animal sacrifice. Some find this completely unjustifiable, while others point out that the sacrificed animals are eaten, and (unlike those in butchers' abattoirs) are ritually honored at the time of sacrifice, adding that this is also the essence of Jewish kosher slaughtering. The dispute is intelligently examined on p. 3 of the Autumn 1993 issue of the magazine *Green Egg*.

One point of view on this is expressed by our friend Wolf-Willi Boepple, a goat-farmer in British Columbia, who is closer to Nature than almost any Pagan we know. She writes:

> Humans who choose not to eat meat are in no way morally superior to the wolf or bear; to assume otherwise is just as arrogant as that of some 'factory farmers' that animals are soul-less commodities. These people view death as annihilation, and humans as so 'unnatural' that *any* partnership with an animal is exploitation. They do not recognize that WE are not completely free, either! Even the most atrociously-kept animal can lie down when it is tired, and that is one freedom which I for one envy greatly. Now: I am in NO WAY defending animal abuse or factory farming! I personally put my goats' needs before mine, consistently. I have seen all kinds of farms, and can vouch for the fact that many animals in 'captivity' enjoy the best of both worlds: meadows and forests to run in, yet safety from predation; their health is cared for, food and shelter provided for them. Many of these animals enjoy strong bonds of love and affection with their human caretakers. It is a personal belief of mine that these animals came to us willingly, out of a compassion so deep we cannot fathom it, knowing full well that many of their kind would be starved, abused, or tortured by humankind. You know, there are not very many wild animals who have traits that would make domestication feasible! I see it as a sacred trust, one which must not ever be abused. Tragically, it has been abused many times, in many places. But, ultimately, they could leave us if they really wanted to. They are NOT soul-less puppets, as the Rightists seem to think; they DO have choices, too. We can manipulate fertility and breeding to a certain extent, but we cannot FORCE them to live and breed, not really. Among other reasons, they are here to teach us respect and compassion and humility.

We would not agree with everything she says; for example, the vast majority of farming livestock do not 'come to us,' they are born as farm property, even when they are happy that way. And not all 'atrociously-kept' animals can choose to lie down—veal calves and battery hens cannot, for example. But in case anyone should think that some of her views are naive fantasy, having watched Wolf-Willi in professional action, we can confirm that she is as skilled and knowledgeable a farmer as one could wish to meet. And she certainly has a rapport with her goats; she can call any one of them by name out of a group at a distance, and that single goat will come to her.

The Ultimate is the creative life force of the Cosmos, but all manifestation is part of the total organism. Our own planet can be regarded as one limb or organ of it, and we ourselves (and all Earth's other creatures and components) as cells within that limb or organ. Our health depends on its health, and vice versa.

That total organism is seen as continuously evolving. Many other religions tend to regard the Cosmos as basically static, and confine their thoughts of progress to that of the individual soul. Paganism regards evolution as Cosmic, with constant mutual feedback between the Ultimate and its manifestation, including ourselves; the stage of an individual soul's progress is within the context of that of the Cosmos.

This belief colors one's own sense of responsibility. It is not enough to kneel down in passive obedience to the Ultimate—to say *inshallah* ('as God wills') to whatever happens. God (to give the Ultimate its usual name) requires more of us than that—namely, creative feedback, an unceasing effort to understand the nature and direction of Cosmic development (in our context, of that of Mother Earth) and to contribute to it.

This attitude determines the basic Pagan motivation: to be a dedicated part of the Terran evolutionary process, and to involve oneself wholeheartedly in carrying it forward by individual and communal feedback with the Source.

How far does this Source, the Creative Intelligence, intervene in the process of evolution and its smaller events? This can be discussed endlessly and interestingly, but most Pagans would agree that on the Cosmic scale, It has complex overall plans which It constantly moves to put into effect. On the smaller scale, detailed intervention depends on genuine reaching-out by humans (and certainly, throughout the Cosmos, by other intelligent and self-aware species); and again, most Pagans feel they have evidence of this. Divine intervention, though, can never be entirely one-way. Cosmic—and in our context, Terran—evolution is a living, continuing, and complex process, and must depend on feedback between manifestation and its Source.

Pagans would agree with Albert Einstein's statement: "God does not play dice with the Universe."

Humankind has a greater responsibility to the Earth than any other Terran species—not merely because our population explosion and industrialization has reached an environmental danger point, but because (as the Gaia Hypothesis puts it) in *homo sapiens* Gaia has developed 'the equivalent of a central nervous system and self-aware-ness.' In other words, we have ended up in the driving seat, and the rest of Nature are our passengers, without safety-belts. Few religions seem to recognize this staggering responsibility, though to be fair many of their believers do. But awareness of it is a keystone of Pagan philosophy.

The monotheist religions tend to have a static rather than an evolu-tionary attitude to the nature of Deity. An interesting example of this was a televised debate at Oxford University in October 1993, on the motion that since Evil exists, God cannot—proposed by an ex-nun, and discussed by distinguished theologians including a rabbi, academics both religious and agnostic, and University students. Many thoughtful arguments were put forward by both sides, but nobody once mentioned the concept of evolutionary Creation, in which the various elements (including intelligent species) develop by trial and error and the learning of lessons, and in which constant and detailed Divine intervention to ward off the 'evil' resulting from mistakes made during that learning would sabotage the whole purposeful development of the process. (To be fair, the rabbi did favor our concept of God changing and developing as we progress.)

Belief in reincarnation also softens the 'unfairness' of being a victim of human evil actions. One is not trapped inescapably in the situation, nor is one wiped off the slate if one is killed by it. One takes a deep breath and starts again.

The creative/evolutionary spectrum is continuous and interdepend-ent. Each individual is of the same nature as the Source, and is capable of being a channel for it.

Jesus said "The kingdom of Heaven is within you" (and he probably said the same about Hell). But official Christianity seems to have ignored this statement, and put Heaven 'up there,' with God looking down upon us across a gulf which can only be crossed after death and resurrection, and with the right union ticket.

On the organic-Cosmos basis we have discussed, Pagans believe that gulf to be a fiction; creation, evolution and manifestation are a continu-ous spectrum. The kingdom of Heaven is certainly within us, and it is up to us to find and attune ourselves with it, here and now.

As Pagans, to ignore ecology and the needs of Mother Earth is to ignore the underlying principles of our philosophy. Many Pagans are already involved with ecology groups, but it is important not to forget that Pagan philosophy starts on our own doorstep and our own home.

Recycling, using phosphate-free washing powder and detergents, and so on is as much a part of being a Pagan as dressing in robes and performing arcane rituals. We must see our role as the guardians and protectors of our Mother, not only spiritually, by doing Earth-healing rituals and so on, but by balancing this with action on the material plane.

Many Pagans have become deeply involved in non-violent, direct action to protect the environment, on both sides of the Atlantic. Recently in England, Pagans were protesting and using direct action techniques to prevent a road being put through a site officially classified as a 'site of outstanding natural beauty.' This work, being carried out by the British Department of Transport, had been deemed illegal by the European Parliament, after petitions and protests against the plans had been ignored; but the British Government ignored the European ruling as well.

The site, Twyford Down in Hampshire, not only had unexcavated Bronze Age burial mounds, but also some of the rarest butterflies and wild orchids in the whole of Britain. Many Pagans found themselves in the position of lying down in front of bulldozers during the day, and acting as priests to the many protesters camped on the Down during the night. Rituals were held to empower those present for the next day's protests and direct action. The authorities employed a private security firm to control the protesters, which was done ruthlessly; one personal friend of ours had acid poured on his hands. The protesters were in fact relieved when the ordinary police took over. The road was built, regardless, but the vigorous protest had made a public issue of it, and one hopes made the Government a little more cautious in future.

Similar events have been occurring in the United States for many years, with protests and non-violent direct action against the unsafe disposal of toxic waste, logging, and many other ecology issues.

Although not all Pagans are in a position to become involved in such actions, they do philosophically have a responsibility to support those who are—be they Pagan, Christian or whatever. This support can take various forms, including joining the pressure groups that exist. Many Pagans are already active supporters of such groups as Greenpeace, Friends of the Earth, and Earth First. Support can take the form of increasing public awareness of the issues and of fund-raising, and these are just as important as being involved 'on the front line' of direct action. As Pagans, to ignore the ecology issues now presenting themselves to us is to deny our own belief in the God and Goddess. We all have a part to play in the future of our world.

10.

Reincarnation

Almost all Pagans believe in reincarnation—as indeed does much of the rest of the world (such as the Hindus and Buddhists) outside Western monotheism.

Reincarnation was in fact an element in early Christian belief. St. Jerome (340-420 AD) said that a form of it was taught in the early Church, at least to a select few; and his contemporary St. Gregory—who was renowned for his strict orthodoxy—wrote: "It is absolutely necessary that the soul shall be healed and purified, and if it does not take place in one life on earth, it must be accomplished in future earthly lives." But when the Church became a hierarchical part of the Imperial State, it regarded the once-only reward or punishment of Heaven or Hell (or the deferred judgment of Limbo) as an essential part of its disciplinary structure. So reincarnation was declared anathema by the Second Council of Constantinople in 553 AD.

The various Gnostic sects, persecuted as heretical by the Church hierarchy, generally continued to believe in it.

The basic belief of reincarnation is that each human soul returns to Earth for life after life, sometimes as a man and sometimes as a woman. To make progress, in each life he/she should learn lessons and correct mistakes, continuing to be reborn until he/she is ready to pass on to the next stage. We cannot fully understand what 'the next stage' may be; if we could, we would presumably be ready to move to it.

The 'spiritual bank balance' which we carry from life to life—of lessons learned or unlearned, of good or harm done, of responsibilities met or not met—is known by the Hindu word *karma*.

(Another Hindu term often cropping up in the reincarnation context is *bodhisattva*. It means a person who has fulfilled his/her karma and is

ready to move on, but decides to continue reincarnating to help humanity.)

Belief in reincarnation involves the concept we have already mentioned—that of Levels of Reality. This concept, as we have seen, is
common to all religions, but in most it merely acknowledges the
Spiritual, the Mental, and the Physical levels. In Paganism and occultism it tends to be more precisely subdivided—into the Upper and Lower
Spiritual, the Upper and Lower Mental, the Upper and Lower Astral,
the Etheric, and the Physical

A human being is seen as consisting of an immortal part, generally
called the Individuality, and a transient part acquired for each single
incarnation, generally called the Personality.

The immortal Individuality comprises the Upper Spiritual level or
'Divine Spark;' the Lower Spiritual, keynoted by one of 'Seven Rays;'
and the Upper Mental of abstract mind, which is also differentiated into
types. The Individuality contains both male and female aspects in
complementary balance.

The transient Personality—the 'suit' worn during a particular incarnation—is either male or female, with the other aspect present but
buried (corresponding the Jungian concept of the anima and animus,
and to the contained spots in the Yin-Yang symbol—see Fig. 1). It
comprises the Lower Mental level of concrete thought, form, and
memory; the Upper Astral of abstract emotions and the desire for union;
the Lower Astral of instincts and passion, and the desire to possess; the
Etheric Level, the tenuous energy-web of near-matter which encases
the physical body and links it with the subtler planes; and the Physical
Plane, the material body itself.

(A note in passing: In recent years, the development of Kirlian
photography has dramatically substantiated the existence and nature of
the Etheric Level.)

On physical death, the 'suit' of the Personality is shed and disinte-
grates, and the Individuality withdraws to a non-physical environment
generally referred to as the Summerlands (a word borrowed from the
Spiritualists). Here it absorbs the lessons of the incarnation just experienced, and communicates with other resting Individualities, particularly
those it has known in the most recent or earlier incarnations. How it
reacts to the Summerlands, and even how they appear to it, depends on
the Individuality's degree of development and state of mind; a warped
soul may feel it is in Hell, and a healthy one that it is in Heaven.

After what should, for the healthy soul, be a period of evaluation, the Individuality withdraws into spiritual solitude to absorb it. When it is ready, it re-emerges to ensoul a new Personality, a fetus awaiting birth in the womb of a new human mother.

Many people's recall experiences suggest that the length of time between physical death and rebirth may vary widely, from months to several years.

Such recall experiences, and the ways in which they occur, also vary widely. One of the most convincing confirmations arises from psychiatrists' normal regression techniques. Time and again psychiatrists, having no previous belief in reincarnation, have found that when they regress a patient under hypnosis to childhood and babyhood to uncover and deal with buried traumas, he or she may suddenly regress further, and start recounting an earlier life. Several of the most interesting books on the subject have been written by such professionals, who were at first taken aback but in due course convinced by the phenomenon. Examples are Arthur Guirdham's *The Cathars and Reincarnation*, Joan Grant and Denys Kelsey's *Many Lifetimes*, and Dr. Edith Fiore's *You Have Been Here Before*.

Needless to say, once one accepts the possibility of reincarnation, one should be healthily skeptical about recall when it seems to occur. One should record it with an open mind, and wait to see if anything else confirms it. But we ourselves, leaning over backwards to be cautious, have on several occasions had unexpected confirmation of apparent recall by later events, involving facts, locations and events which we could not possibly have known at the time of the first recall.

To take one dramatic example, when Stewart and Janet visited Spain for the first time (guests of Spanish television as known witches—a nice post-Franco development) they were taken on a visit to Segovia, a city which has changed little over the centuries, and Janet immediately knew her way around it, in remarkable detail. This triggered an incarnation recall of her life as a courtesan on the fringe of the court of Ferdinand and Isabella. As always, we filed all this away with an open mind; but that was only the beginning. Some time later, in a pub in Ireland, a couple were present with their five-year-old son, whom we hadn't seen since he was a babe in arms. He wandered across to Janet, and said: "Your hair is the wrong color. It ought to be black... And you had those clicky things in your hands... Oh, you're not my mummy now—*she* is—but you were my mummy then. And my daddy wasn't your husband, he was your friend..." And so on and so on, neither of us prompting him at all. Finally he said "Oh well, bye-bye" and went back to his parents.

Coincidence?

One fact which recall confirms again and again is that many souls are repeatedly linked, meeting in successive incarnations. Janet and Stewart have sound evidence for believing they were intimately associated in a life in Ancient Egypt about the time of Rameses II, of which they both have had recall, and details of which were confirmed when they visited that country. Janet remembers Stewart as one of her Segovia clients, though so far Stewart has no memory of this. And Janet and Gavin have vivid memories, mutually confirmatory, of being a brother (Janet) and sister (Gavin) in pre-Christian northern Europe.

People who do not believe in reincarnation, or know little or nothing of the theory, are often puzzled by an immediate reaction, for no evident reason, of liking or disliking someone they newly meet—a feeling which can be inexplicably strong. It may often be that such a reaction is in fact an unconscious incarnation recall. 'Love at first sight'—or its opposite—is often not 'at first sight' at all, whatever the people concerned think.

The effect of belief in reincarnation on one's attitude to Mother Earth, and one's responsibility to her, is obvious. To those who believe in a once-only life here, followed by Heaven, Hell or Limbo, Earth is a temporary stopping-place, an anteroom to eternal reality; and to some of these it is even an evil place, a prison from which one must work for release by salvation (an aspect of the Dualist philosophy which we considered in Chapter 6).

To believers in reincarnation, on the other hand, the Earth is their home for many lives to come, so their attitude to her is bound to be different. Which is one of the reasons why Pagans are strongly environmentalist.

This is not a selfish attitude, either, concerned only with their personal futures. They know it will also be the continuing home of their children and their children's children, and that they owe to them, too, a constant struggle to protect and improve it. Some of the Heaven-or-Hell school, to be fair, are also concerned by the conditions their descendants will have to face; but for them it does tend to be mitigated by the belief that even if those conditions deteriorate, for their descendants too salvation will provide an escape.

One objection sometimes raised to the theory of reincarnation is the population explosion. If reincarnation is true, it is asked, where do all these millions of souls come from? Or has their resting-time in the Summerlands been unhealthily reduced through human foolishness?

The answer to this would seem to be that new souls are being constantly created, for two reasons. First, it must always have been so; if *homo sapiens* has a role to play in Terran evolution, perfected Individualities passing on to a higher stage need to be replaced by others. And second, cosmic evolution is a feed-back process; if we as a species take unwise action (such as the unforgivable Vatican ban on contraception) then we reap the consequences. Cosmic readjustment from the Source, including from Mother Earth herself, is likely to follow, as part of the feed-back, and if it creates problems such as over-population the fault is ours. (It has been suggested, for example, that the newly-arrived scourge of AIDS is such a readjustment, though it would be unwise to take this for granted, or our determination to find a cure might be weakened. 'It's the Will of God' has all too often been used to excuse lack of compassionate effort.)

Once we accept reincarnation, and the existence of young and old souls, many of us find we can often distinguish between the two, by a certain look in their eyes and their reaction to the world around them.

It is fair to add that there are some Pagans who do not believe in individual reincarnation, but think that its apparent evidence, even when genuine in itself, is picked up from the human Collective Unconscious and not from personal memory. This is a minority view which we and most Pagans do not share; but Paganism is a non-dogmatic religion, free from imposed articles of faith. One is not required to believe anything of which one has not become personally convinced. But we have found that holders of this minority view do not lag behind the rest in their sense of responsibility to humankind, Mother Earth, and her creatures.

There are also minor differences about details of the reincarnation process. For example—when does the soul enter the fetus? At conception, or later?

Stewart had reason to wonder about this. His mother had believed in the folk tradition that what one concentrates on while pregnant will affect the child; she was a schoolteacher, and felt she wanted her first child to be a writer. So as she explained to Stewart years later: "While I was carrying you, I read every good book I could lay my hands on." In any event, Stewart could read before he went to school, has never wanted to be anything but a writer, has worked as such all his life (even writing gun drills and training booklets during his wartime Army service), and will only be happy by writing till the day he dies.

Does this mean that Agnes Farrar reshaped the nature of a soul already in the fetus she was carrying—or did her determined concentration invite the Individuality of an already-existing writer to enter that fetus at the appropriate moment? Stewart tends to believe the latter, since he has for example had incarnation recall of a life as an Egyptian scribe, and has the strong feeling that the writer's approach is part of his continuing essence.

Janet's incarnation recalls, time and again, emphasize Pagan, witch, or shamaness activity.

Gavin, from his nursing experience, has come to believe that the soul enters the fetus slowly rather than 'with a bang,' and that the process of absorption of the soul into its new body continues even after a baby's birth.

There is a purely physical argument in favor of this view, too. Humans are unique in that a newborn baby's brain is only one-third of its ultimate size at birth, because the mother's pelvis could not cope with the full size. The brain takes about a year to reach full size. Could it not then be argued that the soul's physical 'home' is not fully ready for it at the fetal and birth stages?

For all three of us, the explanation of the initial entry of a particular soul during pregnancy, rather than at conception, seems to make more sense than what could be the distortion of a soul's nature once it has entered the fetus.

But opinions on all this may well differ.

Opinions also differ—in particular between Hindu and modern Western believers in reincarnation—on the uniqueness of species. Hindus believe a human may reincarnate as an animal, and vice versa. Most Westerners (and we ourselves) believe that each species has its own nature, that every immortal Individuality remains for all of his/her existence within the bounds of that nature, and that a soul's commuting between species would conflict with the Pagan organic view of the Cosmos.

A further disputable question is to what degree individual animals reincarnate as themselves. It is hard to believe in an individually reincarnating mosquito, moth, or even rabbit; a more easily acceptable view is that in such species, a dying individual returns to the species' Group Soul, which continues endlessly to give birth to single-life individuals.

It has also been suggested that in some species—the honey-bee, for example—the colony, the swarm, is an individual in itself, a miniature

Group Soul, an organism of which the fertile Queen, the competing males, and the busy workers are component cells.

But what about the intelligent species, such as the higher primates, the dogs, the cats? There would seem to be much evidence of individual reincarnation among intelligent animals who are in close contact with humans. This is not something to be arrogant about—it is simply that with other intelligent species we have little or no means of accessing the evidence. We have known for many centuries that dolphins, for example, are highly intelligent—and surprisingly friendly with humans—but we have not yet achieved the kind of breakthrough in language communication with them that American researchers have been achieving with chimpanzees.

There is still a great deal to learn, with regard to both humans and animals—but with the new attitudes that are rapidly developing, particularly among Pagans, who knows what we may discover?

11.

The Ancient Roots

Ancient, pre-patriarchal cultures contained the roots from which modern Paganism has evolved, so an understanding of at least the most important of them in the Western world is a great help in understanding today's movement.

The earliest evidence is to be found in prehistoric cave paintings and statuettes. The Paleolithic (Old Stone Age) emphasis was strongly Earth Mother oriented. As Erich Neumann points out (*The Great Mother*, p. 95), of the Stone Age sculptures known at the time he was writing (1963), 55 were female and five male, and the male ones were poorly executed and apparently of minor importance. Typical of the female figures is the one known as the Venus of Willendorf, with huge belly, breasts and buttocks, tapering footless legs, and a faceless head; skeletal remains prove that she was in no way similar to Stone Age women, but symbolized the birth-giving and nourishing Earth Mother.

Paleolithic cave paintings tend to concentrate on the hunting aspect, consisting mostly of pictures of remarkably well-observed deer and wild cattle. Where they include human figures, some seem to represent sympathetic-magic ritual to prepare the hunter for a successful pursuit.

The emergence of written records confirmed the importance of the Goddess—and also the interconnection of the North African, Near and Middle Eastern, and European cultures, as typified by the similarity of Goddess names: the Egyptian Aset (Isis), the Near Eastern Asherat, the Middle Eastern Ishtar, the Teutonic Eostre/Ostara, and others. The whole scene continued to interconnect and emigrate, an example being the Near Eastern Baal and Baalat ('Lord' and 'Lady'), the Carthaginian Baal Hammon and Tanit, the Irish Balor and Danu, and the Welsh Beli and Dôn.

Within all this interconnection and feedback, there were five main religious cultures in this part of the world in pre-Christian times: the Egyptian, the Near Eastern, the Greek, the Northern European, and the Celtic. The Roman pantheon early on became a pale reflection of the Greek, attaching Greek personality and mythology to the corresponding Roman names—that of Hermes to Mercury, of Poseidon to Neptune, of Aphrodite to Venus, and so on. (Unfortunately, the fact that Latin was the international language of literate Europe in the Middle Ages and Renaissance emphasized this takeover, so that the Roman names were used for everything; Botticelli's painting *The Birth of Venus*, for example, precisely depicted the Greek legend of the birth of foam-born Aphrodite, and Shakespeare's *Venus and Adonis* fell into the same trap.)

Egypt

Ancient Egypt—the longest-lasting national culture in the world, apart from the Chinese—seemed to emerge into history about 3000 BC, mysteriously almost fully-formed out of nothing. Very early, it united the various nomes (local states) of the Nile Valley and Delta under one monarchy, and also merged their deities—which explains why some Egyptian Gods and Goddesses appear more complex and many-sided than (for example) the Greek ones, which tend to express what we have called 'aspect-purity.' The merging worked, materially and spiritually; for three millennia Egypt was a fruitful civilization, surviving with few passing interruptions.

And interestingly, there is much evidence that the serious Egyptian priesthood knew perfectly well that all these Gods and Goddesses were in fact aspects of the one Ultimate and that their rich mythology served to strengthen those aspects.

Egyptian religion balanced the male and female aspects; Isis was at least as important as (and in many ways more active than) Osiris, and the complementary temples of Amun-Ra and his consort Mut still stand at walking distance from each other in Luxor and Karnak. And although the male Pharaohs were the nominal rulers, their succession was matrilinear; royal authenticity derived from the Queen and her heiress, which is why so many Pharaohs married their sisters or even their daughters, to validate their right to sovereignty, and why at the very end, both Julius Caesar and Anthony wanted to marry Cleopatra, so that the Egyptian people would accept their rule. (The same principle applied at all levels; peasant property was inherited through the women.)

Isis is probably the richest and most many-aspected Goddess form that any culture has conceived, and during the Ptolemaic period and later, her worship spread throughout Europe and the bordering areas, reaching as far north as York in England. This development is well described in R.E. Witt's book *Isis in the Graeco-Roman World* (see Bibliography). It was methodically crushed as the Church became more powerful, but the symptoms remained; many of the Virgin and Child statues in old Christian churches (particularly in the south of France) began their existence as Isis and Horus, the imagery being identical.

The Near East

The earliest written evidence of Near Eastern religion and legend dates from about 2050 BC, and on a substantial scale from about a century later. The area stretched from Mesopotamia to Anatolia, and included several peoples and languages. The first organized society to emerge was the Sumerian; other major ones were the Babylonian, Assyrian, and Hurrian. All these were Asian in origin; the last to arrive were Indo-European, the Hittites.

Their mythology, as elsewhere, reflected their society and its environment, which is why it laid particular stress on the controlling of primordial Chaos, which (in Assyro-Babylonian myth) the Salt-Water Goddess Tiamat personified, by the Sky God Anu and the Fresh-Water and Wisdom God Ea (see p. 21). These relationships were complex and continuing. For example Bau, another form of the Primeval Dark-Waters Goddess, was said to be Ea's mother, and was later represented as the wife of the Irrigation God Nirsu (Ninurta); their marriage was celebrated at the Babylonian New Year at the end of harvest. All these legends symbolized the achievement of balance between human effort and raw environment, on which successful agriculture depended.

On the Canaanite coast, the same theme appeared in the killing of the Fertility God Baal by Mot, God of Sterility and Death, and the subsequent killing of Mot and revival of Baal by Baal's sister Anat, Goddess of Fertility, Love and War.

(The Egyptian equivalent was the endless confrontation between the fertile Nile Valley, personified by Isis and Osiris, and the threatening desert personified by Set—salt water being virtually irrelevant to Egypt's problems.)

Supreme Mother Goddess of this family of cultures, under her various names, was Inanna (Sumerian), Ishtar (Assyro-Babylonian),

Astarte or Ashera (Phoenician), and Atergatis (Philistine and Syrian). (The similarity of these names to Aset, Isis's Egyptian name, must also be significant.) In her Ishtar form she had many consorts—the Supreme and War God Assur, the Spring Sun and Vegetation God Marduk, the Writing and Speech God Nebo, and the Creator God Merodach; and her lovers included the Seasonally-Dying Vegetation God Tammuz. For 240 of the 360 years that Solomon's Temple stood in Jerusalem, Ashera was worshipped alongside Yahweh (Jehovah) as his bride and sister, and her image was publicly displayed.

Hebrew mythology, in its Old Testament form, is largely a local variant of that of its neighbors; on this, see pp. 42–43.

Greece

The most noticeable characteristic of the Greek pantheon, compared with those of its neighbors and contemporaries, is what we have already called its 'aspect-purity.' To take three examples: the War God Ares is purely and brutally destructive, without the noble-warrior mask or the vegetation-deity roots of the Roman Mars; the Love Goddess Aphrodite represents sexual desire and fulfillment only, indifferent to marriage, childbearing or faithfulness; and Pan is a God of Nature, pure and simple.

This is typical of the fact that Greece was the birthplace of modern scientific thinking. The Egyptians, in their architecture and land division, had conquered simple practical mathematics; they had discovered, for example, that a rope triangle of three, four, and five-unit sides produced a right angle, but it was a Greek who clarified this into the square on the hypotenuse equaling the sum of the squares on the other two sides. And it was a Greek, observing and measuring the angle of the Sun at various latitudes, who not only deduced that the Earth was a globe, but defined its diameter remarkably closely.

> To the Hellenic mind *logos* and *mythos*, 'reasoning' and 'myth,' are two antithetic modes of thought. The former includes everything that can be stated in rational terms, all that attains to objective truth, and appears the same to all minds. The latter includes all that concerns the imagination, all that cannot be subject to verification, but contains its truth in itself or, and this amounts to the same thing, in powers of persuasion arising out of its own beauty.
>
> (*Larousse World Mythology*, p. 97.)

We have said that the Egyptians knew simple practical mathematics; but it is fair to add that the construction of the Pyramids, with their precise astronomical alignments, suggests that their knowledge of mathematics was considerably more sophisticated than they made public, and that they too knew that the Earth was a globe and had a close idea of its dimensions. Babylonian clay tablets also include many of precise mathematical and astronomical records. But it was the Greeks— the somewhat misty Thales, and Pythagoras and Euclid in particular— who introduced the principle of step-by-step logical proof. 'Q.E.D.' is a Greek invention.

Another factor coloring the whole of Greek mythology is its combination of matriarchal roots and patriarchal overlay; in many surviving myths, both these elements can be traced. The earliest Greeks to colonize the Western Mediterranean were matriarchal; the later Indo-European invaders who overran and merged with them were patriarchal. The invaders adopted and modified the local mythology, and also introduced and modified some of their own—an example being their Horse God Poseidon, whom they made a God of the Sea (with which they had been unfamiliar), but who retained his horse symbolism.

Typical of the patriarchalization process was Zeus, the Supreme God; in modified myth, he became the father of practically everybody, whoever their earlier attributed fathers had been. He even himself gave birth to his daughter Athene from his head, after swallowing her pregnant mother Metis—surely a supreme example of a patriarchal takeover.

Zeus's consort Hera, originally a powerful Mother Goddess in her own right, became demoted to a jealous and bitchy housewife, obsessed with frustrating or punishing Zeus's countless amours. (Untypically, her Roman equivalent Juno, consort of the Supreme God Jupiter, retained much dignity and power—doubtless reflecting the respect accorded to the Matron even within that male-dominated society.)

Nevertheless, the persuasive beauty of Greek mythology as a whole, referred to in the Larousse quotation above, has seemed indestructible; and its aspect-purity is a great help to those Pagans who are drawn to using its God- and Goddess-forms.

Celtic

This, closely followed by Northern European, is the model most widely used by modern Pagans.

The Celts appear to have originated in Germany. About the ninth century BC they began to invade Gaul in successive waves up to the second century BC. About the eighth century BC the first Celts settled in Britain, and in Ireland at some time after that. In the sixth century BC they settled in the Iberian peninsula, and in the fourth century BC invaded Italy, actually seizing Rome at the Battle of Allia in 390 BC. They were the 'Galatians' of the New Testament.

The Celts were not a unified culture, so much as a family of related tribes, with a variety of often overlapping tribal mythologies. In many areas, such as Gaul, the Celtic culture was conquered and dominated by the Roman Empire. In Britain, after the Roman withdrawal, it survived and largely merged with that of the later Saxon invaders.

Only on the Atlantic fringe did it remain dominant. Today, Ireland, Wales, Scotland, the Isle of Man, Cornwall, and Brittany in North-Western France are still essentially Celtic in culture and folk tradition, with surviving Celtic languages still spoken by a minority of the population, the survival of those languages actively encouraged by enthusiasts, and in Ireland by the Government. In the Isle of Man and Cornwall, the languages had died in use, but again are being revived by enthusiasts. There are in fact two basic Celtic languages, recognizably related—Q-Celtic (Gaelic) in Ireland, Scotland and the Isle of Man, and P-Celtic in Wales, Cornwall and Brittany. (The two linguistic names refer to dominant sounds, and can be remembered by the word for 'son of'—'mac' in Q-Celtic and 'ap' in P-Celtic.)

Celtic mythology has survived more fully in Ireland than anywhere else. Early Irish Celtic Christianity coexisted reasonably amicably with its Pagan neighbors, until the Vatican took control of it; one symptom of this neighborliness was that the existing oral traditions, which were very rich, were written down remarkably faithfully by early Christian monks. All these writings are still available in published books with opposite-page English translation, such as the five-volume *Lebor Gabála Éireann* (*'The Book of the Taking of Ireland'*—commonly known as *'The Book of Invasions'*), a detailed account of the stages of the occupation of Ireland in the mythological cycle. No other Western or Northern European country has a pre-Christian bibliography on anything like the same scale.

In Ireland, 'the Gods of the old religion' have not 'become the Devils of the new,' as was general throughout Christendom; instead, they became the heroes and heroines of accepted national mythology, with a firm place in folk tradition and practice. Typical of this national attitude was that fact that during the terrible persecution centuries, when anything up to 10 million men, women and children throughout Europe were hanged or burned as 'witches,' in Ireland the victims could be numbered on your two hands. And the *bean feasa*, wisewoman or village witch, while officially frowned upon, has always been respected and consulted—and still is, as Janet can confirm.

Northern European

We have chosen to use this name here, because the usual scholars' label is 'Germanic' or 'Teutonic,' which the ordinary reader may find too localizing. It takes longer to describe because of its complexity; in fact it was a family of cultures, embracing Scandinavia, Germany, Friesland, and Saxon Britain. It also embraced two pantheons, originally rivals but finally merging—the Vanir of the aboriginal agriculturalists, and the Aesir of their warrior conquerors. (Want a mnemonic to remember which is which?—try V for Vegetation and A for Armies.)

The earliest written reference to the religious beliefs of these people was by the Roman scholar Tacitus in 98 AD. In *Germania* he distinguished them from their Gallic, Celtic neighbors:

> As to the Germans themselves, I think it is probable that they are indigenous, and that very little foreign blood has been introduced either by invasions or by friendly dealings with neighbors.

We now know that this was mistaken; they were not in fact indigenous, but were in a continual state of migration. During their travels from the East they had already adopted several Sky Gods which we now know to be of Indo-European heritage. They were also influenced by their Gallic neighbors; for example, it is very likely that the Gallic Thunder God Taranos and the Germanic Thor are the same. Tacitus records these deities using Roman names. He refers to the predecessor of Odin as 'Mercury,' of Tyr as 'Mars,' and finally of Thor as 'Hercules,' all being descriptive of the Gods' roles. (It was during this period that the Aesir were beginning to replace the Vanir.) Tacitus recorded in detail the rites of the Goddess Nerthus (Mother Earth). He also mentioned the worship of 'Isis' in the coastal areas—probably an early form of the Goddess Freya.

After the collapse of the Roman Empire, most of the tribes moved either West or North, and started to develop more pronounced separate cultural identities. The tribe known as the Suebi settled in what is now Sweden and Norway, and later become known as the Norse. They had wholeheartedly accepted the newer Indo-European deity Odin, a fusion of the older Gods Tiwaz and Wodenaz. The older agricultural deities took a definite second place within this culture.

Later the Norse, as the Vikings (which has been translated as 'Pirate,' 'Wanderer,' 'Traveler,' etc.) plundered Christian Europe until the end of the tenth century. They spread their culture as far east as Russia, as far west as Iceland, and as far south as the Mediterranean. Norse explorers reached the New World from about 1000 AD onwards, five centuries before Columbus. The Sagas record in convincing detail, and discovered remains confirm, that they explored the coasts of New-foundland and Labrador, and even established temporary settlements and trading-posts. There is also some evidence of trade links with Native Americans to be found as far south as New England.

It is from the twelfth-century Icelandic scholar Snorri Sturlson that we know most about the Norse myths. He wrote two important works: the *Poetic (Elder) Edda* and the *Prose Edda*. It was in the *Poetic Edda* that the terms Aesir and Vanir were first used, and the 'war' and fusion of the two pantheons explained.

The Anglo-Saxons probably never knew themselves by this name. They were a fusion of several smaller cultures, including the Jutes, Frisians, Franks, Danes, Angles and Saxons, who were settled from northwestern France to the Baltic coast. The Franks were later to push south and conquer Gaul; they are the ancestors of today's French. The Jutes, Frisians, Angles and Saxons crossed into Britain, and pushed its Romano-Celtic inhabitants into Cornwall and Wales during the fourth and fifth centuries. They were later followed by the Danes, who split Anglo-Saxon England in half (hence the marked differences in dialect between Southern and Northern English).

Unlike the Norse, these cultures' deities tended to maintain their agricultural nature, and there is little evidence that they developed into coherent, related pantheons. Their names remained similar to the Norse: Odin was Woden to the Anglo-Saxons, and was seen more as a hooded, wandering figure than the Norse All-Father; Thor, as Thunor, remained a God of Thunder, but took on more importance as a God of Agriculture; Tyr, as Tiuw, was worshipped as a War God and God of Oaths. Little is known of the Goddesses of these peoples, most evidence of them having been destroyed by Christianity within two centuries of settling in England.

The Vanir can be considered the Germanic equivalent of the Celtic Tuatha Dé Danann: they became revered as a Goddess-oriented fairy (or elven) faith. It is probably from this that Anglo-Saxon and Continental German witchcraft developed. This faith became known as Seidr (Norse) or Seith (Anglo-Saxon), and included a form of shamanism carried out by Priestesses known as Vala or Volva. Its principle deity was the Goddess Freya. It was outlawed by Christianity more immediately than other Pagan practices because of its Goddess associations. The Northern European peoples also had their equivalent to the Roman Fates: the Norns (Norse) or as Shakespeare records them in *Macbeth*, the Weird Sisters (Wyrd in Anglo-Saxon). They also developed complex cosmologies based on Yggdrasil (the Norse World Tree) and on Irminsul (the Anglo-Saxon Cosmic Pillar).

This family of cultures achieved several notable things. They were the first to introduce democracy into Northern Europe (see p. 149), and were one of the first to give legal equality to women. They created their own system of letters, the Runes (see p. 71), which was still developing until outlawed by Christianity. Runes are one of the most well-known legacies of this culture among Pagans, being a system of spiritual wisdom and a source of magical power.

12.

The Modern Rebirth

When patriarchalism became terminally ill—the first symptoms of this being evident in the 19th century—the underlying Pagan attitudes which had been suppressed for two millennia began to flex their muscles.

In Britain, for example, as the Church's actual power of dictatorship waned to mere social, political and economic discrimination against the unorthodox, the needs which Paganism meets, and which the Church had increasingly failed to meet, inspired the emergence of actual movements and organizations, such as the Golden Dawn. We have examined the nature of the most important of these movements in Chapter 3.

In the 20th century, the pattern changed further. Two World Wars, and technological advance, greatly weakened the rigidity of the class structure; although they still wielded economic power, the standards and attitudes of the upper class were no longer humbly accepted as the ideal pattern. The middle class became much more influential, standing more and more on its own feet, and the working class was less shackled by round-the-clock labor. Parliamentary membership, which used to be virtually an upper-class monopoly, came to include the whole class spectrum, with the Labor Party, supported and partly run by the trade unions, sometimes actually winning power.

At the same time, young people became more economically independent (a development which revolutionized the music industry, for example) and less likely to accept parental patterns automatically. Cultural differences became increasingly a matter of age-groups rather than of class, a change accelerated by the fact that, for the first time in history, one could no longer always tell a person's class by the clothes he or she wore.

British television, as somebody put it, became 'the least worst television in the world,' and its variety, frankness, and openness to different opinions (including some that would earlier have been regarded as seditious), available in more and more homes, lubricated the increasing fluidity of British thought and openness of expression.

All these changes, however, created a (largely subconscious) spiritual vacuum which the existing religions and philosophies increasingly failed to fill. The time had come for a coherent and expressive Pagan movement to make its contribution.

Gerald Gardner's books appeared at just the right moment.

Gardner himself had no idea of the impact those books would have. He was convinced that witchcraft was dying, and that he was recording it before it disappeared altogether. He lived for ten years after the first of his non-fiction books, *Witchcraft Today*, appeared, so he must have begun to realize how wrong that judgment had been. His system had provided the focus that was needed to fill the vacuum, and to get the Pagan movement into increasingly organized action.

Admittedly (apart from the already-existing organizations such as the Druids) that new movement in Britain was at first purely Wiccan. But once it was in existence and growing, it provided yet another crystallization point—for other forms of Pagan activity to become conscious, to join in public festivals and other activities. British Paganism soon began to become more varied.

It was also exported—to the Continent, to Australia, and above all to America. Americans on the whole are far readier to explore new ideas than most Europeans, so it was not long before what was a British breakthrough became an American explosion.

On this, and on the growth of Paganism in other parts of the Western world, we have more in Chapter 19.

13.

Paganism and Sex

Pagans' attitudes to sex, its problems, its ethics, and its relationships are varied, because Pagans are human beings. But by and large, three essential factors underlie these attitudes.

First of all, they are free of the suspicion and distrust of sex which has underlain Christian attitudes ever since the sexually psychotic St. Paul laid down rules which the patriarchal Church, once it became official, established as dogma. Official Christianity as a whole declares that sex is only permissible within marriage, and both Vatican Catholicism and Christian Science, for example, insist that it is for reproduction only (though the Vatican reluctantly permits a married couple to enjoy it, subject to that proviso). Secondly, Pagans' emphasis on the complementary equality of men and women undermines the pattern which two millennia of patriarchalism have established. And thirdly, as on other subjects, Pagans tend to respect various people's attitudes, instead of regarding their own as the Law of God.

As in so many fields, Paganism merely expresses wholeheartedly the attitudes which have become increasingly prevalent among non-Pagans, including grass-roots Christians. Pressure for the ordination of women has already succeeded in the Church of England. The first 32 women priests were ordained in Bristol Cathedral on March 12th, 1994, fortunately without the disruption by the caveman fringe which had been apprehended. Many of the 32 had been deaconesses for years, and they had very varied contributory experience, from midwifery or nursing to pastoral counseling or child care. The Church of Ireland has had women priests for a few years already—and interestingly, one of them has estimated that about half of those attending her ordination in Dublin Cathedral were Catholics. Desire for ordination is growing steadily among Catholic women, particularly in the United States.

The ban on contraception laid down by Pope Paul VI in his disastrous 1968 Encyclical *Humanae Vitae* (overruling, incidentally, the advice of his own Committee of Cardinals) is increasingly ignored, for example, by the Catholic families of Ireland, where the sale of condoms was made legally possible even before the onset of AIDS made it inevitable. Pope John Paul II reiterated the ban on contraception as part of his Encyclical *Splendor Veritatis* on October 5th, 1993, while this book was being written. Significantly, the *Irish Times*—the Republic's most important newspaper—in an editorial the following morning was critical of the Encyclical, pointing among other things to the effect of the contraception ban on 'the overcrowded slums of half of the cities of Latin America;' and on the Encyclical's wider insistence on obedience as opposed to individual conscience, the editorial commented: "It disturbs through its failure to recognize the profound moral inspiration—'Love thy neighbor'—of many who support new attitudes. In a modern, complex world, formal moral injunctions often clash, and choices cannot be avoided." Such open criticism by a respected Irish newspaper would have been unthinkable at the time of *Humanae Vitae*.

More and more happily-united couples, in both Europe and America, are deciding not to get legally married, feeling that their partnership is a personal decision which does not require State or Church validation.

On the non-religious front, the battle for the equality of women has been steadily succeeding, from the Suffragette days onwards. And this battle includes women's sexual freedom, in both choice and activity.

What, then, *is* the most generally-held Pagan attitude to sex?

First of all, that it is a natural and enjoyable human activity. *Homo* (and *femina*) *sapiens* is more sexually active and motivated than other mammalian species, our interest and activity being continuous, unlike that of the other species, which is confined to periods of 'heat;' in technical terms, our cycle is ovulatory, while theirs is oestral. Nature has decided thus for various evolutionary reasons, so we might as well accept it. The Pagan view of a balanced existence is well summed up in the old Anglo-Saxon slogan: 'Flagg, Flax, Fodder and Frigg'—meaning respectively a roof over your head, clothes for your back, food for your belly, and a happy sex life.

Second, that we are the most self-aware, and socially and technically sophisticated, species on Earth, and that therefore our sexual activity should be governed by mutual respect and consideration, and not merely subject to spur-of-the-moment impulse regardless of its effect on the partner or the possible offspring.

Third, that we are all individuals, and that there is no universal set of rules which must be imposed on all of us. One couple may be happy with a permanent, legally recorded marriage, with no outside sexual relationships. Another may like their partnership to be the central and continuing one, but 'open'—i.e., allowing outside sexual activity. Another couple may prefer to live separately, while having a continuing sexual relationship with each other. A group of three or more may be happy as a sexual 'team,' domestic or otherwise. People change and develop, and the stage in any relationship may be reached where it has outlived its viability, and should end—preferably on amicable terms. And, of course, any individual is free to prefer a celibate life. All but the first and last of these would be regarded by a Christian Church as 'sinful,' but to Pagans they are all acceptable, and deserving of support and understanding—provided that the people concerned are genuinely happy with them.

One thing does disturb us a little; a tendency among some Pagans to think that non-monogamous arrangements are 'Craft' and 'cool,' and that if they are not prepared to plunge into them unthinkingly, they are behind the times. We want to emphasize that domestic and sexual arrangements are entirely a personal matter, depending on the individuals concerned. A couple who are genuinely happy with faithful monogamy are just as 'Craft' and 'cool' as those who are genuinely happy with a triad, a quartet, an open relationship, or whatever. They key word is 'genuinely'—to which should be added 'maturely.' Arrangements which are unconventional by hitherto existing standards (of the culture within which one lives) should only be entered into by people who are emotionally mature and free from serious psychological problems.

The 'open relationship' attitude of established partners has been growing steadily among Pagans, and in many ways it admits honestly what a lot of married couples have been practicing privately since time immemorial (though often, under patriarchy, with the wife tolerating it for the husband but not vice versa). The attitude of happily-united Pagan couples who do practice it is well expressed by a woman friend of ours in New Mexico:

I believe that Love is Limitless, and has a billion forms. As you know, ——— and I have been working on an open relationship for some 17 years, and it has its good times and its bad times, but all in all, I find it to be the right one for the two of us. I also believe that without it, we would cut ourselves off from so much human companionship, relationship, with the loss of the clan and the extended family, and that would be a great loss to our collective soul—and our societies. Be happy, love and cherish one another, and let your friends and loved ones enjoy the reflection of your love.

Children of any kind of relationship are of course a vital question, which we shall deal with separately in the next chapter.

Wise Pagans recognize that there are differences between men's and women's patterns of sexual interest, and that there are evolutionary reasons for these. To over-simplify the differences somewhat, at a primitive level, men are turned on by what they see, and women by how they are treated. The survival of any species, at that primitive level, depends on as many females as possible being impregnated, so males are programmed to find any healthy female, particularly a young one, desirable. On the other hand, species survival also demands that during their vulnerable periods of pregnancy and child-rearing (the latter being exceptionally long in humans) females shall be reliably protected and fed, so females are programmed to select mates who will be dependable as continuing partners, from among the many who pursue them.

Neither sex should regard its primitive programming as 'morally superior' to the other's—but both sexes are entitled to demand that these programmings should adapt to the mutual respect and consideration suitable to the state of evolution to which we have progressed.

(In passing—the use of the word 'wolf' to describe a shamelessly promiscuous man is very rough on wolves! They are models of conjugal fidelity, mating faithfully for life, and both sexes being dedicated parents.)

Evolution has done surprising things to human sexuality, quite apart from the shift from the oestral to the ovulatory cycle. For example—when we went around on all fours, like other mammals, the sexual signal was the female backside. When we changed to moving and standing upright, and to facing each other, Nature had to repeat this signal in front, which is why women have prominent breasts, unlike all other primates and human men. Female gorillas, chimpanzees and so on are flat-chested, yet they feed milk to their infants as efficiently as human women. Women's breasts are purely sexual signals (a syndrome to which women have instinctively contributed by painting their lips red).

Confronting each other face to face was the first step in the humanization of sex, in the sense that it became increasingly person-to-person, instead of merely a genital urge. We also departed from the general primate pattern by becoming almost entirely hairless, with all-over erogenous sensitivity, so mutual and often complex caressing evolved as an important factor in arousal and enjoyment.

Recognizing all this frankly and unashamedly, as most Pagans do, instead of seeing it as Satan's cunning temptation to sin, enables us to combine it with mutual respect and subtle consideration of each other's feelings.

In Chapter 17 we shall consider the dangers and conflicts that can arise from failing to appreciate all these factors.

Some Pagans, in particular some Wiccan groups, often hold rituals 'skyclad'—i.e., naked—and this of course has added to Fundamentalist accusations of 'orgies.' In fact, anyone who has become familiar with nudity, whether ritual or casual, knows how unprovocative it is—less provocative, in fact, than deliberately sexual clothing. In general, the Pagan attitude to nudity is relaxed, and this attitude proves to be a healthy one.

It is an attitude, incidentally, shared by the many thousands of naturists, members of respectable family naturist clubs; and the Fundamentalists never bother to accuse them of 'orgies.' The weapons used are determined by one's feelings about the target.

What about homosexuality and bisexuality? Again, on the principle that we are all individuals, Pagans support the rights and freedom of gays and lesbians, and heterosexual Pagans fight alongside them to ensure those rights and to resist prejudice and persecution. An interesting addition to this supportive attitude is the very recent discovery that homosexuality is often the result of a DNA gene—undermining the common prejudice that it is always the product of psychological disturbance or of New Age 'fashion.'

While Pagans are unanimous in support of gay and lesbian rights, it must be admitted that some heterosexual groups—particularly those which emphasize the polarity of male-female working couples—are unhappy about admitting them as members, feeling that they disturb the clarity of such working. In the first days of running a coven, we tended to feel that way ourselves, but we have since had two gay members. We found that both of them willingly focused on their male aspect during Circle working, and the fact that their male aspect was untypical by conventional standards in no way weakened the polarity-working.

As for homosexual covens and working groups, during our 1991 American tour, we took part in one festival where one of the groups was entirely gay; they performed a lakeside ritual in the presence of all of us, and we found it inspired and indeed beautiful, a real contribution to the festival as a whole. They were friendly with everyone and accepted by everyone.

Doreen Valiente, in *The Rebirth of Witchcraft*, says that when she was being trained:

> If you were a man, you were told that you had to find a woman of sufficient rank to initiate you and then have a female partner to make 'the perfect couple.' Homosexuality, we were told, was abhorrent to the Goddess, and Her curse would fall upon people of the same sex who tried to work together. For a long time I believed this, but today I question it. Why should people be 'abhorrent to the Goddess' for being the way they are? Whether moralists like it or not, it seems that nature has decreed that a certain proportion of the human race shall be homosexual instead of heterosexual. Why this is, I do not pretend to know.

Fortunately, that is one way in which Wicca has progressed since the Gardnerian starting-pistol. We know of no group which would speak of such 'abhorrence' today.

There are more thoughts on Pagan sexual attitudes in the next chapter.

14.

Pagan Families

Until the Industrial Revolution transformed Western society, the extended family was the basis of its fabric. All the generations of a family lived together. Growing boys learned their trade as apprentices to their fathers, and growing girls learned home-running from their mothers. Grandparents were available as reservoirs of experience.

With the dawn of the factory age, this began to break down. Families might still live together—more and more of them in the mushrooming overcrowded urban slums—but increasingly, their daily work separated their daily lives. The old pattern only survived (as it still does) in such things as farming families and small businesses like family shops, blacksmiths and so on. But even today, such families tend to be living separately from other relatives.

Pagans, too, mostly live in their own homes, in touch nowadays (like others) by telephone and car. But we find there is a healthy Pagan tendency to value the extended family more than some others do, and to respect its members of all ages.

'Youthism' is an exaggerated feature of current Western society, and particularly a commercial one. Advertisements of products almost always feature under-30 actors or models. Catwalk models selling fashions are in their teens or 20s, and have an average shelf-life of five years, if they are lucky; the prudent ones have another profession up their sleeves for after that, even if it is only to train or manage their successors, or to design clothes themselves. The idea is constantly pushed that attractiveness, sexually or personalitywise, is confined to the young.

Plastic surgeons flourish on the belief; their services are virtually compulsory for Hollywood actresses who want to continue working after 30.

Moreover, the fashion industry and associated pressures impose narrow limits (literally) on the acceptable standards of youthful attractiveness itself. Unless a girl is thin, she is frightened into thinking herself unattractive, into starving herself, and even into the mental and physical (and often fatal) disorders of anorexia and bulimia. Many catwalk models admit that their anorexia is encouraged by the simple fact that the thinner they get, the more money they earn. This imposed compulsion ignores the fact that women are individuals, and so is their attractiveness; one woman may be slim and attractive, and another plump and attractive, and to try to force anyone into an uncharacteristic pattern is unforgivable.

The same compulsion applies to the youthist image of men, of course, pushing the concept that the tall young Adonis is the ideal of male attractiveness. Though men are slightly less circumscribed than women in this; a middle-aged man, provided his figure is still reasonably trim, is allowed to look 'distinguished'—doubtless because of the factor we have already mentioned, that at a primitive level men are turned on by what they see, and women by how they are treated.

Women today are luckier in one way than they used to be. In Victorian times, and until the women's liberation movement grew in effectiveness, a woman over 30 was expected to dress, behave, and think of herself as middle-aged. Today, more and more mothers of grown children, and even grandmothers—as well as those who used to be branded as 'spinsters'—reflect what may be called the Tina Turner syndrome, refusing successfully to fit into the old (in both senses) pattern.

Many of them are showing increasing confidence in their own attractiveness, and dressing and carrying themselves accordingly—not by being 'mutton dressed as lamb,' but by rejecting 'mutton' as a derogatory concept and showing that it is not necessary for them slavishly to imitate 'lamb' standards to be attractive in appearance and behavior.

"Beauty is truth, truth beauty," Keats wrote. Pagans believe there is beauty in all of us, of both sexes and all ages, whether it is physical, mental or spiritual, or a combination of these; but it is the truth of the individual that expresses it, not any commercially or socially imposed standard. Pagans do not agree with the old French saying *Il faut souffrir pour être belle*—'it is necessary to suffer in order to be beautiful.'

To be fair to the French, they recognize the category *jolie-laide*, 'lovely-ugly,' to describe a woman whose features break all the conventional rules of beauty, but whose individual appearance is oddly attractive.

It is questionable whether it is even necessary to smell the way the advertisers dictate. Two Pagan women friends of ours (one slim/attractive, the other plump/attractive) admitted to us that they found a healthy male armpit, in its natural state, far sexier than expensive aftershaves!

(Which raises, in passing, another point—the cunning of commercial terminology. No one could sell scent to men until someone came up with the name 'aftershave lotion'—or dolls to boys until someone thought of 'Action Men.')

Popular film and television is dominated by youthism; even the Mutant Hero Turtles are teenage. And, for example, *Baywatch* would have us believe that the female users of the southern California beach are exclusively in their teens or 20s, 95 percent bikini-clad, and all 36-24-36. We have been there—and to say the least, they aren't.

Pagans are realists, and it would be hypocritical to deny that youth is visually and sexually attractive, to people of all ages. We may point out that *Baywatch* is statistically unrealistic, but no one can deny that most men (including Pagans) still enjoy watching it; and there are corresponding programs which women enjoy. It is perfectly fair, and natural, to appreciate young people's enhancement of the human landscape— but it is not acceptable to treat them as objects for exploitation or abuse, or to feed the commercial delusion that attractiveness (of a particular restricted definition) is all that matters because it 'sells.'

To which should be added that here, as in other matters, Pagans are not confined by dogmatic rules. Non-Pagan attitudes to age-gap marriages, for example, tend to label them as sugar-daddy-plus-golddigger, or wealthy-widow-plus-toyboy. Yet if two people of differing ages are genuinely attracted to each other, to hell with the 'rules.' Stewart is 34 years older than Janet, and at first they resisted the idea, thinking it couldn't possibly work; but in the end the chemistry won and they gave up resisting, and have now been happily together for 20 years and legally married for 19. And Stewart's brother-in-law is 19 years older than his sister; they have been happily married since the end of World War II, and he has just celebrated his 92nd birthday. (Proving the point seems to run in the Farrar family.)

Employers' emphasis on youth extends beyond 'attractiveness' to the belittling of intelligence and skill. As unemployment rises, getting a job becomes ever more difficult for the over-30s. Younger people are cheaper to employ, believed to be more energetic, and considered easier to train; and if they are to handle customers, their surface attractiveness is wanted. Department heads are also often afraid that if they employ people who are too experienced, they may prove better than themselves and take over. Experience is very much undervalued, or even feared, in the labor market.

Youthism in fact distorts and shackles the true nature and value of youth—as patriarchalism does of men.

This attitude is not only inhuman, it is in the long run damaging to the economy; and it ignores an important and striking new phenomenon—that life expectancy is increasing rapidly. Average life expectancy in Roman times was 22 years; in the Western world in the 1850s it was 45; today it is 75. More and more people are living to their 80s, 90s, and even beyond, and experts confidently predict that this tendency will continue. We are reaching the stage where the under-30s, who were once a majority of the population, will be an ever smaller minority.

For the health of the community (including the young themselves), and of its economy, youthism must give way to a much greater sharing of activity between age groups. And this calls for a clearer understanding of the contributions which the various age groups can make.

The philosophy of Paganism involves this clearer understanding, and Pagans should be doing everything to encourage it—which many of them are. A lot of Pagan groups include a healthy proportion of graybeards and grandmothers, as well as people of middle age.

The contribution of experience which older people can offer has been greatly increased in this century by the phenomenal rate of change. In earlier centuries, on the whole one died in the sort of world one was born in. No longer. It was dramatically summed up by Patrick Moore, the British television astronomy program presenter, when he said the changes in his lifetime were symbolized for him by the fact that he had personally met both Orville Wright and Neal Armstrong.

Stewart has a similar example in his own family. The first sentence spoken by voice radio across the Atlantic was "Can you hear me, Picken?"—and Picken was Stewart's uncle Jim, who worked with Marconi from the start, and whom Stewart knew well when he was a teenager. Stewart's mother remembered how the family thought Jim was mad when he told them that soon they would be able to sit at home and listen to the commentary on a cricket match in Australia while it was being played. Now color vision, with perfect sound, is instantaneous around the world (and you can even set the video to record the cricket match so that you can watch it later).

Stewart, and millions like him, have lived through a fundamentally changing world. So apart from the wisdom which they hope they can offer, they can certainly contribute a wider perspective to their younger friends who have only lived from black-and-white to color television. If they are sensible, they do not contribute it loftily or pompously, but are fully aware that the feedback is two-way, and if they keep their minds open to those younger friends, they themselves will remain flexible and receptive of new ideas. We are all like Russian dolls; the 10-year-old self, the 20-year-old, and so on, are all still alive within the 50-, 60-, or 70-year-old; and if we are wise we will listen to them.

Expressive of the Pagan attitude to the spectrum of age-groups is the concept of the Triple Goddess—an archetypal Trinity found throughout both ancient and modern Paganism. It even survives in Christian folklore, for example in Provence, where the Virgin Mary, Mary Magdalene, and Mary Cleopas were said to have landed after Christ's Ascension at Les Saintes Maries de la Mer on the Mediterranean coast; worship of the Three Maries persists strongly in southern France, if regarded uneasily by the Vatican. In Irish tradition, St. Bridget is popularly said to have been 'three holy sisters of the same name.' Both Isolde of the Tristan and Isolde story, and Guinevere of pre-medieval Arthurian legend, appear as three women of the same name.

The concept survives, too, in Islam as Al-Lat, Al-Uzzah, and Manah, condemned in the Koran (Surah liii: 19-23) as 'empty names, which ye and your fathers have named goddesses'; yet they are still known in Moslem tradition as 'the Three Daughters of Allah.'

Many an ancient Pagan Goddess had one name but was said to be three—such as Hecate of the Three Faces, the Greek pre-patriarchal Hera, the Slavonic Zorya, and so on. In contemporary Eastern Paganism, the Hindus have Bhavani, known as the Triple Universe and portrayed in three forms: youthful, mature, and aged; Chinese Buddhists have the Triple Pussa; and so on.

The idea seems ineradicable.

The Triple Goddess is Maid, Mother and Crone—symbolized by the waxing, full, and waning moon, and by dawn, noon, and sunset.

The Maid is Enchantment, Adventure, the promise of new beginnings. She is Springtime, her frank eroticism dangerous if abused but fulfilling if respected. She is the bright flame of Youth, giving a sparkle to the world. She is the primrose and the daffodil. The male principle is her lover and her fellow-pioneer.

The Mother is Ripeness, Nourishment, the molding womb and the guardian of growth. She is Summer, fertility at its height, feeding, rewarding enterprise and reprimanding irresponsibility. She is the rose in full bloom. She is the radiance of the hearth fire, giving warmth to all. The male principle is both her husband and her son.

The Crone is Experience, Wisdom, the accumulation of all that has gone before. She is Autumn, when the riches of summer are gathered and stored for all to draw upon. She is the fruit-laden tree. She is the glow of sunset, illuminating the darkening landscape. The male principle is her complement in the weighing of knowledge.

The message, through the millennia, is clear: the Three are One and the One is Three, inseparable and complementary. Just as every real woman, at heart, is all Three.

Talking of the complementary male principle, we feel that it is time to consider the concept of the Triple God, if only to reinstate the fullness of the God-aspect which has been crippled by two millennia of patriarchalism, and to restore the Grass Widower to his true partnership.

The three faces of the Triple God might be named the Hero, the Father, and the Sage.

The Hero would be the youthful Adventurer, dedicating his pristine energy to the exploration of new ideas and possibilities, and discovering with his partner the Maid the true nature of their complementary balance.

The Father would be the mature Organizer, protecting the Mother's environment and enriching the education of their offspring by complementing her right-brain function with his own left-brain emphasis.

The Sage, like the Crone, would be a reservoir of experience and wisdom—but he, too, would amplify what they have to offer by the complementary nature of his approach.

The emphasis, as soon as one begins to consider the idea of the Triple God, is inevitably on complementarity; and investigating the concept of the Six should increase our understanding of each of the two Threes.

The Germans used to define the role of women as *Kirche, Kinder und Küche*—church, children and kitchen. With the growing liberation of women, this insistence has rapidly lost ground, in Germany and elsewhere. Pagans in particular live by the principle that we mentioned in the last chapter—that the nature of any man/woman partnership should be determined by the nature of the partners, and not by any imposed set of rules.

There are many couples where the woman is happiest with an outside job, and the man is a natural 'househusband'—and this can apply to their respective roles as parents, too. Even though they love their children equally, and express that love to them, the father may be better (and again, happier) than the mother at handling the details of looking after them at home, and the mother better and happier with an outside professional job. If these conventionally-reversed roles are natural to the couple, and they live them lovingly and well, most children will also accept them as natural, with no more and no fewer problems than parent/child relationships give rise to anyway.

Sadly, in Britain at least, statistics show that the divorce rate is higher among such couples than the general rate. But this is probably due, not to any inherent instability of the arrangement, but to the pressure of conventional attitudes.

In the Western world as it stands right now, Pagans with children face problems and dangers. Most of them have the ideal of bringing up those children to understand their parents' religion, but also to realize that when they are mature enough to decide, they will be free to choose their own path—which may or may not be the same.

As one of our own initiates—herself a mother and a school governor—said when asked on a British television program whether children should be taught religion: "Children should not be taught religion; they should be taught *about* religion."

Such an approach is incomprehensible to many non-Pagans, and certainly to all Fundamentalists. The official Christian view is that children must be christened, baptized, and trained exclusively as Christians from the start, to ensure their salvation. Extremists even still believe that a baby who dies before being christened will be confined to Limbo till the Day of Judgment. These attitudes, whether extremist or merely 'official,' lead inevitably to the belief that Pagans and witches are endangering their children's souls.

In some places—particularly in some American states—this has led to Pagans' children being taken away from them and put into care. The parents are rarely given the chance to appeal or to explain their attitudes; and we know personally of at least one case where two small children, a boy and a girl, were ruthlessly questioned, and physically examined, in an (unsuccessful) attempt to prove child abuse—with understandably traumatic effects on them.

We cannot resist reporting one heart-warming exception. In a southern state, a social worker called on a mother and told her: "We're going to take away your children because you are witches." Surprisingly, the mother was able to sit the social worker down for a few minutes and talk with her—and lent her one of our books to take away and read. The worker did so—brought it back and asked for more—was given them, and read them too—and finally came back and said: "You're all right; you can keep your children."

Such a chance to explain and discuss is unhappily rare; but it does emphasize yet again the importance of local Pagan movements sinking their differences, acting together, obtaining legal recognition of their religious standing, and intervening vigorously on that basis in parents' defense.

Even where official persecution is less of a danger, as it is in Europe, there are still problems. Children of known Pagans—particularly of witches—may be teased and bullied at school; and even if the parents' religious views are not publicly known, small children in all innocence may give them away.

Friends of ours who run a coven in Dublin tell us:

> When we had our children we decided that we would not bring them up as witches, as we felt it would set them apart from their peers. Our feelings are that children dislike being different, and to bring them up in a country where the Christian religion, both Catholic and Anglican, plays such a huge part of everyday life, we would bring them up as their school friends are being brought up. When the children are older, then we will tell them what we practice. When they reach the age of 18, should they decide that they would like to be initiated, we would probably try to find a coven for them to work with rather than with us, as we feel that working with us could cause tension and restraint on their part.

On the other hand, a high priestess in Missouri tells us:

> Children may be admitted to ritual, provided they are in the company of their parents or legal guardian. Full membership may be gained when the child is 16, if a notarized statement of consent and permission is obtained from a parent or guardian (this saves us from the legal ramifications of 'contributing to the delinquency of a minor' suits. Yes, I have seen this happen, believe it or not!) Otherwise, the person may gain full membership when he reaches the age of adulthood as decided by the State of the Union in which he resides. Currently the age range in our group goes from 19 to 43.

And an Ontario high priestess writes:

> Our minimum age for initiation is 18. Besides being the legal age of consent, we require a level of maturity that is not often present in teenagers. Most teenagers are still exploring who they are, and I consider it irresponsible to ask someone to devote themselves to a particular spiritual path when they are still trying to find who and what they are... Our youngest member is 26, the oldest is 43.

In Britain, the Sorcerer's Apprentice Occult Census (see p. 48) found that 62% of its sample had children, and concluded from their replies that:

> It seems evident that involvement in occultism does NOT destroy the accepted social and family bonds which are considered 'normal' within our society.

Where children can be relied upon for discretion, a fairly general practice on both sides of the Atlantic is to let them take part in festivals, and in seasonal Sabbats which are purely celebratory, but to exclude them from working Circles. Even more general is the acceptance of 18, or sometimes of the local 'age of consent,' as the minimum age for initiation; few teenagers younger than that would be mature enough to choose their path soundly.

The whole situation of Pagan parenthood varies from place, but almost nowhere is it totally easy. (What parenthood is, one may ask?) It will only become gradually easier when the true facts of Pagan philosophy and action are understood by our sensible non-Pagan fellow-citizens. And this state of affairs must always be a central Pagan aim, patiently and methodically pursued.

One alarming backlash of dying patriarchalism has been growing recently, particularly in the United States: the replacement of normal birth by caesarian, which is becoming more and more the standard practice, whether there are emergency reasons for it or not. This is partly motivated by the male medical hierarchy's jealousy of the midwife, which has persisted since the centuries when the relied-upon midwife was in fact the witch. Today (witch or not) she is being increasingly edged out, in spite of the fact that she is highly qualified and experienced, and knows when it is necessary (as it rarely is) to call in the doctor.

But a more immediate cause of the caesarian trend, in the United States and Canada, is doctors' growing fear of being sued for malpractice if a normal birth goes wrong, and it can be claimed that a caesarian delivery could have avoided the trouble. More and more American doctors are deciding that for their own protection a caesarian is the safer bet, for a first birth at least.

Many impartial experts are worried that this trend may have evolutionary effects, reducing the ability of women to have natural births. The growing caesarian fashion is a disturbing symptom which Pagans should watch carefully, and take a stand on where necessary.

15.

Pagans in the Community

Pagans are citizens, active members of the community as a whole, aware of their responsibilities to it and of the contribution they can and must make. They are not anarchistic drop-outs.

Homo et femina sapiens are social animals, and that is the strength of our species. Like wolves, some apes, whales and dolphins we achieve by group action far more than we could by individual effort, even more so than the other social species, because language and community-wide communication have enabled us to outstrip them.

Humanity has another unique feature: we progress by the confrontation and interaction of different views and philosophies. At the negative extreme, such confrontation can mean violence and war; but on the positive side, it can mean (on the thesis-antithesis-synthesis principle) successful adaptation to changing needs. So it is vital for the Pagan movement to contribute to this essentially human interaction.

Chrys Thorsen, Director of the American Buddhist Congress, wrote a very thoughtful 'Open Letter to the Pagan Community' (published in various journals and read aloud at the Grand Council of the Covenant of the Goddess) on the occasion of COG's sponsorship of the World Parliament of Religions. Chrys is also Director of the International Buddhist Meditation Center, the oldest American Buddhist Temple, and her husband is a Wiccan in the Norse tradition.

If you wish to defuse the automatic negative reaction that the average religious group or citizen has when they hear the word 'Witch' there are certain things you must know and do... Wake up and smell the coffee. Our entire society is being pulled inexorably into a single community. We are already a global village aided by both technology and the growing consciousness of world crises. There is no benefit but rather detriment for a large growing body to attempt to hide and not be part of this renaissance movement... If you seek the recognition you deserve, you must go about it in an approachable manner. You have got to win personal trust and let people know that you're ordinary folks like them... As you're initially trying to make contact, don't smokescreen people with excessive costumery at interfaith events. Don't dress up and play Witch. I was disappointed to see some of this at the Parliament. Perhaps many Pagans are still in that militant mode that is a normal part of 'coming out.' This is expected and quite alright but really is an early phase and should eventually be matured past... You have a number of good friends already and more can be identified and loosely organized. With further introductions and personal dialogues, this will accelerate into a slow but steady chain reaction. People on a personal level will be able to say to their colleagues, 'The Wiccans? Oh, yeah. I know them. They're good people.' Believe me when I say that Paganism can eventually become acceptable enough to mainstream America. You won't have to fear for your lives, jobs, homes and children. The road will be very long and hard, but not impossible.

It is not only on religious issues that Pagans form links with other concerned members of the community. For example, it is not surprising that Pagans are particularly active in the animal rights movement, and this often brings them into confrontation with various commercial interests, and with the 'sporting' elements.

The confrontation is particularly marked in Britain at the moment. Scotland Yard, the London police headquarters, has a department called the Animal Rights National Index, which contains the names not only of those protesters who have technically infringed the law (by breaking into laboratories, for example), but also of the leaders and membership of animal rights organizations which have never broken the law—and of people who know them. These records are not open to inspection, even by the long-standing and respected Royal Society for the Prevention of Cruelty to Animals.

British police are increasingly active against the movement. Peaceful demonstrators trying to be present with their posters when a fox-hunt is gathering are kept at a distance, often by posts with tapes, on the excuse that they will cause 'a breach of the peace.' The present Conservative government is actually considering legislation to make such protests illegal in themselves.

(To be fair, many individual policemen—not only animal lovers, but also those who know what damage fox-hunting can do to farmland and so on—are unhappy about the job they have to do.)

Public feeling against stag-hunting is far more general than against fox-hunting, doubtless because stags, unlike foxes, are no threat to farmers or poultry-keepers. Several English counties have banned it. But the Quantock Staghounds appealed to the court against Somerset County Council's ban, and on February 9, 1994, they won their case, the judge ruling that the ban was illegal and that "it was not for the Council to impose their moral standards on others." Somerset Council announced that they would appeal against the ruling, but meanwhile other Councils fear that their own bans are in jeopardy.

Stag-hunting, incidentally, results in many hounds being maimed by the stag defending itself.

Police activity where animal rights are involved is often farcically disproportionate. When a department of Oxford University complained that £2,000 worth of mongrel dogs kept by them for experiment had been illegally set free, a major police operation was allotted to the case, with many officers and a temporary command headquarters. Whereas a householder who reported a £2,000 burglary would be lucky if a couple of officers came along to examine the broken window and look for fingerprints.

More than one leader of an animal rights group has been taken into a police station for questioning, been kept there for a few hours till the police told him or her that they were satisfied no law had been broken—and then gone home to find the place has been thoroughly searched and membership lists and other documents taken away. The 'questioning' was merely a maneuver to make this possible.

Admittedly, some well-meaning enthusiasts do infringe the law in dangerous and foolish ways—for example, by breaking into a laboratory and releasing animals into the wild which have been injected with viruses, which can spread fatal diseases such as rabies among the animals of the surrounding countryside. This is self-defeating and cannot be justified—and what is more, it is used by the authorities to excuse even heavier measures against the peaceful activists who are the great majority.

There are, in fact, differences of opinion among animal rights campaigners on the degree of animal experimentation that is permissible. Some argue for example that experiments on rats which can result in the saving of human children's lives can be allowed, under proper supervision. But even those who would permit such experiments insist that they should be done by one Government-controlled laboratory, instead of as at present by a string of independent ones, often doubling up on each other's programs.

And there are arguments in favor of rabies experiments on animals with the intention of protecting the animal population as a whole (and the release of such laboratory animals by protesters, particularly in rabies-free Britain or Ireland, could have disastrous results).

But on one thing all animal rights campaigners are certainly agreed: laboratory experiments on animals by cosmetic firms are in no way permissible.

This is a time of widespread public activity on ecological issues; of growing impatience by grass-roots members of various religions with dictatorial hierarchies; of campaigning on many fronts for women's freedom and equality; of growing insistence on freedom of speech and opinion; and so on. Pagans share all this motivation; but it is important that they should do so in cooperation with their non-Pagan neighbors, and not in splendid isolation. They will then be recognized more and more as allies in things that matter, and will be increasingly understood and accepted.

16.

The Global Village

The birth of the Global Village, now undergoing its labor pains, is a major turning point in human social evolution. It is mainly due to four developments: the collapse of Soviet and other communisms and the resulting end of great power military confrontation; instant world intercommunication perfected by modern technology; increasing economic interdependence arising from that same technology; and the increasingly global nature of ecological phenomena.

Those labor pains are complicated, and at the present state of Global Village development, both positive and negative symptoms are evident. An extreme example of the negative side was the disastrous situation in the former Yugoslavia, with its shameful motivation of 'ethnic cleansing'—reminiscent of Nazi activity, even down to the prison camps with their record of starvation and torture. Others were the civil wars in countries like Angola, which achieved nothing but economic paralysis and innocent deaths—in Angola's case, about 400,000.

On the positive side (quite apart from the collapse of communism and the Cold War, which launched it all) there are such developments as the totally unexpected peace agreement between Israel and the Palestine Liberation Organization, making it possible to end decades of unresolved strife, in spite of minority hard-line opposition on both sides, which at the time of writing was still making fulfillment a slow process.

For us, a pleasing positive symptom—small, perhaps, but typical—was the atmosphere of the World Athletic Championships in Stuttgart in August 1993. That event showed a healthy blend of national effort and pride with mutual respect and even affection, in noticeable contrast to the Cold War undercurrents of earlier Olympics and other events of this kind. (Significantly, all the athletes taking part were of course young.)

Pagan thinking is entirely in tune with the positive elements, and strongly opposed to the negative ones. So Pagans at all levels have a healthy contribution to make to the encouragement of the first and the restraining and resolving of the second.

In terms of this contribution, perhaps the most notable positive development while this book was being written was the inclusion of a Wiccan delegation to the Parliament of World Religions held in Chicago, Illinois, in September 1993. The Parliament is held once per century; at the last one, in 1893, the Buddhists made their first formal mission to North America. This time, the Covenant of the Goddess (see p. 160) undertook to co-sponsor the Parliament on behalf of all Wiccans. Not all the delegations were happy about the inclusion of the Wiccans; the Southern Baptist and the Greek Orthodox representatives walked out in protest. The substantial and varied remainder adopted a 'Declaration of a Global Ethic,' which the Wiccan priestess the Rev. Deborah Ann Light endorsed as representative of the Covenant of the Goddess, Circle Sanctuary, and the EarthSpirit Community. The text was as follows:

The Declaration of a Global Ethic

The world is in agony. The agony is so pervasive and urgent that we are compelled to name its manifestations so that the depths of this pain can be made clear.

Peace eludes us…the planet is being destroyed…neighbors live in fear…women and men are estranged from each other…children die!

This is abhorrent!

We condemn the abuses of Earth's ecosystems.

We condemn the poverty that stifles life's potential; the hunger that weakens the human body; the economic disparities that threaten so many families with ruin.

We condemn the social disarray of the nations; the disregard of justice which pushes citizens to the margin; the anarchy overtaking our communities; and the insane death of children from violence. In particular we condemn aggression and hatred in the name of religion.

But this agony need not be.

It need not be because the basis for an ethic already exists. This ethic offers the opportunity of a better individual and global order, and leads individuals away from despair and societies away from chaos.

We are women and men who have embraced the precepts and practices of the world's religions.

We affirm that a common set of core values is found in the teachings of the religions; and that these form the basis of a global ethic.

We affirm that this truth is already known, but yet to be lived in heart and action.

We confirm that there is an irrevocable, unconditional norm for all areas of life, for families and communities, for races, nations and religions. There already exist ancient guidelines for human behavior which are found in the teachings of the religions of the world and which are the conditions for a sustainable world order.

We declare: We are interdependent. Each of us depends on the well-being of the whole, and so we have respect for the community of living beings, for people, animals and plants, and for the preservation of Earth, the air, water and soil.

We take individual responsibility for all we do. All our decisions, actions and failures to act have consequences.

We must treat others as we wish others to treat us. We make a commitment to respect life and dignity, individuality and diversity, so that every person is treated humanely, without exception. We must have patience and acceptance. We must be able to forgive, learning from the past but never allowing ourselves to be enslaved by memories of hate. Opening our hearts to one another, we must sink our narrow differences for the cause of the world community, practicing a culture of solidarity and relatedness.

We consider humankind our family. We must strive to be kind and generous. We must not live for ourselves alone, but must also serve others, never forgetting the children, the aged, the poor, the suffering, the disabled, the refugees, and the lonely. No person should ever be considered or treated as a second-class citizen, or be exploited in any way whatsoever. There should be equal partnership between men and women. We must not commit any kind of sexual immorality. We must put behind us all forms of domination or abuse.

We commit ourselves to a culture of non-violence, respect, justice and peace. We shall not oppress, injure, torture, or kill other human beings, forsaking violence as a means of settling differences.

We must strive for a just social and economic order, in which everyone has an equal chance to reach full potential as a human being. We must speak and act truthfully and with compassion, dealing fairly with all, and avoiding prejudice and hatred. We must not steal. We must move beyond the dominance of greed for power, prestige, money, and consumption to make a just and peaceful world.

Earth cannot be changed for the better unless the consciousness of individuals is changed first. We pledge to increase our awareness by disciplining our minds, by meditation, by prayer, or by positive thinking. Without risk and a readiness to sacrifice there can be no fundamental change in our situation. Therefore we commit ourselves to this global ethic, to understanding one another, and to socially beneficial, peace-fostering, and nature-friendly ways of life.

We invite all people, whether religious or not, to do the same.

With this impassioned Declaration, endorsed by a worldwide spectrum of religions, all Pagans must surely agree; and the Pagan movement has its own unique contribution to make to its fulfillment.

Some people are nervous that the Global Village will mean the swamping of national and local cultural identity. (This nervousness is evident, for example, among those who resist the development of a united European Community.) In fact, the opposite is likely to be the case; as we point out on p. 157, for all its faults, the United States is a model of federal unity plus flourishing state identity. California and Connecticut, Nevada and Nebraska, Massachusetts and Missouri, are all very much American and very much themselves.

Cultural identity is difficult to swamp, and any level. The most successfully united families consist of very different personalities, whose individual natures each contribute to that success.

Pagans can wholeheartedly support and work for the Global Village, confident that greater communication and cooperation between its many cultures will produce not uniformity, but an enrichment of the total spectrum by mutual understanding and respect.

This is not wishful thinking; it will prove more and more to be a fact of life.

17.

Watch It!

Every movement, particularly when it is expanding rapidly, has its aberrant or excessive fringes; and the Pagan movement is no exception.

One element which has been hampering the healthy development of that movement (though Pagans as a whole are becoming more and more aware of its hampering effect) is what may be called Pagan Fundamentalism—the insistence that one's own particular 'path,' its dogma, and even its hierarchy is the only 'right' one.

This is entirely contrary to the basic nature of Pagan philosophy.

Some areas have suffered from it more than others. To take the United States as an example; when we visited one particular state in 1991, we found the Pagan movement there torn and paralyzed by sectarianism, backbiting, calculated dirty tricks, and personal ambition—most of it traceable directly to one source. As a result, it was achieving nothing except a lot of individual misery.

We are glad to say that sensible Pagans there have since become impatient with the situation, and are refusing to bow down to that dictatorship, which is becoming more and more isolated. Cooperation there seems to be growing healthily.

At the other extreme, in Washington State the Pagan movement had long achieved mutual tolerance and cooperation. Among the results, at the time of writing Washington has at least one officially appointed Wiccan prison chaplain; and the long-existing State Council of Religions—which used to consist of three Christians, three Jews, three Moslems, and so on—now includes three Pagans. Such things could never have been achieved by a disunited movement.

Healthy Paganism encourages individual choice, and one result has been the growth of a multiplicity of 'paths'—some of them only distinguishable from each other by minor points of detail—which we discussed in Chapter 4. Essentially, this is as it should be; but it can contain a vicious-circle element. We have heard one group telling another that "your third degree is only equivalent to our second," or insisting on a 'valid' genealogy of initiations, and so on.

The only 'validity' of any path is its genuine acceptance by the people who practice it—even if they sprang from nowhere and initiated themselves, or do not believe in formal initiation at all. Personal suitability of belief and practice is the essence of Paganism. Pagan Fundamentalism is incompatible with that essence.

Confrontation and argument—some of it vehement—is a natural and inevitable, and basically healthy, element in any rapidly growing movement. It is the proof of its vigor, and it is from this that the movement gradually finds its true nature and shape. But it should be about principles and practice, and should constantly develop into discussion and agreement. It should not be the expression of personal ambition, one-upmanship or jealousy; and a continuing watch should be kept to keep these under control.

We would re-emphasize what we said in Chapter 5—that respect for all religions, Pagan or non-Pagan, is obligatory for Pagans; and they must at all costs avoid tying simple, one-category labels round any of them. Criticism of imposed dogma or dictatorial hierarchy is legitimate and necessary; condemnation of, or hostility towards, ordinary worshippers who are themselves the victims of such dictatorship is not.

Neither is invasion or misuse of other religions' holy places. A sad example of this was in Bristol, England, in 1993. Monica Sjöö wrote, in replying to our Questionnaire, telling us of

> … an action which we as feminist Goddess women undertook at the cathedral in Bristol, when on a Sunday during full Mass a group of us, during a women's conference in Bristol on May 8th and 9th, 1993, walked into the cathedral and sang 'Burning Times,' and facing the congregation. We felt that this was a sacred act and enormously powerful. There was no aggro or confrontation apart from this.

She was surprised at the 'whole spate of misogynist and horrendously anti-woman letters and articles' which this prompted in the local magazine *Pagan Voice*. She told us "you may quote me if you like and by name as long as you also do *not* misrepresent what I have just written." We have quoted her exact words to avoid being charged with any such misrepresentation. But we are absolutely certain that Pagans as a whole will be appalled at the action which the women took, and will fully understand the local Pagan anger about it. The invasion of the cathedral showed total lack of respect for another religion; it was in reality sheer 'aggro and confrontation,' and the only effect it could have would be to inflame resentment against local Paganism. It could not have had any educative effect on the cathedral worshippers whatsoever. How would Monica have felt if a group of Christians had invaded a serious Pagan ritual and started intoning the Catechism?

We understand from a British source that one result of the women's action will be that Pagan representatives will not be admitted to the Bristol Inter-Faith Council.

Many Dianic or women-only groups are healthy and fruitful in their work, and cooperate with men on matters of common interest. But there are unquestionably some radical feminist groups who are hostile to men, and this attitude is as negative as the patriarchalism it claims to fight against. True Paganism insists on the complementary equality of men and women.

Fortunately, the exaggerated attitude of such 'rad fem' groups puts them beyond the pale for most Pagans, and indeed for the general public; if anything, it turns them into a joke. But one of their propaganda claims is more widely if unthinkingly accepted—that the public and media display of female sexuality, from scantily-clad girls decorating commercial advertisements at one extreme to porno films at the other, is 'exploitation of women.'

Sometimes, of course—when the women concerned are doing it reluctantly, because they need the money—this is true. But it overlooks the fact that in many cases the women enjoy doing it, through pride in their own strength.

In today's situation, when patriarchy is doomed but still fighting, some Pagan women play down their attractiveness in defiance of it, while others emphasize their attractiveness as a challenge to anyone who dares exploit it. Often neither is truly happy with the roles they have cast themselves in, though most of the emphasizers are.

Sexual parading is a built-in element in all mammal (and bird) behavior; without it, species would die out. And humans share this instinct—powerfully so, because as we saw in Chapter 13, *homo et femina sapiens* are the sexiest primates on Earth. Both men and women display and pursue; choice emerges from this exchange of behavior. Also, the nature of this display and pursuit may vary with the fashion of the period, and the customs of the culture involved.

To insist that a woman should not be proud of her own attractiveness, and even earn her living by it while it is at its peak, is to ignore reality. Pagans accept reality, while tempering its phenomena with civilized mutual compassion and consideration. And this acceptance should be accorded, for example, to the pin-up whose self-respect is enhanced by what she chooses to do.

Another lesson which some Pagans need to learn is to do their homework. Understandably and quite permissibly, many groups and individuals are attracted by traditions and pantheons with which they feel in tune, and base their symbology and their rituals on them.

But some such groups tend to let their enthusiasm run away with them, and act on the little they actually know of the culture concerned. As a result, they develop systems which, however well-intentioned, are often confused and bear very little relation to the actuality of that tradition. This can of course lead to their work having little, or unintended, effect—and incidentally to justified mockery from non-Pagans who happen to be genuine experts on the subject.

Adopting the symbology of an ancient tradition, such as Egyptian, Greek, Middle Eastern, Nordic, or Celtic (the major ones of the Western World) calls for careful and deep study, the reading of authoritative books on the subject—and even, if possible, visiting the countries where the roots of that tradition are still alive. This is hard work, but if one is not prepared to face it, one should stick to the symbology of the environment where one is living. Doing this at least some of the time is a good idea anyway—it helps keeps one in touch with the Earth Mother as she is where you are—and there is no harm in variety, provided the elements are not mixed in one ritual, and provided all of them have been thoroughly studied.

We three, for example, sometimes practice in Celtic symbology (since Janet and Stewart are both more than half Celtic, and we have lived for 18 years in a Celtic country); sometimes Nordic in its Anglo-Saxon form (since Gavin is of Saxon tradition and a profound scholar of the subject); and sometimes Egyptian (since Janet and Stewart have visited Egypt, and studied the subject thoroughly); and sometimes entirely in twentieth-century symbology to tackle specifically twentieth-century problems. But we would never mix any of these on the same occasion; that would be as discordant as playing jazz, folk music, and a Beethoven symphony simultaneously.

There are groups which actually define their path as Eclectic, drawing on several traditions and even adding to the selection as they go along.

This is fine, and can enrich the multi-dimensionality of their vision—provided that they are well-informed on the traditions they are drawing from, and that the elements on any one occasion are harmonious and self-consistent. We know of one well-intentioned, Goddess-oriented group in Ireland who will invoke everyone from Kwan-Yin and Kali to Danu and Demeter not only in the same ritual, but even in the same sentence, and the result is mere confusion, detracting from the power of their intent.

We met one native Hawaiian priestess who was appalled at Western Pagans' mixing of such invocations, particularly in regard to her own volcano Goddess, Pele. "She is powerful, and dangerous if you don't approach her carefully," she told us. "Mix her with those others, and she just won't understand." A very practical warning, this; too many visiting Pagans climb Pele in careless enthusiasm, even in flowing and inflammable ritual robes, forgetting that she is active and unpredictable. Some have even died as a result.

To return to the matter of doing one's homework, take the Nordic tradition as an example. That tradition (which is really a spectrum of traditions, embracing Scandinavian, Teutonic, Dutch, and Anglo-Saxon forms) is often especially prone to lack of genuine study. Two factors in particular have affected this.

First, the Viking image. Too many people identify the Nordic tradition with the Viking record of invasion and pillage, not realizing that most such Vikings were younger sons with no land to inherit and therefore going abroad to grab—while the families at home, the real Nordics, were peaceable agriculturists. It should be added that even the Vikings often settled down as active traders and farmers—as they did for example in Dublin, which became a fruitful fusion of two cities, Celtic and Viking. It was Norsemen, fleeing royal Christian tyranny, who established the first democratic republics in Europe—in Iceland in 930 AD, and in the Isle of Man in 979 AD (whose parliament is still known by a Norse name, the Tynwald).

And second, the Wagnerian image which followed on Christianization (and which was enthusiastically adopted by the Nazis) romanticized the warrior aspect, and caused it to be accepted too widely as a true picture of the Nordic tradition.

The original Odin was admittedly a warrior, but he was a much more complex figure than that; he was also shamanistic, a psychopompos (conductor of the dead), God of magic (runes), and a God who sacrificed himself in pursuit of wisdom (the Hanged Man of the Tarot). Frey and

Freya were deities of love, fertility and prosperity. Thor was loved by the peasantry, often with an affectionate twinkle in their eyes. Even Loki was originally probably more like the Native American Coyote, a constructive trickster, not the malicious saboteur which Christianized legend made him.

In short, the true basic Nordic tradition is that of peaceful farmers, struggling for prosperity in a hard northern environment. Wise Nordic-path Pagans should study these roots—and wear gumboots, not jack-boots.

One other point on the adoption of traditions—most American Pagans know that they should be good neighbors to Native Americans, attend their festivities when invited (the genuine ones, not the tourist-traps), and strive to understand their traditions. But they also know that they should not attempt to copy them; Native Americans, struggling to rescue and re-establish those traditions (which may vary widely from tribe to tribe) after centuries of oppression, compulsory Christianity, and decimation, understandably resent such imitation. "Our spiritual-ity," as one of them told us, "is not for sale"—and this feeling should be respected.

A small but important point to remember: pouring libations of wine or beer on the Earth is a long-established European tradition. But the whites' introduction of alcohol to America was disastrous for the indigenous tribes, whose metabolism is unable to handle it. So Native Americans do not like it poured on American soil. Placing offerings of corn or tobacco on the ground is their equivalent of libation; and it would promote harmony for white American Pagans to adopt the same prac-tice, or to use fruit juice. Blue corn is traditional, and should be soaked in water first, so that it swells up *before* birds or animals take it into their stomachs. (Some tribes did brew their own forms of herb alcohol, to which they were not allergic, before the white man came; but it would be wise not to use this fact as an excuse for libation.)

Our final point in this chapter may be considered pedantic, but as writers, loving and respecting language, we feel entitled to make it. Like most religions, Paganism, and perhaps Wicca in particular, tends to use archaic English in certain rituals: 'O thou Circle, be thou a meeting place...' and so on. There is often a poetic beauty in this, emphasizing the special nature of the ritual. But if you are going to use it, *get it right*. Apart from anything else, using it clumsily will disturb participants who do know how it should go, and distract them.

The two commonest faults are (a) muddling singular and plural, when using 'thou, thee' and 'ye, you,' and (b) muddling the subject and object of a sentence.

'Thou' and 'thee' are singular; 'ye,' and in archaic English 'you.' are plural. Time and again we have heard 'Ye Lords of the Watchtowers of the East, we do thank thee...,' which is nonsense.

'Thou' and 'ye' are nominative, the subject of a sentence (or vocative, addressing someone, as in 'O thou Circle...,' or imperative, as in 'be thou a meeting place...'). 'Thee,' and in archaic English 'you,' are accusative, the object of a sentence. It should therefore be 'Ye Lords of the Watchtowers of the East, we do thank you...,' and 'Thou art welcome' but 'We do welcome thee'.

One other thing to remember, in the traditional couplet 'Eight words the Wiccan Rede fulfill, An it harm none, do what ye will'. 'An' here means 'if,' not 'and,' so it should not have a 'd'.

While we are at it, we might as well go the whole way and voice the complaint we felt when Magickal Childe published two of our books under the title *A Witches Bible Compleat*—quite apart from the repeated confusion with Gavin and Yvonne Frost's book. There is some excuse for 'Magickal,' from Crowley's distinction between true magic and conjuring. But 'Childe' for 'Child' and 'Compleat' for 'Complete' are pointless affectations, and the absence of an apostrophe at the end of 'Witches' is sheer illiteracy.

...All right, pedantry over!

18.

Go On, Smile

All too many believers in a religion ban humor from anything related
to their faith. Wit and laughter are for them entirely secular; to allow
such things to trespass on holy territory would be sacrilege, an offense
to the (presumably humorless) God.

Most Pagans do not share this attitude. They regard humor as an
essential factor in human self-evaluation, a safeguard against pompous-
ness.

Pagans tend to make fun of themselves, of each other—and even of
their beliefs, to see if they will stand up to such treatment. People who
are over-solemn, they feel, are in danger of losing a sense of proportion,
and thus of reality. Valid convictions should be able to survive mockery
and be reaffirmed by it. Even their jokes about other religions are, on
the whole, good-natured—though they can be scathingly satirical about
self-interested hierarchies and imposed dogma.

(To be fair, many followers of other religions take the same attitude.
An excellent example of this is W.H. Davies' poem *Ducks*.)

With all this in mind, we have collected together a few examples of
Pagan humor.

Three well-known Pagan high priestesses—let us call them Ann,
Betty, and Carol—were driving together to a Festival being held on an
island in a river. But when they reached the river, they found heavy rain
had flooded it.

Ann said "No problem," and walked across the water to the island.

Betty said "If she can do it, I can," and walked across after her.

Carol thought "If they can do it, I can," stepped in—and sank like a
stone. A couple of strong lads swam across and rescued her on to the

island. They pumped her dry, and when she could talk, she asked the other women: "How did you manage it?"

Betty asked: "Didn't you see the stepping stones?"

And Ann asked: "What stepping stones?"

What is the difference between a nurse and a nun? A nun only has to bow down to one God.

Monday's witch is foul of face,
Tuesday's witch is a disgrace,
Wednesday's witch is long of nose,
Thursday's witch has extra toes,
Friday's witch bakes poisoned pies,
Saturday's witch has evil eyes;
But the witch that was born on the Sabbath day
Tends to smell—so keep away!

(Malcolm Bird)

The two leading Glasgow football teams are Rangers, which is Catholic, and Celtic, which is Protestant. A Glasgow friend of Stewart's was on holiday in the Isle of Man and found himself drinking with another Glaswegian in a pub. The other man started talking about football, and asked "D'ye support Celtic?"

Stewart's friend, not wishing to get into a heated discussion, replied: "No, I don't."

"Oh, ye support Rangers, then."

"No, I don't support Rangers, either."

The man frowned. "What are ye then, a bloody atheist?"

A man passing a pet shop saw kittens on sale as 'New Age Kittens, $1.' A week later he passed it again, and saw the same kittens on sale for $5.

Curious, he went in and asked why the change. "They're worth more now," the shopkeeper said. "They're Pagan Kittens since they got their eyes open."

"And do all plants have Latin names, Professor?"

"They do, madam."

"Isn't Nature wonderful!"

A missionary in Africa found himself facing a lion. He fell to his knees, and prayed to God for protection. To his surprise, the lion knelt too, and was obviously praying.

"Bless you, Brother Lion," the missionary said. "We are all God's children, and it moves my heart to kneel with you..."

And the lion said: "Shut up while I'm saying grace!"

Disraeli, on his deathbed, was asked if he wished Queen Victoria to be brought to him. "I don't think so," he replied. "She'd only give me a message for Albert."

The difference between New Age and Pagan is one decimal point. A New Ager will charge you $100 where a Pagan will charge you $10. *(Isaac Bonewits)*

Holy Mary, conceived without sin—help me to sin without conceiving. *(Graffito in Dublin ladies' rest room)*

How many Gardnerians does it take to change a light bulb? Thirteen, consisting entirely of man-woman working couples.

How many Rad Fems does it take? Seven: one to do it, two to organize the creche, and four to debate the meaning of the word 'unscrew.'

How many Crowleyites does it take? They can't; Uncle Aleister didn't leave any instructions.

How many Chaos Magicians does it take? They don't need to—they're used to working in the dark.

How many Satanists does it take? They can't; they are unable to get bulbs with left-hand threads.

How many Fundamentalists does it take? They won't, because their original bulb was the only *right* one.

Comment from a New Mexico witch, up to her eyes in laundry: "I think I must be working off a karmic debt, for having been cruel to a washerwoman in a past life."

At a moot a few weeks ago I met a particularly sad specimen of a Crap Witch. Actually this poor disillusioned sod started out as a devil worshipper. But being dyslexic it was a while before he realized he had mistakenly sold his soul to SANTA. Shame really. *(Pauline, England)*

Hymie fell on his knees and prayed: "Dear God—please let me win the lottery!"

No luck that week, so next week he prayed again: "I'm desperate. *Please* let me win this week!"

No luck again. He groveled, begging: "Dear Lord—I don't know which way to turn. *Please, PLEASE* let me win this time..."

And a voice came out of the heavens: "Hymie—meet me halfway. Buy a ticket?"

European occultists recognize four Elements—Earth, Air, Fire and Water. In America, there are five—Earth, Air, Fire, Water and Chocolate.

A priest and two nuns were playing golf. At the fifth, the priest missed a two-foot putt, and muttered: "Oh, damn!"

The nuns drew themselves up. "Father, if you're going to blaspheme, we'll call this off."

"I'm sorry, sisters. Heat of the moment. May God strike me dead if I do it again."

The nuns calmed down, and all went smoothly till the fourteenth, when the priest missed an eighteen-inch putt. He forgot himself and spat: "Oh, damn!"

The three of them froze, horrified. Overhead a huge black cloud gathered, and out of the cloud came a bolt of lightning—which killed the two nuns.

And out of the cloud came a deep voice: *"OH, DAMN!"*

Let us all worship Freya
She is certainly a stayer,
And all the Gods obey her
So she's good enough for me!

Let us all worship Horus
He was here long time before us,
But he certainly won't bore us
So he's good enough for me!

Let us all worship Kali
She has come here for a parley,
And she rode here on a Harley
So she's good enough for me!

Let us all worship Pele
I have seen her on the telly,
She has fire in her belly
So she's good enough for me!
(and so on, verse after verse, in chorus)

A Catholic priest who died found himself at the Pearly Gate, and an
angel told him: "I'm sorry, Father—there's an epidemic down there,
so there's rather a queue to clear. Would you mind if I put you in the
waiting room for a while?"

After half an hour, the impatient priest knocked on the door of the
waiting room and the angel came in to reassure him that the delay
wouldn't be long. "Make yourself at home, Father. There's a drinks
cupboard, and some magazines."

So the priest poured himself some ambrosia, and leafed through *The
Celestial Inquirer*, but soon he was bored again, and went to look out
of the window at the golden streets. A minute later the gate was flung
open, and in came an escort of motor-cycle angels with a red sports car
in the middle, driven by a well-known Wiccan high priestess.

Furious, the priest banged on the door and told the angel: "I have
been a servant of the Lord for thirty-eight years—celebrated Mass,
heard confessions, buried the dead, done all my duties—and here I've
been waiting over an hour, and that witch comes straight in..."

The angel interrupted him: "I can sympathize, Father, but you don't
understand. She's only had that car for two weeks, but in that time she's
put the fear of God into more people than you did in your entire career."

A favorite satirical event performed at some Pagan festivals in
America is that of the Ancient and Honorable Order of Bill the Cat (the
name being taken from that of a popular cartoon character). It involves
a Circle ritual which from start to finish is a blatantly crude caricature
of a serious Circle, with hilariously coarse substitutions for all of its
elements. The enthusiastic participants are genuine Pagans, who find
that this letting down of their ritual hair reinforces their understanding
and appreciation of the serious occasions. In this, it is not unlike the
Saturnalian Midwinter revels of Ancient Rome, where all the normal
rules of behavior and precedence were reversed for a few days with a
similar lesson in mind. (See also Discordianism, p. 35.)

19.

Around the World

U.S.A.

The United States is not a country, it is a continent, about 2,700 miles between the coasts of Maine in the East and Washington State in the West (twice as far as from England to Greece) and nearly 1,600 miles from the Canadian border with Minnesota in the north to the tip of Texas with Mexico in the south (slightly farther than from Madrid to Warsaw). And these dimensions do not include its two distant states of Hawaii and Alaska. Even some of the individual states are huge by European standards; California, for example, is about 730 miles from north to south, almost twice the length of mainland Britain.

The Union consists of states differing widely in cultural traditions, history, environment and climate—even though it must be credited with having created, in spite of inevitable strains and conflicts, the most successful federation in history. We have visited 26 of the 50 member states, plus Washington DC, and have found the Pagan scene to be as varied as the states themselves.

To describe that scene comprehensively would take a book in itself; the most we can do here is to describe a selection of the major organizations. For a virtual encyclopedia of the American Pagan movement, we recommend Margot Adler's excellent book *Drawing Down the Moon* (see Bibliography).

We would point out one thing, however. The modern witchcraft revival, and the general Pagan emergence to which it gave birth, were at the start a British phenomenon. But the British spark has become an American explosion. America today is beyond question the spearhead of the expansion of the Pagan movement. Its membership is greater, its festivals are larger and better organized, it publishes more journals than any one person can get around to reading, and more and more Pagan-owned festival areas are springing up, such as Circle Sanctuary in Ohio and the Gaea Center in Kansas; several more are being planned and purchased as we write.

Americans had a flying start in that freedom of religion was one of Uncle Sam's foundation stones, and remains Federal law. As the First Amendment to the Constitution laid down two centuries ago states:

> Congress shall make no law respecting an establishment of religion, or prohibiting the free practice thereof; or abridging the freedom of speech, or of the press; or of the right of the people peaceably to assemble, and to petition the government for a redress of grievances.

So Churches of Wicca and other Pagan religious bodies can apply for, and cannot be denied, legal status. (A moving experience for Stewart was when he conducted a legal wedding, with a Pagan hand-fasting ritual, in Tennessee, as the Rev. Stewart Farrar, recognized minister of a legal religion.)

A major factor in the development of the American Pagan movement has been the use of computer bulletin boards. Virtually every state in the Union has more such Pagan bulletin board members than exist in the whole of Britain; and the state networks link up with each other, so information about events and developments is universally and quickly available. The importance of this setup in the growth and efficiency of the movement cannot be over-emphasized.

The United States has become the focal area of the Pagan explosion; and Pagans in other countries should not resent the fact, but respect, support, and even learn from it.

The Church of All Worlds

Without doubt this is one of the largest Pagan organizations in the United States. Otter G'Zell, the Primate of the Church, was very cooperative in sending an immediate reply to the questionnaire we sent out to him regarding the Church. Here are extracts from his reply:

> The Church of All Worlds is specifically Neo-Pagan, implying an eclectic reconstruction of ancient Nature religions, and combining archetypes of many cultures with other mystic, environmental and spiritual disciplines. Indeed, we were the ones who first proposed, in 1967, that the term 'Pagan' be adopted to apply to the newly-emerging movement of Nature-based and revivalist pre-Christian religions. But we in CAW are not

merely trying to recreate a Paradise Lost; we are actively involved in trying to save the present world as well as working to actualize a visionary future. With roots deep in the Earth and branches reaching towards the stars, we evoke and create myths not only of a Golden Age long past, but of one yet to come...

The CAW Mission statement is: 'to evolve a network of information, mythology and experience that provides a context and stimulus for reawakening Gaia, and reuniting Her children through tribal community dedicated to responsible stewardship and evolving consciousness.' We are fairly all-embracing in promoting general Pagan and Gaian lifestyles and values. We advocate basic feminist and environmentalist principles, including freedom of reproductive choice, ordination of women as Priestesses, sacred sexuality, alternate relationships, gay and lesbian rights, protection and restoration of endangered species, wilderness sanctuaries, green politics, etc...

Our mythology is based on the Gaia Thesis—that all earthly life, us included, comprises a single great organism, the living body of Mother Earth, known as 'Gaia' to the ancient Greeks. Our Goddess is the very Soul of Nature!

CAW presently has about three dozen regional 'Nests,' which is what we call our local congregations, or Circles. These are indeed member groups, as are the several subsidiary 'branch' organizations that we have created and chartered to focus on particular areas of concern. These include: Nemeton—fundraising, marketing and publishing; Forever Forests—tree planting and environmental action; Ecosophical Research Association (ERA)—research and exploration into origins and actualizations of myths and legends; Lifeways—education and personal development; Peaceful Order of the Earth Mother (POEM)—dedicated to children and child nurturing; Holy Order of Mother Earth (HOME)—developing magical and ritual structures and techniques.

We are worldwide, including seven Nests in Australia, where we are the first legally recognized Pagan Religion (as we were the first in the U.S.). A third of our Nests are in California, reflecting the greatest concentration of our members. We have individual members throughout the world. Nests require a minimum of three registered due-paying members of at least Second Circle meeting at least once a month. Total number of CAW members of at least Second Circle is approximately 500 (as of October 1993), and growing rapidly. We don't keep records on the numbers of First (outer) Circle people involved, but I would estimate at least another 500 of those. (CAW membership is organized in a system of nine concentric circles.)

We hold seasonal, annual and one-shot events, ranging from as few as 30 people for the annual Eleusinian Mysteries, to 300 at our 30th anniversary Grand Convocation in 1992. In addition, our various Nests around the

U.S. and Australia also put on Festivals and other events, and some of these have had over 100 attendees.

We publish a number of periodicals. The most important of these is *Green Egg*, the foremost journal of the New Paganism for over 25 years. We also put out a magazine for Pagan kids called *How About Magic?*, a members-only newsletter, *The Scarlet Flame*, and our Inner Circle newsletter, *The Violet Vision*.

We have created a new Tribalism, where we relate to each other as members of a tribe, with interconnecting clans and families. And in turn, our tribe is one of the Nations of Earth Religions, bound together by our common love and reverence for our Mother, the Living Earth.

CAW's eclectic approach has allowed it to open up new avenues for the Pagan community in the United States. Most interesting is its fascination with science fiction, which it declares to be 'the new mythology of our age.' Robert Henlein's novel *Stranger in a Strange Land* is almost compulsory reading for those joining the Church.

Covenant of the Goddess

This organization defines itself as "a league of congregations, or covens, from all over the United States, with members in Canada and abroad." In 1975 a large group of covens and solitary witches met in California to form the Covenant, which was then established as a legally recognized Wiccan Church. There are six articles within the Covenant's charter, the most important being Article IV: Powers of the Church, which permits the autonomy of individual member covens while allowing the Church to implement a system of local councils, ministerial credentials, and a system of by-laws. This in itself is quite a feat considering the diversity of traditions and coven structures which exist in the U.S. The Preamble to the Covenant charter lays out the organization's philosophy of diversity and cooperation:

> In the fullness of time and by the providence of our Lady, it seems good to us that we covenant with one another, as members of an ancient and honorable religion, to establish a Church that will further our mutual interests and purposes in the service of our Lady and our Lord, in order to be better able to serve the religious needs of the lay members of our religion, and to be better able to assist one another in the training of our clergy and in all other matters that may benefit from improvements in our communication.
>
> We are agreed: that we worship the Goddess and recognize the Old Gods; that we are ethical persons, bound by the ethics of the traditional Laws of

our religion; and that we recognize one another as being members of the same religion.

We are also agreed that we are not the only members of our religion. If the members of a local congregation choose not to join this Covenant and the Church thus created, their choice creates no presumption that they are not members of our religion.

We are agreed further that the reality of our religion lies within each local congregation, of whatever Tradition, and that there is no sovereign authority in our religion outside each local congregation. Therefore the local congregations which enter into this Covenant with one another cede to the Church thus created only as much sovereignty as the Church will need in order to function effectively as an instrument of their joint will.

The Covenant of the Goddess has broken new ground in establishing an organizational form which satisfies the decentralized nature of Wiccan covens. It has also accepted all-female covens as valid; one of the first Craft organizations in the U.S. to do so. It was also the first Pagan organization (along with Circle and the Fellowship of Isis) to be invited to send a representative to the Council of World Churches, held in Chicago 1993 (see p. 49).

Ar nDraiocht Fein

Probably the most successful of the Druidic organizations in the United States. It was set up by P.E.I. (Isaac) Bonewits, best known in the Pagan community as the author of several books, after his involvement with the Reformed Druids of North America. Ar nDraiocht Fein (ADF) is Irish Gaelic for 'Our Own Druidism.' The Organization describes itself as:

> ...An independent tradition of Neopagan Druidism. We don't make any phony claims about an 'unbroken line' going back to the Stone Age, nor insist that we're the only 'real' Neopagan Druids—just (we think) the best. We're researching and expanding sound modern scholarship (not romantic fantasies) about the ancient Celts and other Indo-European peoples, in order to reconstruct what the Old Religions really were. We're working on the development of genuine artistic skills in composition and presentation in the musical, dramatic, graphic, textile, and other arts. We're designing and performing competent magical and religious ceremonies to change ourselves and the world we live in. We're creating a nonsexist, nonracist, organic, and open religion to practice as a way of life and to hand on to our grandchildren.

We're integrating ecological awareness, alternate healing arts, and psychic development into our daily activities. Together, we're sparking the next major phase in the evolution of Neopaganism and planting seeds for the generations to come.

ADF is now the largest Neopagan Druid organization in the world. We have legal status as a Nonprofit Religious Association. Groves and Protogroves are being organized all over the USA. Songbooks, informational pamphlets, a polytheological dictionary, and other Druidic publications are in the works. Regional gatherings are being held. In short, although our long-range approach is 'as fast as an oak tree,' we're growing more rapidly than any of us ever expected.

The ADF runs on a local level with Groves and Protogroves which are chartered by the Board of Trustees as local congregations. These regularly organize regional gatherings for its membership and must celebrate all eight major festivals (it is compulsory for some of these to be semi-public and open to the rest of the local Pagan community). It also enrolls some of its membership in what it considers to be "the toughest Neo-Pagan clergy training program in existence."

News from the Mother Grove is published by the ADF every other month. It gives information on individual Grove activities, changes in ADF organization and policy, and general news. *The Druids' Progress* is put out twice annually and generally goes into more detail, reviewing the previous six months.

Circle

This was originally conceived of as a resource center for 'Wiccans, Neo-Pagans, Pantheists, Goddess Folk, Shamans, Druids, Seers, Eco-Feminists, Native American Medicine People, Wizards, Mystics, and others on related paths.' It was founded by Selena Fox and Jim Alan in 1974 as Circle Sanctuary, a 200-acre Nature preserve in the Wisconsin hills.

From the Sanctuary is run Circle Network. This acts as an information exchange and contact service. It publishes its own source book *The Circle Guide To Pagan Resources*, which includes information on various groups, centers, and contacts in the United States. It also publishes *Circle Network News* quarterly, containing articles, rituals, news and contacts.

The Pagan Spirit Alliance is an internal association founded for members of the network who are 'attuned to certain ecumenical concepts of Spirituality,' and who wish to share their personal experiences through correspondence. It also publishes its own newsletter.

Circle Sanctuary itself regularly runs presentations—a variety of seminars and workshops throughout the year on such subjects as magic, Tarot, herbalism, psychic development, shamanism, feminist politics, etc. It also runs specific courses for the 'Pagan Ministry' and a course on 'Wiccan Shamanism.'

At the major festivals, Circle regularly holds festival gatherings and conferences. The highlight of the year for Circle Sanctuary is the week-long International Pagan Spirit Gathering. This attracts hundreds of Pagans from all over the United States.

The Ordo Templi Orientis (OTO)

Although originally formed by an Austrian industrialist in 1895, it did not really become well established until Aleister Crowley became head of the Order in 1922. The Order then based its principles on Crowley's *Book of the Law*, which was 'transmitted' to Crowley in 1904. This book is said to announce the transition into the 'Aeon of Horus' and the 'New Age.'

The OTO practices yoga, meditation, ritual magic, Cabala, and other disciplines of the Western mystery traditions. These are taught through a rigid degree structure which corresponds with the Hindu Chakra system. One of the Order's most important rites is the OTO Gnostic Mass. Crowley called this "the central ceremony of its (the OTO's) public and private celebration."

After the death of Crowley in 1947, the title of Outer Head of the Order went to Karl Germer (Frater Saturnus X), and the central base of the Order moved to New York; but Germer did nothing except publish Crowley's books. He died in 1962. In his unprobated will Germer directed that the property of the Order be divided among the 'Heads' of the Order. This led to a period of confusion within the OTO, with many claimants to Germer's legacy. In 1970 Major Grady Louis McMurty (Caliph Hymenaeus Alpha) reactivated his authorization from Crowley as Grand Inspector General of the Order, and it quickly grew under his leadership.

Major McMurty died in 1985, and the leadership of the Caliphate was assumed by Caliph Hymaenus Beta (taking that name out of respect for his predecessor). Since 1970 the OTO has established Lodges, Camps and Oases in the United States, Canada, Britain, South America, Germany, Norway, New Zealand and Australia. It continues to publish

Crowley's works and those of many of its members, and is well known for its publication of the journal *The Equinox*. The International Grand Lodge of the Order remains based in New York.

PAN

To avoid confusion—there are four separate North American organizations using the initials PAN: the Pagan Alliance Network of Stratford, Connecticut; the Pagan Allied Network of Madeira Beach, Florida; the Pagan Arizona Network of Phoenix, Arizona; and the Pagan Affirmation Network of Calgary, Alberta, in Canada. (Addresses on pp. 233–234.)

Canada

The Pagan scene in Canada is heavily influenced by its larger neighbor, the United States. It is not unusual to find Canadian Pagans attending Festivals in the northern U.S. and vice versa. The Covenant of the Goddess and The Church of All Worlds (see United States) have long-established groups in Canada. The Ordo Templi Orientis (OTO) has approximately a dozen groups, one of which publishes its own magazine *Aurora Borealis*. There are also several local groups (including the Covenant of Gaia, based in Calgary) and two larger organizations.

Wiccan Information Network

Founded by a practicing police officer, the Wiccan Information Network is one of the major anti-defamation organizations in North America. It is in contact with Wiccans and Pagans throughout the world and regularly organizes lectures and anti-defamation workshops. It was one of the first groups to produce a booklet, *The Law Enforcement Guide to Wicca*, aimed at dispelling the widespread misconception within police departments that Satanism and Witchcraft were the same, and that witches were involved in occult-related crimes,

Wiccan Church of Canada

Initially based in Ontario, The Wiccan Church of Canada has gone on to establish associate Temples in Hamilton, Toronto and Ottawa. Since its formation in 1979 by Richard and Tamara James, it has remained the focus of controversy due to its rigid organizational structure and its established division between 'Priesthood' and 'laity.'

The church practices its own system called Odyssean. This includes an extensive and often time-consuming training program for its priesthood, which may take years to complete. Most of the controversy revolving around the church comes from its belief in being totally open to all. It believes it is vital that Wicca is publicly recognized as a legal religion and has therefore sought media coverage to fulfill this aim. Its 1987 By-Laws refer to the church's objective as being:

> ...to provide an opportunity for Pagans and Wiccans to receive religious services such as matrimony, funeral, confession, baptism, etc., within their own faith...

The Wiccan Church of Canada has been incorporated by the Government of Ontario and legally provides all the above services, as well as prison chaplains.

Britain

From the early 1950s to the late 1960s the Pagan revival was largely dominated by the Gardnerian tradition, until the arrival of Alex and Maxine Sanders and the Alexandrian tradition. Ritual Magic Orders and the Druidical Orders were also well established, both having roots in the turn of the century, but being noticeably less accessible than Wicca. The success of the Alexandrian tradition can very much be attributed to its more open attitude to initiation compared to the Gardnerian. This, combined with the 'Swinging Sixties' and the increased interest in the New Age and alternative forms of religion, guaranteed its growth and success.

Even in the late 1970s the term Pagan was very much synonymous with the term Wiccan, and it was taken for granted that you could not be one without being the other. The 1980s saw a growth in what some called 'Neo-Paganism,' and a questioning by many as to whether Wicca and Ritual Magic were the only available Pagan traditions. The changes in the scene in Britain are best explained by the history of the major Pagan organizations which have come into being, how they began, and how they have adapted to meet the continuously changing face of the revival.

Britain remains the center of the Pagan revival in Europe, most of its major organizations having members in neighboring countries. Unlike the United States, Britain has been slow to embrace the new technology of computer bulletin boards, mainly due to the cost. In 1994 things had begun to improve with the first Pagan system, CompuServe's 'Black

Dog,' being launched in London. Many of the Pagan periodicals have encouraged more Pagans to go 'on-line,' but computer communication between Britain and the United States was still slow in 1993.

The Pagan Federation

The Pagan Federation is one of the best-known, and longest-running, of the Pagan organizations in existence. The formation of the Federation came out of the publication in 1968 of *The Wiccan*, which called itself 'A Newsletter of the Old Religion of Wisecraft and Pagan comment.' At this point it catered exclusively for members of several Wiccan covens, although it quickly expanded its readership. On September 30, 1971, the publishers, elder members of four Wiccan paths, due to increasing demand from its readership, established the Pagan Front, 'a real attempt to overcome the fragmentation bequeathed to us by the Christian Church of past centuries, and any existing undercurrent of hostility from this or any other source.' Its main intent was to provide information and to counter misconceptions about Paganism. Doreen Valiente chaired the inaugural meeting, which took place on Beltane 1971 with a memorable, and still relevant, opening address:

> Unity is strength; and I welcome the fraternal unity of all sincere people of goodwill who follow the Pagan path. We may not always agree with each other, but we must support each other in our struggle for our right to follow the religion and the lifestyle of our choice in the modern world. We rejoice in being heretics, because a heretic means 'one who chooses.' That is, we choose our own way to live, to think and to worship; not only because it pleases us, but because we believe that human society needs the old Pagan wisdom to restore it to health and sanity, in what people are increasingly recognizing as a very sick world.

Membership of the Federation was, and still is, by yearly subscription which includes quarterly editions of *The Wiccan*. Members had to agree with three principles:

(1) Love and kinship with Nature, participation in the cosmic Dance of Goddess and God, Woman and Man, Yin and Yang, rather than the more customary attitude of aggression and domination over Nature.

(2) The Pagan Ethic, 'Do what you will, but harm no-one.' This is a positive morality, not a list of thou-shalt-nots. Each person is responsible for discovering his or her own true nature and is committed to developing it fully in harmony with the world.

(3) Reincarnation in some form, as taught by many faiths throughout time, including Druids and witches. What we are is the substance of this Nature, this world, not of some far-off beyond.

When first established, the Federation mainly catered for those in well-established Wiccan traditions, and during the mid to late 1970s broadened to include those in other established paths including Ritual Magic, Druidism and Asatru, although membership of Pagans within these paths still remained minimal, and the scene was still dominated by Wicca, including the still-growing Alexandrian tradition. Even up to the mid 1980s *The Wiccan* newsletter and the Federation's information packs catered almost exclusively for those with an interest in modern witchcraft. Contact work consisted of putting individual members in touch with established covens through the committee, the majority of its members being Wiccan. The committee was very much a closed shop, and the external membership of the Federation had no say.

By the late 1980s the Federation was facing increased criticism for its lack of democracy, and its inability to cater adequately for members who followed other paths than Wiccan. It was becoming noticeably left behind in the field of networking and contact work by the newly-formed Paganlink, which was providing for the much wider range of Pagan paths which had come into being. The number of members within the Federation had been growing slowly since the late 1970s, but in the space of five years the numbers of those active in Paganlink had surpassed it. Many within the Federation now realized the need for change.

If the Federation was a tree, it had now been putting its roots down deeply for twenty years, and the early 1990s were to see it finally coming into blossom. The decision was made to introduce gradually a democratic voting system for the committee, by the election of two committee members a year. It was believed this slow process would prevent any disturbance to its running. It began to cater for a broader Pagan community; its information packs now outlined all the major paths including Druidism, Asatru and Shamanism. It started to establish local contacts and representatives, and a program of networking. There was increased cooperation between the Federation and Paganlink, and at the Federation conference in 1992 the Federation's council voiced the view that the two organizations were complementary and wanted to create greater liaison between them regarding events and contact sharing. (Gavin acted as a contact for both during this time.) Some felt the name of *The Wiccan* should change, but this motion was defeated when put to a vote. Membership of the Federation was still 50 percent Wiccan, and the majority of the members were in the southeast of Britain.

Interestingly, after these changes membership of the Federation increased. In 1991 it stood at just on 1000, and by the end of 1993 it had increased to an estimated 2000. This confirms to many that there had been a definite need for change in the Federation, and it is likely that its membership will continue to grow and will confirm its place as the most important Pagan organization in Britain. At present the Pagan Federation is applying for registration as an educational charity and is in dialogue with the Home Office to establish Wiccan prison chaplains.

Paganlink

Whereas the Pagan Federation originally came into being to provide support for the established Wiccan community, Paganlink was formed to support those attempting to revive European shamanic practices and the growing eclectic traditions. More importantly, it was formed to act as an open network for communication between Pagan groups and individuals within Britain, something which up to then had not existed.

The idea of Paganlink was originally conceived of by the late Rich Westwood, owner of Prince Elric's (an occult supply shop in Birmingham) and publisher of *Moonshine* magazine, and it effectively came into being in 1986. The first step was to set up a network by a coalition of already-existing Pagan magazines and news sheets, and encourage others to similar forms of communication. Printed advertisements by groups looking for members, and individuals looking for groups, soon caused new groups to form and communicate directly with those already existing. At this point Rich Westwood stood down as the central coordinator and left the network in the hands of the individual group coordinators. Paganlink became decentralized and anarchic in nature; there was no central committee, only regular moots or gatherings of coordinators or contacts.

One of the major advantages of Paganlink's structure (or rather lack of it) was that the emphasis was put on 'empowering' the individual Pagan to organize events. This could also be one of its disadvantages, leading to periods of apathy. Eventually two individuals were to step forward to counter this by acting as national facilitators and coordinators, and in 1991 an executive council was formed to handle the press and the organizing and financing of contact lists.

Unlike the Federation, the majority of whose members were in the southeast, the interest in Paganlink came initially from the Midlands and the north, the first groups to form being in Oxford, Leeds and of course Birmingham. As time progressed many London groups formed and allied with Paganlink. These included The House of The Goddess, which became well known for its regular Pagan Moon and Samhain festivals held at the Commonwealth Institute and later at London University. In the southwest, Bristol was to become the focus for Pagan activity, and to host the moot which decided on the need for some form of executive, this decision being made due to the large Pagan community which had grown up there.

By 1988 the network had over 30 listed contacts, and the first open national moot and festival was held highly successfully in Leicester. Its success was to result in regular, openly advertised events, small and large, up and down Britain. The following year saw the festival repeated in Leicester (at which the three of us were present) and even though adverse press coverage caused the withdrawal of the indoor venue, it was again a success—partly because a Christian farmer who objected to the press bigotry lent land to accommodate it. A Pagan Federation conference was held there. The larger open festivals continued until 1991, when press handling of the festival at Kings Bromley, Staffordshire, accusing those present of child abuse, resulted in the confidence in open festivals temporarily being shattered. The festivals were recommenced shortly after, and more care was taken in future regarding the press.

The controversy over the 1991 festival, and changes in both Paganlink's and the Pagan Federation's organizational structures, have resulted in closer working ties between the two; both are currently involved in supporting each other in environmental issues. Many had theorized over the possibility of a merger, as they grew more similar to each other. By the end of 1993 Paganlink had very much returned to its roots, after several attempts to organize a central council similar to the Pagan Federation's. As it stands it remains a contact network, complementary to rather than in competition with the Pagan Federation.

The Pagan Hospice and Funerary Trust was set up to look after the needs of the community regarding provisions for terminal illness and death. It provides information about hospital visiting, appropriate passage rites, and legal matters. It regularly prints its own newsletter.

Hoblink acts a support group for the homosexual and bisexual members of the community. It was formed originally within Paganlink to encourage the integration of that part of the community within the whole by providing information and acting as a contact group.

Pagan Animal Rights provides support for those involved in animal liberation, anti-hunt, and anti-vivisection activities as part of their Pagan philosophy. It too prints its own newsletter.

The Odinic Rite

Formed by John Yeowell (known as Stubba), the Odinic Rite is the major Asatru/Odinic organization in Britain. It was originally conceived in 1973 as 'the committee for the restoration of the Odinic rite.' The five aims of the committee read as follows:

1. To restore the body of ritual and ceremony pertaining to the Odinic religion, based upon the books of wisdom comprised in the Eddas, on sources contemporaneous with them and on approved critical works relating to them.
2. To reconstitute a teaching order of gothar (Priests).
3. To publish the ritual, ceremonial, laws and other supporting works that the committee may approve.
4. On the completion of the foregoing aims, to cause to be instituted on a permanent basis a body which shall be responsible for the recruitment, training and examining of gothars as well as for interpretation and extension, whenever and wherever necessary of Odinic faith, principles and practice.
5. To further public knowledge of Odinism by all means available.

By 1980, with the majority of these aims achieved, the Odinic Rite was formed. The Rite's first national moot took place in London in 1987, and by 1992 it had registered as a charitable organization. There are now over a thousand members of the Odinic Rite in Britain, and approximately nine Hearths. It publishes a quarterly magazine *Odinism Today*, and a monthly newsletter, *The Moot Horn*. It also publishes several educational pamphlets about itself and aspects of Odinism. It runs its own teaching program, the Circle of Gothar, and has established a runic study group, the Runic Guild, under the auspices of Freya Aswynn.

In recent years it has been involved in environmental action to protect the White Horse Stone (an ancient monument in Kent marking the site of the Battle of Aylesford and the death of Horsa, the Saxon leader) from the Channel Tunnel link, and has been successful in campaigning to restore the Westbury White Horse in Wiltshire. It regularly holds festival gatherings and 'Blots' (rituals).

Odinshof

Although younger and with a smaller membership than the Odinic Rite, the Odinshof has quickly established itself within the wider Pagan community by promoting strong links with both the Pagan Federation and Paganlink. In its constitution it defines its objective as:

> To promote the ancient teachings and philosophy of Odin (Odintru), and to advance education.

Like the Odinic Rite it has several Hearths, which generally have autonomy on decision making from the central Witan assembly (although they agree to abide by the constitution and its more important rulings). It is very active environmentally, and in 1992 set up the Land Guardian scheme. Its first campaign was to protect Oxleas Wood, the last surviving piece of wild wood in the London area. This was being threatened by the building of a major link road. It has registered itself as a charity and is currently promoting its land fund scheme to buy the wood and other endangered areas. It intends to establish them as conservation sites.

Order of Bards, Ovates and Druids

The Order is the largest Druidic organization in the United Kingdom and Europe, and traces its origins as far back as 1717. It considers Druidry to be a tradition which has continued to evolve and develop since early times, and is therefore dedicated to presenting the Druid way in a fashion that is relevant to today's needs.

It is actively involved in ecological and spiritual issues within the wider Pagan community, and regularly holds workshops in Britain, France, Holland and the United States. There are currently over a thousand members in over a dozen countries worldwide, and in over thirty Groves or Seed Groups.

The Order has two main aims:

1. To help the individual develop their potential—spiritual, intellectual, emotional, physical and artistic.
2. To work with the natural world, to cherish and protect it, and to cooperate with it in every way—both esoterically and exoterically.

It achieves these aims through its three grade system of training. The first grade consists of Bard, and the training of the initiate centers around basic Druidry. The lessons involved are both practical and academic, with the intention of stimulating the initiates personal growth.

The Ovate grade follows the Bardic grade and its main emphasis is on introducing the initiate to the Healing and Divinatory skills required of a full Druid. He/She also commences study of the Arthurian cycle to encourage further development of the inner self.

The final grade is that of full Druid, which is bestowed on completion of all the aforementioned training. The individual is then considered capable of leading their own grove with the approval of the Order. They are expected to continue to study the Arthurian and Grail myths and to develop spiritually and intellectually.

All their teachings are presented formally, and this is supported by audio cassette tapes and workbooks for each grade. It publishes a monthly newsletter, which its members are encouraged to contribute to on a more informal level. The Order is currently promoting a campaign for individual ecological responsibility and a sacred grove and tree planting program.

Council of British Druid Orders

Only recently formed, this Council has representatives of all the major Druid orders in Britain, including the Order of Bards, Ovates and Druids, the Glastonbury Order of Druids and several smaller organizations. It also has representatives of the PADRAS (Pagan and Druidic Rites at Stonehenge) organization, which is fighting to have the stone circle in Wiltshire reopened for religious and ritual use.

The Green Circle

Formed in the early 1980s by the writer Marion Green, the Green Circle was started to act as a forum to encourage dialogue between the practitioners of all esoteric systems. As such it is not strictly Pagan, accepting Christian mystics and those interested in more 'New Age' and Eastern paths. Its publication *The Green Circular*, regularly includes articles on Paganism and witchcraft. On joining the Green Circle (by paid membership) you are expected to take part in its self-initiatory path working. Many of its members have formed active groups up and down Britain as well as on the Continent.

The Ordo Templi Orientis (OTO) and other Ritual Magic organizations

Britain has several well-established lodges throughout the country and some 'hive offs' from the original organization. Several more secretive organizations (who would prefer us not to mention their names) also exist.

A number of Golden Dawn societies are currently functioning; interestingly enough these are found around the more well-known university towns.

Ireland

Ireland (the Republic, that is, not the until recently strife-torn North) is an exceptional place for Pagans to be publicly active in. It is almost entirely Catholic, but its Pagan past is deeply embedded in its chromosomes. As one young County Clare farmer put it to us: "Scratch the topsoil of Irish Christianity, and you come at once to the bedrock of Paganism"—and in eighteen years of living there, we have found it to be true.

Celtic mythology and folk customs are in the Irish air you breathe. This is partly because Ireland, almost uniquely in Western Europe, was never part of the Roman Empire, so its native culture was not subjected to centuries of transformation by foreign rulers in pre-Christian times. Even when Christianity came to Ireland, it coexisted remarkably harmoniously with its Pagan neighbors—so much so that Celtic Christianity worried the Vatican, which in the end had to bring it to heel.

Eight centuries of British occupation and rule made Irish traditions an integral part of the resistance; and when England became Protestant under Henry VIII, Irish Catholicism was also driven underground, where much of the surviving Pagan tradition tended to merge with it.

The Republic has now been independent of foreign rule for over 70 years, but the strange blending of Catholicism and Paganism is too deeply embedded to disappear.

In most lands, it can be said that 'the Gods of the old religion have become the Devils of the new,' but not so in Ireland. The Gods and Goddesses of the Pagan Celts have become legendary heroes and heroines, surviving in such things as place-names. County Louth, for example, is in Gaelic Contae Lú (the County of Lugh), and County Wexford is Contae Loch gCarman (the County of the local Goddess Carman). And visiting Pagans often find it strange that the months of May and November in Gaelic are Bealtaine and Samhain respectively.

Pagan attitudes do not merely survive in such names; they persist in folk-custom as well. A typical example in our own experience was a retired building worker who told us how when he was a child in the west of Ireland, his parents used to take the entire family out at midnight on May Eve to dance naked round the newly-sown crops. The children were told this would protect them against colds for the coming year, but we suspect that was in case the priest came to hear of it. In fact, of course, it was an unashamed Pagan fertility rite, and the parents would certainly have known it. Yet this was a good Catholic family, who went to Mass regularly and without conscious hypocrisy—as our retired friend still did.

That is just one of countless examples we have come to accept as a natural part of the Irish scene.

As for the public activities of committed, non-Christian Pagans like ourselves, although there is of course a rigid minority which disapproves of and even fears them, by most people they are accepted with remarkable tolerance. The Irish tend to love eccentrics; and provided you are a good neighbor—and if someone pulls your leg, you grin and pull his back—you can believe and say what you like. The only thing which is not easily tolerated is a chip on the shoulder (an exception with which we are inclined to agree).

We (Janet and Stewart) are known throughout Ireland for what we are, having appeared on television and radio and in press interviews many times; Dublin taxi-drivers tend to say "Oh, you're the witches, aren't you?"—and to chat from there on till they drop us. We once received a letter simply addressed to 'The Witches, Ireland' which the Post Office delivered. And a year or two back, a couple of days before Christmas, our local Catholic priest turned up on the doorstep smiling and said: "I don't know what you lot do at this time of the year, but have a good one anyway." Naturally we wished the same to him.

In unhappy contrast, Northern Ireland at present suffers from Christian Fundamentalism at its worst—within Christianity itself. At the one extreme, there is Dr. Ian Paisley, the Democratic Unionist leader, proclaiming the Pope to be the Antichrist. At the other, a sad example is the Protestant minister who was forced by his Elders to resign his job because on Christmas Day he crossed the road to the Catholic church to wish a Happy Christmas to their Catholic neighbors.

We know a few Pagans in the north—and at least one newsletter, *Pschitt*, which contains a lot of Pagan material and published an interview with us—but it seems they tend to be ignored as irrelevant to the main confrontation.

We asked a well-informed Pagan friend who lives in the north (one of our own initiates) if grass-roots northerners of both traditions were fed up with the extremists of both kinds, and he answered very emphatically: "Without a shadow of doubt."

In the Republic, fortunately, one may be friendly with somebody for years without even knowing whether he is Catholic or Protestant, unless one happens to go to church in the same parish. And although the Republic is 90 percent Catholic, both Dublin and Cork have elected highly respected and successful Jewish Lord Mayors. While in December 1992 County Clare, traditionally one of the most conservative areas in Ireland, elected to the Dáil (Parliament) as a Labor member Dr. Moosajee Bhamjee, an Indian Moslem psychiatrist from South Africa who came to Ireland ten years earlier to escape Apartheid, and who earned local respect for his community work.

The southern Irish tend to judge people as people, instead of tying category-labels round their necks.

It must sadly be admitted that, in spite of the Paganism embedded in the Irish chromosomes, the modern Pagan revival movement there has so far failed to unite. We know of at least three organizations claiming to be focal points for such unity, but all ignoring each other—and, incidentally, our own activities. One of them (not, we hasten to add, the Fellowship of Isis described below) has claimed, in public advertisements, to be "the only organization representing Irish Paganism," and even though it is run by a Wiccan couple, it insists that Wicca has no part to play in Irish Paganism. We had a long correspondence with them about these nonsensical claims, but they refused to withdraw them.

We know two covens and three solo workers who have regretfully withdrawn into isolation through weariness with this situation. As one of the solo workers said to us: "I came into the Craft for fellowship and communication, not to have my time wasted by organizations and individuals bitching behind people's backs."

The Fellowship of Isis

Although its foundation Iseum is based at Clonegal Castle, Enniscorthy, in the Republic of Ireland, it claims to have 12,000 members worldwide in over 76 countries. These members include not only Pagans, but also Christians, Buddhists and others. Its organizers spoke at the Parliament of World Religions in Chicago in August 1993, due to its international membership. It has regularly held conferences for its many independent Iseums and Lyceums in London. Here are key extracts from its Manifesto:

> Growing numbers of people are rediscovering their love for the God-dess... Thus, one hears such inquiries as, 'How can I get initiated into the Mysteries of the Goddess? How can I experience a closer communion with her? Where are her nearest temples and devotees? How can I join the priesthood of the Goddess?' and many other questions.
> The Fellowship of Isis has been founded to answer these needs. Member-ship provides means of promoting a closer communion between the Goddess and each member, both singly and as part of a larger group. There are hundreds of Iseums and thousands of members all over the world, since the Fellowship was founded in 1976 by Lawrence, Pamela and Olivia Durdin-Robertson. Love, Beauty and Truth are expressed through a multi-religious, multi-cultural, multi-racial Fellowship. The good of all faiths is honored.
> The Fellowship is based on a democratic basis. All members have equal privileges within it...There are no vows required or commitments to secrecy. All Fellowship activities are optional and members are free to resign or rejoin at their own choice...
> The Fellowship reverences all manifestations of Life. The God is also venerated.The Rites exclude any form of sacrifice, whether actual or symbolic. Nature is revered and conserved.
> The Fellowship accepts religious toleration, and is not exclusivist. Mem-bership is open to all of every religion, tradition and race. Children, listed as 'Children of Isis,'are welcomed, subject to parental consent.
> The Fellowship believes in the promotion of Love, Beauty and Abun-dance. No encouragement is given to asceticism.

The foundation Iseum based at Clonegal Castle regularly holds open rituals on the main festival dates. Beneath the Castle the wine cellars have been converted into a Temple dedicated primarily to Isis; this is where the indoor celebrations normally take place. Within the Temple there are also shrines to numerous other Goddesses from around the world.

Brazil

The living Pagan mythology and practice in Brazil is that imported by African slaves, the Yoruba people from Nigeria, and variously referred to as Brazilian Voodoo, Santeria, and Orisha. For example, the

Sea, River and Lake Goddess Yemaja is very widely worshipped; her festival is on New Year's Eve, when thousands of people place offerings on the beach at Copocabana and elsewhere for the sea to claim for her. But this is almost entirely confined to the very poor, and the original deities and mythology of the indigenous Brazilian natives have been virtually forgotten.

Alceu Dias de Oliveira quotes the saying 'Brazil is a country without memory,' and tells us:

> Many important happenings in this country are forgotten by the mass. If you walk the streets to ask about these deities, apart from the African ones and some more popular like the Werewolf, the Saci or the Boto, very probably no one will be able to tell you anything about the deities. When not destroyed by the oppression of Catholicism and other Christians (who saw 'God' in Tupan, the Storm God of the Tupi-Guarani tribe, and the 'Devil' in Jurupari, the tribe's principal God, and still today try to teach Indians to cover the 'shame' of their nudity), the deities, in the major centers, in the last decades of more information and intellectual enlightenment are still victims of a new kind of oppression: the contempt of 'thinking' people and the spread of a materialistic approach to life, which reacts against the religious oppression of the past but sees our cultural past as naive and useless.
>
> The words 'religion,' 'God,' etc. are almost always related to Catholicism in Brazil; very rarely do you find someone who would dare to refer to his/her belief in the Orishas, or practices related to it, as religious commitment; and almost never would such reference be made by someone not involved in the practices. In other words, this is not considered 'religion' in the true sense.

Scandinavia

Most activity centers around Norway where the major organization for Scandinavia, the Nordic Pagan Federation, is based. Within Norway at least three Wiccan covens now exist, alongside approximately four Ordo Templi Orientis (OTO) groups, and some diverse Shamanic and Dianic oriented groups. In Sweden there exist several self-initiated and eclectic groups, but there appear to be no Alexandrian/Gardnerian covens. Denmark is similar to Sweden, and both countries have OTO groups. Finland has at least two Wiccan covens and one Fellowship of Isis Iseum.

Nordic Pagan Federation

Based in Bergen, Norway, this is the only organization covering specifically all of Scandinavia. It was set up following the formation of several Wiccan covens in Norway by Vivianne and Chris Crowley, both being committee members of the British Pagan Federation. It follows the same three principles as the Pagan Federation and currently has approximately 100 members in seven groups. Although not directly affiliated with the Pagan Federation, it fosters close ties with them and with the Wiccan-Pagan Press Alliance of the United States. It publishes its own magazine, *Nye Gaia*, two to four times a year.

Generally each of the groups organizes its own open festivals, and the main organization has hosted the Pan-European Wiccan Convention in Norway; some of its members have attended these when held in Britain and other European countries.

Iceland

An interesting country, in that is the only one in Europe where Paganism has equal standing with Christianity as the State religion.

An English-language Pagan newsletter, *Huginn & Muninn*, is edited by Thorsteinn Gudjónsson (address on p. 231). The editorial board have been criticized by some Icelandic Pagans for writing it in English, but they point out that it is intended for 'the various Asatru groups all over this planet,' very few of whom of course understand Icelandic.

France

France remains very much in the shadow of Britain. Several covens of Gardnerian and Alexandrian heritage exist, alongside its own home-grown organization/tradition. Druidism has also recently experienced a revival in France. This revival has been centered around Brittany, which is steeped in Celtic/Druidic history, and has a Celtic local language closely related to Welsh.

Wicca-Française

Wicca-Française has attracted controversy since its formation, mainly due to its embarrassingly open sexual attitudes, typified by its rather saucily illustrated periodical *L'Étoile*. It has strong contacts with French Canada.

L'École Druidique des Gaules

This group is probably the largest Pagan organization in France. They are monist in nature (believing in one totally supreme being as opposed to Christianity's God/Satan dualism). They are generally involved in supporting freedom of religion, and the protection of surviving Celtic culture and prevention of its suppression.

Germany and Austria

In Germany several Alexandrian covens now exist of recent heritage. These covens have strong links with Britain and the newly-formed Norwegian covens, many of their members having attended the Pan-European Wiccan Conventions and having hosted one in Germany. The term 'Pagan' is generally not used by German Wiccans, as it has become associated with the growing Neo-Nazi movement from which they wish to distance themselves. Many of those with an interest in Asatru face the same problem, and tend to be quiet about their beliefs. OTO and Fraternitas Saturni have several well-established lodges in both Germany and Austria, and there is also growing interest in Chaos Magic.

No actual major Pagan organizations exist, although the Arbeitsgruppe Hexen (Witches' Working Group) and the Deutsche Wicca Netzwerk (German Wiccan Network) have now been established for some time. The Wicca Netzwerk regularly sends out a circular contact letter. One periodical called *Der Wicca-Brief* is currently being published in Hamburg. In Austria there also now exists the Foundation for Shamanic Studies based in Vienna.

The Netherlands

The Dutch Pagan community consists mainly of Wiccans of Gardnerian or Alexandrian descent. The British Green Circle is well established in Holland, and has close contacts with the only substantial home-grown organization.

Silver Circle (Centrum voor de Oude Religie)

This is not so much an organization as a coven with a very large Outer Circle. The central group has about 50 members, and there are outer court groups. Silver Circle runs discussion meetings (by invitation only) for people with an initial interest in Paganism, arranges 'picnics' during the summer months, produces information leaflets, and puts out the only Dutch Pagan magazine, *Wiccan Rede*. This is published in English and

Dutch; but then the Dutch, being a small but economically active country sandwiched between big lands speaking English, German or French, are habitually multilingual, so it is arguable that such a magazine would (a) be understood by the Dutch, and (b) be a means of foreign communication.

The Baltic States

Since Lithuania, Latvia and Estonia became independent of Soviet rule, their strong Pagan traditions have begun to emerge, though so far the organizational pattern is not fully apparent. Up-to-date information can be obtained from American organizations of Baltic heritage, listed under 'Baltic States' on pp. 229–230. They may well be able to provide information also on the still obscure Pagan situation in Russia.

Australia

Australia's native Pagan tradition is obviously that of the Aborigines. This is very shamanistic in nature, and is becoming of increasing interest both to the European Pagan community and to the New Age movement.

In Queensland and the southern Australian states, anti-witchcraft laws are still on the statute books, although hardly ever enforced. New South Wales did not repeal its Witchcraft Act until 1971. There were reports of witches' meetings in Canberra in the 1920s, but these have never been confirmed.

Australia's best-known witch was Rosaleen Norton. She was an artist whose provocative paintings of half-animal, half-human forms caught the public's attention, and resulted in a lengthy court case in 1955. This resulted in her being found guilty of obscenity charges. In their book *The Occult Experience*, Nevill Drury and Gregory Tillett describe her as:

> ...no mere 'witch.' She lived in a world of magical beings and astral entities which manifested in various degrees in her remarkable paintings. There is no question that Rosaleen Norton was one of the forerunners of Australian occult exploration.

The occult has a strong history Down Under, dating back to the turn of the century. The Theosophical Society, Rosicrucians, and the Ordo

Templi Orientis (OTO), are all very well established. Paganism and Wicca, though, did not really become established until the mid to late 1960s. With the migration of many new English to Australia during this time, came Wicca in the form of the Alexandrian and Gardnerian traditions, both being now very firmly rooted (the first Alexandrian coven was formed in Perth in 1962).

With the advent of computer technology, and the use of electronic-mail systems and Bulletin Boards, the Pagan community has forged strong links with the communities in the United States. The American Church of All Worlds now has at least seven Nests or Proto-nests in Australia, and has its own section for these Nests in *Green Egg*. We came across one High Priestess in the United States teaching a 'computer coven' in Australia. Up to 1993 they had relied on U.S. Bulletin Board systems, but now have their own system based in Canberra called 'In Gaia We Trust.' This is part of the PODS (Pagan Occult Distribution Service) Network. The U.S.-based Rune Guild also has a group based in Canberra.

Several Pagan magazines circulate in Australia, including *The Wiccan*, first published in 1979, and based on the Pagan Federation's magazine of the same name. As far as we know, only one major organization exists—The Pan Pacific Pagan Alliance based in Sydney.

Many of the early Wiccan groups in Australia adhered automatically to the eight Sabbat dates of the year traditional in Europe and the United States (see p. 96), while others were quick to point out that these were six months out of step with the Southern Hemisphere, where one could hardly celebrate (for example) the rebirth of the Sun at the Australian Midsummer at the end of December. On the principle of relating to the Earth 'as she is where you are,' Australian Wiccans have now all accepted this obvious argument, and evolved their own systems. Many of them also cast the Circle anti-clockwise, this being the direction in which their Sun travels, and attribute the Elemental Quarters on the basis of Earth South, Air East, Fire North, and Water West—reversing the Earth and Fire attributions customary north of the Equator.

Japan

The majority of Japanese still continue to practice their native Pagan tradition of Shinto (see p. 36). The similarities between Shinto and modern Paganism have been recognized by the Japanese for some time. In 1974 the High Priest of the Kodama-jinja, at Enoshima, sent a telegram to the British Odinist committee (later to become the Odinic Rite):

> May success attend your noble efforts to reintroduce sacred words and beliefs of your ancient gods to the people of Britain. Followers of the Kami, hail Sons of Odin.

Over recent years an interest in modern European Pagan practices has begun to grow, particularly in Wicca. Japanese interested in Paganism have not faced the same intolerance as those in Europe or America, mainly due to the influence of Shinto. This has resulted in the translation of several books (including our own *Eight Sabbats for Witches*) into Japanese, and widespread media coverage of the subject in recent years. Obviously the Pagan scene in Japan is still in its infancy compared to the United States or Britain, but there are already plans to start a network. This is the goal of the only Pagan organization in Japan, The Pagan Project, which plans to cater for both the Japanese Pagans and the foreign Pagans living in Japan.

20.

The Way In

Because Pagans believe that all sincere religions are different paths to the same truths (however much dogmatic hierarchies may try to distort them), and that what suits one person's 'wavelength' may not suit another's, they do not proselytize. They confine their efforts to explaining the true nature of their philosophy, so that their non-Pagan neighbors will understand it, instead of being deceived by Fundamentalist propaganda.

However, people who feel they are naturally in tune with the Pagan outlook are constantly seeking for local contacts so that they can meet and work with others of like mind. We receive letters from readers of our books asking for such contacts almost daily.

Such people are entitled to the guidance they ask for.

So you think Paganism is for you?

There used to be an argument by two separate camps within the Wiccan community over whether Witches were 'born' or 'made.' Over the years we have discovered neither to be true, rather that Witches discover what they are for themselves. We believe this to be equally true for all the Pagan paths. The commonest answer we have received when asking people how they became Pagans has been: "Oh, I've always been a Pagan, I just didn't know I was until I (read a book, saw a documentary on it, got invited along by a friend to an open meeting, etc.)." Many people, before discovering Paganism, have already formulated for themselves the spiritual nature of deity, the universe and Nature. It is not unusual for them to have explored other spiritual paths, particularly Buddhism and Taoism, and to have found parts of those traditions they agree with and other parts they don't. Normally they incorporate this knowledge with their own instinctive feeling about spirituality, and later 'discover' that what they have created is the basis of Pagan philosophy. Many have expressed this to us as a feeling of 'coming home.'

Many also find Paganism after a period of dissatisfaction with Christianity, although this must not be confused with rebellion against it, as rebellion in itself is not a good reason for choosing Paganism. If you are now considering Paganism and have not explored other spiritual paths, you should! Paganism does not believe it has a monopoly on spirituality, and you may find yourself better suited to another religion. This does not mean you cannot still explore Paganism, and if you still believe, after looking at the other options, that it is for you, you will have gained valuable insight into the nature of religion as a whole.

Finding your path

There are numerous paths in Paganism, enough to suit the most spiritually hungry. We have listed the commonest paths in Chapter 4, *The Rainbow of Paths*. The decision to name it that is appropriate, because just as there are numerous combinations of colors within a rainbow, there are numerous combinations of Paths within Paganism. There are Wiccans who practice Ritual Magic; Ritual Magicians who also practice Asatru; Druids who practice dowsing and Earth Magic; and so on *ad infinitum*. Paganism is a personal religion, and so is a person's path. No two Pagans' paths are exactly the same. Only you can find your own, nobody else. It is a personal journey into your own spirituality, and as such can be hard work.

So how do you find your path? Through information and experience. Read as many books on the subject you can get your hands on. Even though you may already be drawn to one specific path, read up on as many of the other paths as you can. Books have been published on all the major Pagan paths, many on the same subjects giving different viewpoints and opinions. These are the most useful, as they encourage you to think for yourself and make up your own mind. Always remember that most books on individual paths give the writer's subjective viewpoint, and are not Holy Writ; and that although books contain a lot of knowledge, they don't contain experience and the wisdom that comes from it.

Write off and subscribe to some Pagan journals. There are hundreds of publications throughout the world catering to Pagans. It is not unlikely one is being produced within a hundred miles of you. Many such journals advertise in the astrology magazines found in your average newsagent's. They are also quite incestuous, and once you have brought one journal you normally find several others advertising in the back of it. Pagan journals give a good insight into your local Pagan community, as the majority of them are produced by local groups. They should give you an idea about the present issues which concern Paganism and a grass-roots view of different paths.

The next step from reading books and magazines is finding people. Contact networks for Pagans now exist in various developed countries, and again these are advertised in most Pagan publications. Networks mainly consist of small local groups which hold regular, open meetings. Most of these groups consist of a number of Pagans following different paths, although in some cases they may have a setup where they are an 'outer circle' for a more formal coven or grove. The more varied the people that attend, the better. Talk to the Pagans there and find out about their particular paths. Don't be afraid to ask questions; always remember they have all been in exactly the same position as you are in now. Do you find you have something in common with some and not with others? Do you agree with some about their particular path and not with others? Find out about other Pagan contact groups in your area; most groups keep in touch with each other and vary slightly in their emphasis.

Experience, and experiment. If you are interested in ritual and get invited to an open ritual by a group you feel comfortable with, go to it. Get as much experience about different paths as possible, attend Earth-healing rites with the Druids on Tuesday, and open Sabbat celebrations with the Wiccans on Wednesday. Explore aspects of various paths for yourself. Experiment with different paths by yourself; spend time in the countryside, close to Nature; conduct your own mini-rituals in the privacy of your own home; next time a friend has a headache, try healing it.

Always remember that an individual's path is dynamic. It never remains static, but continually evolves and adapts to its surroundings. It may take time for you to find your own path; but have patience and confidence.

But also remember something else: you are out to find the path you are at home with, and to dedicate yourself to it. The search itself should not become a permanent habit, or you may turn into a 'religion-hopper'—a type with which Paganism is all too familiar, and which ends up wasting everybody's time.

Finding a Group

After working solo for a while you may decide that you wish to work with a more formal group such as a Wiccan coven, a Druidic grove or a Pagan hearth. In the past such groups could be difficult to find, and generally people took what was available in their area (for Gavin this meant joining an eclectic Ritual Magic group even though his chosen path was Wiccan). In some places where individual Pagans are still closed off and no community as such exists, this still applies. In this case make the best of the experience and have patience. If you have managed to find an open Pagan contact group in your area, they are likely to know of several local practicing formal groups and may be able to arrange an introduction. The Pagan press also carries advertisments from covens, groves and hearths, although most Pagan groups try to avoid proselytizing while doing this.

When you approach a group for potential membership, there are several things to remember. First of all, the ball is in your court to make contact, and there is no guarantee they will wish to meet you; and if they do, you may still be refused. If they are not interested in you, don't be discouraged; carry on trying to make contact with other groups.

If you are accepted as a potential member for a group, it may be some time before you are initiated into it. If they do want to accept you into full membership immediately, ask yourself why? Most groups are quite tight-knit, and prefer to know the people who are joining them reasonably well. It may be several weeks or even months before you are formally accepted into it—whether by a Wiccan First degree initiation, or by a corresponding passage rite of the tradition concerned.

When accepted into a group, you go into it on their terms. If you are not completely happy about the running of that group, its ethics or anything else, don't join. This is why groups have a waiting period. Don't expect to join a group and change it; this will only result in conflict.

Probably one of the most useful things you can do while deciding to join a group is to evaluate them using Isaac Bonewits' Cult Danger Evaluation Frame. This was first published in his book *Real Magic* and has since appeared in several other Pagan books. The Frame lists fourteen things to watch for in a group, and it is also useful for groups to monitor themselves regularly with. One thing particularly to watch out for is groups who show Fundamentalist tendencies. They normally claim to be 'true Craft' or the 'only real Pagans/Witches in the area,' or the only ones teaching the 'true mysteries,' etc. Leaders of groups using these terms are normally involved in controlling the power of that group, rather than (to quote a term used by Starhawk) 'empowering' their members. Beware of those claiming to be 'Gurus'; these do not exist in Paganism, and are against its philosophy. Give credit to those who do teach, and remember they are sacrificing their own time and energy to do it.

Cult Danger Evaluation Frame

1. INTERNAL CONTROL: amount of internal political power exercised by leaders over members.

2. WISDOM CLAIMED by leaders; amount of infallibility declared about decisions.

3. WISDOM CREDITED to leaders by members; amount of trust in decisions made by leaders.

4. DOGMA: rigidity of reality concepts taught; amount of doctrinal flexibility.

5. RECRUITING: emphasis put on attracting new members; amount of proselytizing.

6. FRONT GROUPS: number of subsidiary groups using different names from that of main group.

7. WEALTH: amount of money and/or property desired or obtained; emphasis on members' donations.

8. POLITICAL POWER: amount of external political influence desired or obtained.

9. SEXUAL MANIPULATION of members by leaders; amount of control over sex lives of members.

10. CENSORSHIP: amount of control over member's access to outside opinions on group, its doctrines or leaders.

11. DROPOUT CONTROL: intensity of efforts directed at preventing or returning dropouts.

12. ENDORSEMENT OF VIOLENCE when used by or for the group or its leaders.

13. PARANOIA: amount of fear concerning real or imagined enemies, perceived power of opponents.

14. GRIMNESS: amount of disapproval concerning jokes about the group, its doctrines, or its leaders.

To use this frame, mark the potential group you wish to join between 1 to 10 against each of the fourteen categories. If you get anything over a low to moderate score (say over 60) we recommend that you avoid that group, or at least ask more questions.

Hiving Off

Many new groups are formed by members leaving the group in which they were trained to found their own. Preferably this is amicable, arising because the departing members feel ready for it, or because they are moving to another area, or even because they want to concentrate on a particular kind of work.

In the Wiccan three-degree system, the general rule is that the hivers-off (or at least one leader of them if they are more than a working couple) must be Second or Third Degree. If the leader is Third Degree, the new coven is immediately independent; if Second Degree, the 'umbilical cord' is retained from the parent coven, who give guidance till they feel the new coven is securely on its feet, and then give the leader(s) the Third Degree to establish independence. Other paths may have similar rules.

Unfortunately, of course, the split is not always amicable; it may result from a clash of personalities, or from serious differences over practice. If this happens, one should always strive for agreement to differ, mutual respect, and communication where necessary. One group split off from our coven several years ago, in heated argument; in due course they and we realized there had been mistakes on both sides, and we became loving and cooperative friends.

Starting your own Group

This is not something you should take on lightly, and we recommend that you should have exhausted all possibilities in finding and joining a well-established group before even considering it. Starting your own group can be hard work, particularly if you intend something as formal as a coven or grove. If there is no similar group in your area, you may consider approaching a group outside it for guidance. It is now not unusual for covens to support groups out of their area as a form of sponsorship.

When you start a group, the first thing you need is people. A group can be anything from two upwards. If it is to be just an open meeting group, the number of people within in it doesn't matter so much; but if you are starting a formal working group, you should avoid exceeding six participants before you are well established. They should all know each other quite well, with a good level of trust already formed.

Set your ground rules before you start. Even though everything may seem fine at first, agreed rules and guidelines prevent and settle arguments later. As time progresses, you may have to amend some of these—but always by total agreement. The most important rules you should cover are listed below. These are for the formation of a formal group, but some points are just as applicable to open-meeting groups.

1. ETHICS: Most Pagan and Wiccan groups adhere to 'an it harm none, do what thou wilt.' This, although appearing a simple ethic, puts responsibility on the individual for his or her actions. It is a subject that should be thoroughly discussed before starting a group.

2. DECISION MAKING AND INTERNAL POLITICS: This covers the subject of leadership within the group. Some groups use a democratic system where all decisions are by a majority vote; others insist that all must agree; and some use a system of leadership based on degrees or by rotating the responsibility. All of these work as long as the group obeys its own ethics and guidelines consistently; but we do recommend that newly-formed groups start by using consensus of opinion. If you later opt for a system of leadership (it is not unusual for a natural leader to emerge), remember that it takes maturity, and involves accepting responsibility—and most important, the ability to listen and understand the needs of others. Good leaders continue to use consensus of opinion, and only make a unilateral decision if they have to. Egotism and self-interest have no place in leadership. Many groups find it works well to distinguish between actual Circles or other rituals, when the acknowledged leader has command, and all other times, when decisions are democratic.

3. GOAL SETTING, PASSAGE RITES AND DEGREES: A lot of misunderstanding and pomposity has grown up around degrees. The degree system used by many Pagan groups is nothing more than a system of levels of achievement, validated magically by a passage rite. There are advantages and disadvantages to using them. The main advantage is that they give individuals and the group something to work towards. Without a defined set of goals, a group can quickly turn in on itself and disintegrate. Goal-setting can take the form of reading assignments, research, meditative and magical exercises, and individuals

passing back that information to the others in teaching sessions. Once individuals have been considered by the group to have achieved their goals, they can pass through the appropriate passage rite. The main disadvantage of the degree system is that, if taken dogmatically, it can become hierarchical. There is always a danger of this once a recently-formed group begins to accept new members, who may 'pedestal' the older members for their supposed knowledge and wisdom, with the older members allowing their egos to become carried away.

4. MEMBERSHIP: It is best to avoid accepting new members until the group is well established and confident in itself. This may take anything from a couple of months to a year. It is wise to keep to yourselves during this period; there are always people who feel they have the right to interfere, which can cause disruption if the group is not yet stable. Once you have decided you are ready for new members, resist the temptation to advertise for them. Paganism is not a religion that proselytizes, and it could get your group a bad reputation in the Pagan community. Allow potential members to come to you. If you want to remain semi-public, this is best done by letting members of open-meeting groups know of your existence, and they will point people in your direction—or tell you about them, which has the advantage of your being able to say 'No' without even meeting them. Never on any account accept would-be members into a group straight away. There should always be a waiting period when you get to know them and they get to know you. Make sure they understand how your group functions, what will be expected of them, and your rules and guidelines. Never compromise on these just to get them into your group. They should be presented with a 'take it or leave it' situation. This sounds a bit harsh, but it prevents any discord later, and ensures that new members know where they stand.

5. MEETINGS: Decide how often and where you are going to meet. It is best that a new group meets fairly regularly in its early days, until it is confident in itself. Meeting weekly is a good idea, and this does not necessarily have to take the form of a formal ritual. It can be just a reading and education session. A group should at least meet once a month, and hold one ritual during this period, to establish a 'group mind.'

When setting up a group, always be aware of potential pitfalls. The commonest is allowing egos to become carried away, and for members to find themselves in competition with each other. (This generally tends to involve the younger male members.) Be prepared for arguments and disagreements. These happen in groups which have been established for years, and are an indication of growth within that group. Growing pains always happen in new groups, and regular frank discussions, rather than arguments, can avoid conflict; if you have established your ground rules, this should be easy. Most new groups argue over trivial things, and a compromise is always at hand if you look for it. It is useful for a new group to refer periodically to Isaac Bonewits' Cult Danger Evaluation Frame, quoted above, to see if it is developing well.

Becoming a Priest/Priestess

Two trains of thought are current on the place of Priests and Priestesses. The first, the New Age approach, suggests that as we enter the Age of Aquarius we all become our own Priest or Priestess, conducting our rites and rituals for ourselves, family and friends. This means that the role is not continual, and finishes when the Circle is closed. The second approach favors a permanent Priesthood administering to the needs of the community. The idea of an established Priesthood is not new to Paganism, and has existed within every culture: Druidism is such a Priesthood, based on the maintenance of the Celtic mysteries, and we know that Druids acted as a spiritual and political focus within their settlements. Discussion between adherents of both viewpoints continues within the Pagan community.

The New Age approach works well in insular groups which have little contact with the general public, and where all the members have the same level of commitment. It is based on the principle that everyone should take responsibility for their own spirituality. In a perfect world this would be true, but there will always people who require spiritual guidance from someone who is trained and/or experienced to give it.

The second approach, that there is a need for a trained Priesthood, makes up for this inadequacy. For example, Janet regularly gives Tarot readings for members of the local public. As such she is counseling, and therefore acting as a Priestess outside of the Circle—a role that entails a lot of responsibility. Poor counseling could do more damage than good, breaking the first ethic of the Craft 'An it harm none...' etc. A Priestess of long standing whom Gavin used to work with, once heard a conversation in a small occult shop which infuriated her. A girl of about 18 had recently become a member of a well-known organization and had decided she was now a 'Priestess,' and had the know-how (even though she had received no training whatsoever) to counsel rape victims and 'reconsecrate their wombs.' Gavin's Priestess immediately turned on her and rebuked her for it. The girl had no training in counseling and certainly no life experience. The damage she could have done was incalculable. Such examples give credence to the need for a trained Priesthood.

In the United States and Canada some large Pagan organizations already run extensive courses for training their own Priesthoods. But such formal training within organizations is not essential. What really makes a Pagan Priest or Priestess is the fact that it is a vocation. We could name many people whom we have met, on both sides of the Atlantic, who fit into this category, standing out by their dedication and the fact that they are a Priest or Priestess 24 hours a day. Many are in occupations which support their role, such as nurses, professional counselors, alternative therapists, psychotherapists, authors, occult shop owners, and so on, though being a member of such a profession does not in itself necessarily make a good Priest or Priestess.

As we have said, it is vocation and dedication that makes a member of a Priesthood. This means willingness to study anything that is appropriate to the role, and does not necessarily mean knowing how to conduct a ritual. It is, above all, about serving humanity and the natural order. This means being willing to be directed by fate and your deities. The Anglo-Saxons called this Wyrd, and other European cultures had similar philosophies.

To call Wyrd 'fate' would be to trivialize it. In many respects it is akin to the Taoist principle of Wu Wei—to yield to circumstances and allow intuition to guide you. This is best described as sailing a boat on the sea of life. Instead of trying to sail against the winds and currents (the adversities of life) you learn to use them to your advantage, by tacking (using intuition). The concept of Wyrd incorporates this, but also concepts of time and space. In his book *The Way of Wyrd*, Brian Bates' central character, the sorcerer Wulf, describes it thus:

> Wyrd existed before the gods and will exist after them. Yet Wyrd lasts only for an instant, because it is the constant creation of the forces. Wyrd is itself constant change, like the seasons, yet because it is created at every instant it is unchanging, like the still center of a whirlpool. All we can see are the ripples dancing on the top of the water.

When Pagans become Priests or Priestesses, they are agreeing to allow deity to direct them on the web of life. To use the boat metaphor again, they are agreeing initially to take a pilot (their personal deity) on board to navigate them past life's hazards, while being trained how to sail. They are then expected to help others by teaching them what they have learnt.

Many Priests or Priestesses have a particular personal deity whom they serve—normally a reflection of the type of activity that they most perform, and thus usually an aspect deity (see pp. 18–21). Most would say that the deity 'picked them' rather than the other way round, and many would describe having mystical experiences related to the deity. In the Shamanistic path there are also 'power animals' to consider. In the boat metaphor, these could be described as the dolphin or sea bird showing you the way the sea and air currents are flowing.

We would recommend most Pagans to adopt the New Age approach for at least several years before considering commitment to the ideal of Priesthood (if at all). To those who find that they are drawn to the role of a Priest or Priestess, we would ask them to remember that it is a vocation. It involves dedication and hours of serious study, being prepared when necessary to put the needs of others before your own, and being willing to submit to the will of your particular God or Goddess. It is a life decision, and one that should not be taken lightly.

21.

Questions and Answers

To present an accurate survey of the Pagan movement worldwide is probably impossible at this moment in time. Paganism by its very nature is dynamic and continually evolving. In the past several years there has been unprecedented growth worldwide, which has continued during the writing of this book. The purpose of this census was to show the potential trends which are occurring and how they will affect the Pagan movement in the future. We also felt it was important to allow the ordinary grass-roots Pagans a chance to voice their views, and we have tried in this chapter to give a good cross section of quotes from the community as a whole.

Originally we sent out a sample survey of 51 Questionnaires to selected individuals, groups and organizations from our database. We sent out three types of Questionnaire to Pagans in several countries: No. 1 to organizations catering for groups or individuals; No. 2 to groups or covens; and No. 3 to solo workers. The information for Questionnaire No. 1, to organizations, was used purely for research purposes, and this information is contained in Chapter 19, *Around the World*. Information from Questionnaires No. 2 and No. 3 has been used in this census and again, some of it provided us with useful research.

Wording Questionnaires for surveys can be difficult. This is particularly true when sending them out to a very eclectic (and potentially pedantic!) Pagan public. We therefore used a mixture of open-ended and closed (Yes/No) questions, which we felt was the best compromise. We sympathize with one reply which stated:

> ...to try to answer your questions, I immediately come up against a number of difficulties. The principal one, of which the others are sub-sets, is that I see myself as a traveler, a voyager on a spiritual journey, a quest

which is continually taking me to new places, in each of which I am learning different lessons. Your questions, on the whole, assume a certain settled, defined set of practices, whereas my own answers to the 'Do I do this?' type of question tend to be 'I have done' or 'I might' or 'Not yet'.

Katy J., Oxfordshire

Of the original 51 Questionnaires we sent out, 20 were No.1; 19 were No.2; and 12 were No.3. Of these only approximately 50% replied. From a sociologist's point of view, this is a good return from such a sample survey. In the foreword to each Questionnaire we asked the participant: "If you have contacts who could also usefully contribute, we will glad to send you as many (Questionnaires) as you need." In reply to this the Pagan Federation circulated all three Questionnaires in their periodical *The Wiccan*. This resulted in a further 110 replies (and explains why the response from Britain was the largest). The Canadian Pagan magazine *Songs from the Dayshift Foreman* also circulated all three, resulting in another seven replies. In the United States several Pagans posted Questionnaires on bulletin board systems. This resulted in another 35 replies. We sent out a further nine Questionnaires to other interested parties. By mid-October we realized our chances of conducting a neat orderly sample survey had been scuppered by the enthusiasm of the Pagan community! This alone gives an indication of the amount of communication which now exists within the Pagan community worldwide.

Distribution of Replies Internationally, and Totals

Country	Organizations (1)	Groups (2)	Solo (3)	Total
Australia	1	1		2
Belgium			1	1
Britain	4	38	79	121
Canada		6	7	13
Finland		2		2
France			1	1
Germany		1	5	6
Ireland	1	1		2
Italy			1	1
Japan			1	1

Country	Organizations (1)	Groups (2)	Solo (3)	Total
Lithuania	1			1
Netherlands		4	1	5
Norway	1	1		2
Portugal		1		1
South Africa		1		1
Spain			1	1
Sweden			1	1
United States	2	20	30	52
Totals	10	76	128	214

Because many of the questions are repeated on both solo and group Questionnaires (e.g. questions No.7 Solo and No.11 Group *Do you use Cabala in your working?*) we have combined these results below where marked. We have also renumbered the questions for ease of reading.

The Survey Replies

1. (Combined group and solo question) Do you consider your group specifically Wiccan, Ritual Magician, something else, or simply Pagan?

The majority of those replying to this survey were Wiccan, 60%. There are three possible reasons why this should be so:

a) Most practicing Pagans in the community label themselves as Wiccan.

b) Better communication exists among Wiccans than any other path; e.g. the majority of readers of *The Wiccan* magazine are Wiccans and therefore completed more Questionnaires; and the majority of bulletin replies from the United States and Canada came from Wiccans.

c) We ourselves know more Wiccans than any other path, and to this degree our distribution of Questionaires was biased.

It was noticeable that there was a lack of replies from other defined Paths such as Druidism (4%), Asatru (2%), Shamanism (2%) and Ritual Magic (3%) even though we had been careful to include these groups.

The majority of those who called themselves Druid were solo. We received only one reply from a Druidic group:

> The group I run is through the Order of Bards, Ovates and Druids, but within the Order the understanding is that Druidry is not a religion and the structure is such that there a wide variety of paths within it, from (aspiring) Druids who are witches to those who call themselves Celtic Christians, and those who follow it for the personal development rather than the spirituality (perhaps these will go on to spirituality?). Because there are a number of Wiccan orientated people within our group, effectively it tends towards being Pagan.
>
> Nemeton Seed Group, Reading, Britain

Some of those defining themselves as Wiccan also stated interests in other paths, as did some of those who merely called themselves Pagan (26%). Some also labeled themselves according to their situation:

> I usually think of myself as a Pagan, although initially I called myself Wiccan. I prefer the term Pagan as I feel it means getting in touch with the Earth in a simple way, whereas Wiccan infers more ritual and magic. This is only my interpretation, of course, and to me the dividing lines are quite blurred. I tell most people I am a Pagan, occasionally I will say Wiccan and sometimes I use the term 'white witch' if people don't understand the implications of Pagan or Wiccan.
>
> Sue F., Chelmsford. Britain

Labeling is one of the issues within the Pagan community that should be looked at carefully. It is easy to label yourself (or someone else) without really looking at what that labeling means, and what practices are involved. This can result in prejudice and a 'them and us' situation. Many of the Pagan paths are beginning to overlap, particularly as the community grows. Hopefully this will increase understanding between the different paths, otherwise there is a danger of excluding many like-minded people just because they call themselves something different.

Wicca remains the 'spearhead' of the Pagan revival. This must be attributed to better communication, and more willingness to communicate.

2. (Combined group and solo question) If you are Wiccan, how do you define your path—e.g. Gardnerian, Alexandrian, Gardnerian/Alexan-

*drian, Traditional, Hereditary, Eclectic, Dianic, Shamanistic, etc.? Or
do you prefer not to use a path name, and simply call it Wiccan?*

This was aimed at Wiccans to show the changes occurring in one
particular area of the community. The largest groups were the Wiccans
who labeled themselves Eclectic (24%), and Gardnerian/Alexandrian
(18%). Gardnerians replying came to 12%, followed by Alexandrian at
7%, and Traditional/Hereditary at 7%. A modern term, Hedgewitch,
also did surprisingly well with 3%; this derives from Rae Beth's book
of the same name, about traditional country witchcraft. Other path
names were used by 14%, such as Dianic, the American New Reformed
Orthodox Order of the Golden Dawn, and Georgian. Several others
chose labels meant to describe their practices, such as the 'Celtiphilic
Eclectic Erisian Witches' (Circle Dragonmist, California). Eleven percent did not feel it necessary to use any label other than Wiccan.

Wicca is certainly becoming more eclectic, and is losing some of the
dogma attached to Gardnerian and Alexandrian attitudes in the early
days. Many Wiccans now label themselves Gardnerian/Alexandrian,
reflecting the realization that these two traditions (which in the 1970s
were at loggerheads with each other) are basically the same:

> Gardnerian/Alexandrian. Although we have lineage in both styles, we are
> primarily Alexandrian in attitude and habit. Because of the similarity of
> the two paths, we usually call ourselves Traditional Wiccan.
>
> Quicksilver Coven, Ottawa

What effect this swing towards eclecticism will have on Wicca in the
future is debatable. Obviously many find it an important part of Wiccan
practice, typified by the common phrase: 'If it works, use it!' Others
fear it may result in Wicca losing its identity, which drives some to
emphasize their tradition's roots:

> We are definitely Alexandrian. As a matter of fact, we're working hard
> to reconstruct some of the Alexandrian tradition we feel has been lost to
> eclecticism. We half-jokingly, half-seriously have begun to call ourselves
> Classic Alexandrian Reconstructionists.
>
> Morven's coven, Massachusetts.

Four percent (all solo) called themselves Shamanic. Although some
replies indicated interest in Ritual Magic, those calling themselves

Shamanic were the only replies who considered it possible for a major path to be also an individual path within Wicca. Shamanism itself is a solitary path by definition (see p. 28), and some solo practitioners now clearly recognize the important similarities between solo Wicca and traditional Shamanistic practice.

3. (Group only) How many members does your group have? Are they divided into an Inner and Outer Circle?

Only 37% of the groups that answered were split between Inner and Outer Circles or similar structures. The main reasons given for this were for teaching purposes, or for practical working depending on a level of commitment between the group's members:

> We have an Inner and Outer Circle, but the Outer Circle is for candidates to the coven, students and others who wish some level of affiliation with our group, but cannot commit to the coven due to time or other pressures.
>
> Quicksilver Coven, Ottawa.

Among the majority who did not use a division, some were uneasy with the idea of splitting a group in this way, and felt it to be counter-productive, resulting in a 'them and us' situation and the possible development of a hierarchical structure. They felt it was better to instruct new group members during magical workings, rather than to exclude them.

The main argument for a division came from groups involved in teaching in excess of eight members, when one-to-one instruction became impossible. They found it easier to teach a larger group in this way, dividing the members by their level of knowledge. These groups generally used a system of degrees to mark the attainment of knowledge. A secondary argument for division was that large numbers of untrained members present at a magical working may disrupt it. Many groups at some point must make a decision on what is more important to them, growing in numbers or maintaining personal intimacy.

4. (Solo only) Were you initiated by someone else, and if so what was his/her path? Or were you self-initiated, using what kind of ritual? Or did you regard initiation as unnecessary for solo working? Is the practice hereditary in your family?

Thirty-eight percent of those that replied had not been initiated, 35% had performed their own self-initiation or dedication ceremonies, 25% had been initiated by someone else, and only 3% were hereditary. Solo Pagans were divided equally between those three classes. Some replies were very thought-provoking:

> I was first initiated into an Alexandrian coven. At the time it seemed like a good idea. I now believe that 'initiation' as such is something that happens over a period of time through experiences rather than ceremonies.
>
> Catmye, Stourbridge, Britain.

> I have had an initiation by Phillip Carr-Gomm, arch druid of the OBOD, but I withdrew myself.... Through this experience of having an initiation, I think it is unnecessary for solo working.
>
> Anon Druid, Belgium.

> Self dedicated, following Raymond Buckland. I don't think the practice is obligatory, though maybe I will (become initiated) one day. As Scott Cunningham says, 'There are only two people qualified to initiate, namely the God and the Goddess, and I can't think of anyone who is better qualified.'
>
> (Wrote "Quote me, quote me" and then forgot to enclose name!)

Many of those who had been initiated now felt it was unnecessary for solo working. Others who stated that they had not been initiated (self or otherwise) had dedicated themselves instead and were waiting to find a group to be initiated into.

Although it took a long time for self-initiation to be accepted (particularly among the more traditional Wiccans), it now seems to be considered by the majority of solo practitioners as irrelevant to solo practice, and been replaced by the rite of self-dedication. This conclusion was best expressed in a reply from Gwydion Wolf of Ireland;

> I was initiated by someone else. They themselves were self-initiated and were at the time calling themselves Wiccan. I don't think that initiation is absolutely necessary if you are content to remain a solo practitioner, but I do think that some sort of self-dedication ceremony should be undergone, if for no other reason than being polite to your personal Gods and Goddesses. If, on the other hand, you intend to form your own Coven at

a late date, then being initiated by someone else and working with other people can be an advantage to your magical experience.

5. (Group only) Is your membership confined to, or predominantly consisting of, a particular category—e.g. university students, health workers, police officers, sailors, media workers, etc.?

Most groups had members from mixed social and occupational backgrounds. We received only one reply where members belonged to a single occupation—a campus networking group consisting solely of students. Thirty-one percent stated that their membership came from noticeably well-educated middle-class backgrounds. All but one of these groups were Wiccan.

Generally, groups did not feel they were influenced by the candidates' background when accepting them. Some tried consciously to maintain a mixed membership:

> We like to aim on a coven population as mixed as possible. We have found out that the more difference you have the more creative you can be. It is the best way to learn from each other—to be different.
>
> Jetske and Maurice, Alkmaar, Netherlands.

One reason why some Wiccan groups tend to have members from a specific social and occupational background may be to do with their close-knit structure. Proselytizing and recruiting are widely considered taboo. This, combined with the fact that most groups prefer secrecy, can result in potential new members being already known to the group, and therefore more likely to come from the same educational and social background.

As time goes by, the gap between two people of supposedly different class backgrounds becomes more and more blurred. In the end it becomes a subjective decision. Pagan philosophy leaves little room for social distinctions among the different paths or between individuals. Janet and Stewart once had an Asian princess and a building worker in the same coven, and any initial nervousness quickly evaporated.

6. (Group only) Is it female-led, male-led, or does it avoid the concept of leadership as far as possible?

Groups led by a joint leadership of both sexes polled 38%, followed by female-led at 33%. Only three groups that replied were male-led; one because there was no suitable High Priestess, and another being an Asatru group. Twenty-five percent avoided the concept of leadership, and were run by consensus of opinion or democratic process.

Traditionally Wiccan covens have been High Priestess led, with the High Priest in support. Many Pagan groups have followed this pattern, on the premise that as society was patriarchal, emphasis on the Goddess principle, and thus on the High Priestess, was needed to restore balance.

> The group is female led; from our group perspective the Goddess is the ultimate authority. We don't avoid the concept of leadership—our High Priestess gives out gold stars!
>
> Temple of the Earth Mother, Britain.

Most sensible High Priestesses in this position consult with their High Priest and coven on important decisions, only using their final say as a last resort.

Many groups now disagree with this form of leadership, feeling that there is a need for balance. This can be attributed to the fact that women's role in society has now changed, giving them more equality with men. In practice this means recognizing the God and Goddess, and therefore the High Priest and Priestess, as equals.

Groups who rejected the concept of leadership were against the idea of hierarchy. Most of them were eclectic in nature, or just listed their path as Pagan. Some of these groups 'rotated' leadership:

> The ones who put on the meeting, ritual, Esbat or Sabbat lead the gathering, but have no special rights at all. The 'leader' is whoever of those putting on the meeting, who wants to start with whatever discussion is going on.
>
> Black Eagle and Silver Moon, Arlington.

Obviously there is no wrong or right answer to this question. The replies made clear the varied ways in which a group can be successfully run. The question of leadership and hierarchy within groups is still under debate in many areas of the Pagan community, with many loudly voicing their disapproval of these concepts. With this in mind, here is a final word in defense of it:

Our group is led by a High Priestess. I would like to have a High Priest to co-lead the group, but since I don't have a steady working partner, I lead the group, and the male elders of our group act as High Priests when needed. A lot of people are against hierarchy, but let's face it: hierarchy is part of life. We can refuse to acknowledge it in our covens, or use the coven as a place to learn how to make hierarchy work. We can learn to lead well and to be led well. I hope that in my coven people both learn how to govern graciously and also how to accept authority, but without losing self. In my coven, they should learn how to question things that make them uncomfortable, but to do it in a way that makes both of us feel good. That's a very valuable skill to have in this lifetime. Just think of how it could help them in their jobs if they learned how to gently get a manager to listen to their points of view. Or think about how a good coven leader must graciously and patiently answer the repeated questions of neophytes or deal with harsh emotions. Wouldn't those skills come in handy in interpersonal relationships, even parenting?

Morven's coven, Massachusetts.

7. (Group only) Is your membership of both sexes, exclusively female, or exclusively male? If of both sexes, do you accept gay or lesbian members?

Only three groups that replied had members all of one sex—these three being all-female. Thirteen percent of groups had gay or bisexual members, including one which included a formerly male transsexual. In all 95% felt that they would have no problems accepting bisexual or homosexual members.

Within the wider Pagan community the conclusion must be that the majority of groups consist of both sexes, followed by all-female groups. All-male groups exist, but remain a minority. Magical dogma has always dictated that all-male groups tend to be unproductive magically, although the existence of male homosexual groups puts this is doubt (we unfortunately received no replies from such groups, although we know of several). All-female groups (generally Dianic) sometimes face problems from their local Pagan community, particularly with stereo-typing:

Dianics are seen automatically to be lesbians whether we are or not, which can be irritating. There are also many heterosexual and bisexual women who prefer to worship with other women. As a wild guess, I'd say the Dianics in Vancouver are about 65% lesbian, 20% heterosexual, and 15%

bisexual—at least among those who will tell you! But the women's circles I attend are far less about sexuality than about mothering, taking care of the older generation, work and prosperity, recovery and healing—the responsibilities of life common to all of us.

Marga, Vancouver.

Homosexuality within Paganism (particularly Wicca) had been a controversial subject for a long time, although our survey indicates beyond doubt that homosexuality is now widely accepted. We received no replies which could be called blatantly homophobic, and only 5% of groups would not accept homosexuals as members. Their reasoning was basically the same:

We do not accept gay and lesbian members, not because we have prejudice against them, but because we feel the polarity of Wicca should be pure as in the Great Rite and the consecration of wine and cakes.

Jan and Barry, Telford, Britain.

The problem seemed to center particularly around the working of polarity magic—one of the keystones of Wiccan practice. Obviously many groups have found an answer to the problem of polarity-working with homosexual and heterosexual members. Often such a mixture was found, not only not to hinder magical working, but also to open up new avenues of thought:

Our coven membership is of both sexes—this energy balance is (for us) vital! At the moment we have three gay members, and it has been they who have stimulated discussions on this topic within the group. All three feel comfortable working with a female partner, and even emphasize that it is necessary to be able to. They have no disadvantages within the group and their sexuality plays no particular role. Two would even like to have a sort of handfasting ceremony done and we feel this is possible, although the focus of the ceremony, and relationship in general, is somewhat different than that of heterosexual couples. It is time Pagans wake up! Homosexuality is nothing new to our society, only it has been suppressed over the centuries, like the innate power of Woman. It is our duty as Pagans and Witches to help design the New Age, and to exclude minorities would be to hinder the expansion of a new world consciousness. The Power of the Witch is not based on sexuality, but on inner strength, enlightenment and dedication.

Heide, Lollar, Germany.

8. (Group only) Do you have a degree structure, and of what kind?

The idea of degree structures within the modern Pagan revival originates with the magical orders of the 19th century. Gerald Gardner adopted the system into Wicca, with the help of Aleister Crowley, after his hive-off from the New Forest coven. It has been part of Pagan group practice ever since then, adopted by many different paths apart from just Wicca.

In our replies 42% of groups were still using the basic three-degree system. Thirty-three percent had discarded the idea of degrees altogether. Twenty-five percent worked different systems related to their own traditions (e.g. The Pagan Way only has a two-degree system) or had adapted the original to produce their own:

> We do not have degrees, but we do have three levels of transition: Dedication, Initiation and Ordination. Dedication recognizes a commitment to learn about the Craft. Initiation recognizes that the person is familiar with the Wheel of the Year, the aspects of the Moon, the Gods and Goddesses, has some grasp of the Mystery, and is capable of running a ritual from beginning to end. Ordination recognizes the readiness to found a coven, practice pastoral counseling, perform handfastings and wakes, etc.
>
> Circle Dragonmist, California.

Many did not use a degree system on principle, finding it hierarchical. Others felt that it served no real purpose:

> One either is or is not a Crafter. After commitment it is only a degree of experience.
>
> Dave and Tricia, Brandon, Britain.

Some of those that did use degree systems were aware of both of the above arguments:

> We do not see the degrees as signs of hierarchy, but they mark stages of development, and should mark significant changes in one's life.
>
> Ariadne and Lupus, Cardiff, Wales.

The degree system is still obviously widely in use. Many of those using it do not see it as a form of hierarchy, the main argument against its use. Those that have felt this way, but also have recognized its positive benefits, have adapted it accordingly. It is unlikely that the degree system will disappear completely in the future, but adaptation of it to a particular group's needs is quickly becoming the norm.

9. (Group only) Do you admit children to some or all of your rituals? What is your minimum age for full membership? And what is the actual range of ages within the group?

We have given more quotes from replies to this question on pp. 134–5.

This has been another contentious issue among the Pagan community, particularly in recent years with accusations of ritual abuse. Fifty-one percent never allowed children in rituals; 44% allowed them only on specific occasions, usually open celebrations rather than magical work and 5% allowed them in Circle all the time.

One reason given for not admitting children was that they might be a distraction for their parents, and be frightened by the ritual:

> We regard the involvement of children in ritual as wholly inappropriate. The combination of children's psychic sensitivity and their lack of understanding of what's happening makes for a potentially frightening and disturbing experience for the child and also disrupts the adult participants' concentration.
>
> Anon. Wiccan coven, Telford, Britain.

Obviously this applies mainly to magical ritual rather than to celebrations. One other reason for not allowing children to attend rituals was the feeling it was wrong to involve them at an impressionable age:

> I've been to a ritual at a friend's house, with an eight-year-old and a ten-year-old present, and found it very uncomfortable. I believe children should not be 'indoctrinated,' and just being present means that they are.
>
> Deborah, Fleetwood, Britain.

Those who lived in areas where there were more problems with religious intolerance were less likely to admit children to rituals, magical, celebratory or otherwise. The majority of those who never allowed children in ritual came from countries where Paganism had no legal status. In the United States, even though in some areas religious intolerance towards Paganism was incredibly high, the idea of children attending Pagan functions seemed to be more widespread than in Britain. The same seemed to apply to Holland, which has always had a reputation for tolerance. Again, they differentiate between the different types of function:

> Children are not admitted to full-scale rituals, although especially during the summer months we have outdoor 'rituals' where children often attend. These are conveniently called 'picnics,' and that word reflects the general atmosphere better than 'ritual.' Instead of calling up the Lords of the Watchtowers, we invite the four winds to attend. The main section of the ritual often includes an individual meditative walk through the woods to find materials to make a corn dolly or a sun wheel, and when we come back to the ritual area we all work together to make a symbolic representation of the season, of the God and Goddess. Sometimes we dance or circle around. Magical work is not usually part of these outdoor rituals, although individual candle magic might be done, or something like writing a wish on a dead leaf and burning it. Our daughter who is now eight, and the other children who attend, are quite conversant with these small spells and have taken to them quite naturally.
>
> Merlin and Morgana, Al Zeist, Netherlands.

The minimum age for membership of groups varied considerably, ranging from below 18, with parental permission, to 21. Those who accepted under-18s made up only 7%. The majority of groups accepted members at 18. Age ranges within groups varied, although there was a noticeable tendency for groups to be of a particular age range. Groups tended to fit into two distinct categories; those of members from 18 to 30, and those of mid-30s and above (these were in the minority). The oldest member of any group was in his mid-80s.

Children are our future, and there is no doubt that this was foremost in the minds of those who answered this question. We sensed more of a move within Paganism to accept children as valid members of the community, and not to exclude them from its activities, though there is little doubt that the involvement of children in situations in which they feel uncomfortable is undesirable, e.g. complex magical workings. The other question is: do we have the right to indoctrinate our own children?—something we regularly accuse monotheistic religions of. Possibly the answer is our friend's which we quoted on p. 133: not to teach our children religion, but to teach them about religion.

10. (Combined group and solo question) Do you lay special emphasis on particular aspects—e.g., gay and lesbian rights, vegetarianism, animal rights, environmentalism, politics, women's rights, etc.? Or is your emphasis all-embracing?

There was an even split here between solo and group workers, with neither likely to be more all-embracing or have a special emphasis than the other. The exceptions to this were those involved in anti-defamation or promoting religious tolerance; which seemed to be very much a group activity. Sixty-two percent of group and solo Pagans had no special emphasis, or were all-embracing, although some of those felt quite strongly about the issue:

> We do not concern ourselves, generally, with political or social topics such as gay and lesbian rights, animal rights, women's rights, etc. We are witches, not socio-political activists, and we think there is a difference between the two—though we recognize others may feel differently.
>
> Caer Dunraven, North Carolina.

Others felt that being 'socio-political activists' was an important part of their Pagan practice:

> By nature, the Craft is inclusive of all people, as the divine resides within everything in the natural universe. So, I can't see how (or why) a sexist would be attracted to a Pagan faith. The Gods love all people and so do we. Of course I feel this applies to reverse bigotry as well (for example, women hating men or blacks hating whites). I believe that we must be actively interested in politics for our very own survival. After all, how many states attempt to outlaw Witchcraft even though it is a valid expression of religious faith? We get fired, evicted, and have our children taken away from us; we cannot afford to be politically passive.
>
> Morrigan Aa, Woodbridge Township,
> New Jersey.

Specializing in more than one of the issues mentioned seemed to be the norm. The issue on which the majority, both group and solo, laid special emphasis was (not surprisingly) ecology and environmentalism. This totaled 25%. Healing came second with 12%, followed by feminism with 10% and animal rights at 7%. Other issues mentioned included gay and lesbian rights, anti-defamation and religious tolerance, and finally research into the mysteries, magic and religion. Direct involvement by Pagans, particularly in ecology, is increasing, causing concern by some that the movement will be seen as political. Most Pagans see the risk as unavoidable. As one reply put it:

> I lay special emphasis on the environment. If we don't worry about that, will there be anything left to worry about in the end?
>
> Sabin, Fuis, Netherlands.

11. (Combined group and solo question) Do you charge payment for Tarot readings? Healing work? Spells? What is your view of the practice, in each of these categories? And do you differentiate between work done by the coven in the Circle, and work done outside it by individual members?

Charging for magical work has traditionally been considered unethical, although with Tarot reading, astrology, and other forms of divination it has always been thought acceptable. The replies confirmed this: 63% did not charge for any form of 'Craft'; 32% were willing to charge for forms of divination; and only 5% charged for magic and healing. Several reasons were given by those who felt it necessary to charge, but even some of them had doubt:

> I have charged occasionally for all three. Those who make their living from such work are, in my opinion, entitled to charge an appropriate fee. It also stops one being abused. Charging a fee stops people becoming over-reliant, or asking for a reading for something which they themselves could solve with a little effort. Sometimes I have been offered 'payment in kind' as opposed to money, which I also find acceptable. The two hang-ups I have about charging are (1) it can be exploited, and (2) not all people can afford even a nominal sum.
>
> Anon. Wiccan, Breisgau, Germany.

Many of those who did not charge saw no problem about charging for magic and healing as long as it was to cover costs of materials and time employed:

> We do not charge for the use of magic at all. We consider it be a violation of the Laws of the Craft. We do allow charging for materials and time, but not for use of magical powers. If the Gods are invoked or the personal magical power of the person doing whatever work is used, we cannot ask

payment for it. For example, we can charge someone a reasonable fee for making a wand, but not for imbuing it with magical power.

Quicksilver Coven, Ottawa, Canada.

The exploitation of magic and healing for profit is considered highly unethical by all except a very small minority of the Pagan community. We received no replies condoning such practices. Many even felt uncomfortable about charging for time and materials. One reply was from an artist and another from a psychotherapist; neither could differentiate between their magical or healing practices and what they did for a living. They also felt that there was pressure to conform to the ethics of the rest of the Pagan community:

> I am an artist and I have noticed that the process of art involves magic (in the strong meaning of the word). I make and sell art; at other times in my life I have made and not sold art. These decisions are personal. I have no objection to traditions or covens taking a collective decision on this, but I do wish that people would be more respectful of the rights of others to take a different decision.
>
> Caril, Hazelton, Canada.

As the Pagan community grows, this is likely to become more of an issue. Some feel it will come under increasing commercial pressure in the future, and may find itself prostituting itself to capitalism.

One issue which was not addressed in this question was charging for teaching. This has always been considered unethical, for face-to-face teaching, and heavily frowned upon by the majority of the Pagan community, though the past several years have seen paid-for postal courses in Wicca, both in the United States and in Britain. Organized Churches in the United States are being caught up in both face-to-face and postal-course charging. Money is needed for their continued running, and they find themselves charging for courses, services and the training of Priesthood, as a necessity.

The Pagan community will have to differentiate carefully between necessary charging for time and material, and the exploitation for profit of spiritual services. Many have already applied this to magic, healing and divination. In the future they will find they have to apply it to even more issues.

12. (Combined group and solo question) Do you use the Cabala in your working?

The majority, 64%, did not use the Cabala at all. Eleven percent used it continually in their magical practices, and 25% only used it occasionally. We found that Groups were more likely to use it than Solos. Cabala has always been the main magical system used by Ritual Magicians. Not surprisingly all the Magicians that replied were using it. The other major users have been the Alexandrians, who (due largely to Alex Sanders himself) were strong advocates of its use in the early 1970s. They made up the majority of those who used it all the time, and a fair percentage of those that used it only sometimes. Several reasons were given by those who did not use it:

> My neighbor the Rabbi assures me that study of the Cabala is for married men who have fathered children and have passed their fortieth birthday. I defer to his understanding of the rules of Judaism. For me to use the Cabala, or advocate its use, would be to perpetrate a robbery of someone else's faith.
>
> Branwen Stonecipher, Calgary

> I do not use the Cabala. I intend to study it eventually; but I am not certain that, being a Jewish text, it is applicable to Pagan-orientated Witchcraft.
>
> Pictus, Orlando, Florida.

Other reasons were given for its non-usage. Some felt it had Christian overtones which worried them; some that it was too complicated, preferring simpler 'natural' magic; others just felt 'uncomfortable' about its use. Those that did use it agreed on the reasons:

> We do use Cabala in our workings. We also do pathworkings on the Tree of Life. We incorporate Cabala into our training and work because we feel that it is the most comprehensive magical system that we (that is, the members of the Western Mystery Tradition) have. Cabala and Cabalistic teachings often explain the 'why' behind the 'what' in Craft practice.
>
> Caer Dunraven, North Carolina.

There is little doubt that the Cabala is moving towards becoming practiced solely by the Ritual Magicians in the Pagan community. Many Wiccans that did use it are now looking at other 'home-grown' magical

systems to work with. Shamanism, Druidism, and even Asatru are being
explored as replacements. This was borne out by the answers to Question 2, and is probably due to an increase in published research by
academics and Pagans over the past several years on these subjects.
Pagans are beginning to ask more about their native Pagan traditions,
and to question the validity of accepting ones from foreign cultures.
Even so, Cabala has become heavily Westernized over the centuries
and can no longer be considered purely Jewish. It is unlikely to disappear totally from Pagan practice.

*13. (Combined group and solo question) Do you practice skyclad—al-
ways, often, sometimes, or never?*

The majority of Pagans practiced skyclad sometimes, often or always, making up 63% (sometimes or often 51%, always 12%). Those
that never went skyclad made up 37%. We found that groups were more
likely to practice skyclad, and those that did were more likely to be
Wiccan. Solos were the least likely to do it all the time.

Those that never went skyclad generally gave two reasons:

> Never, two reasons: (1) North Yorkshire isn't the warmest place; and (2)
> we believe if the energy you are harnessing is so weak as to not get through
> your clothes then it's time to give it up. We feel it unnecessary.
>
> Maggie, Thirsk, Britain.

Very few Pagans now say that clothes block psychic energy, and most
find that statement irrational as a reason for going skyclad. Hardly any
that did practice skyclad felt the need to justify their actions. Several
replies, particularly from Northern Europe, mentioned cold weather,
stating that they only worked skyclad indoors:

> Always skyclad. Women with heavy periods wear gowns; I did when I
> was heavily pregnant (odd really!) and guests are never forced into
> anything they feel uncomfortable with. If a new member felt unable to be
> skyclad (except for initiation) they could wear a gown. Outdoors we do
> wear clothes often—in fact I wear thermals!! I have had the misfortune
> to see my husband once in cowboy boots, a cloak and a vest and nothing
> else—outdoors! I felt more mirth than reverence during that ritual (well,
> you try invoking the Horned God like that!!).
>
> Deborah, Fleetwood, Britain.

One thing everybody seemed to agree on was that nobody had the right to force anybody to go skyclad against his or her will (although some felt it was a necessity for initiation). None of the replies attacked the right of others to go skyclad. It seems that the majority of Pagans have experienced going skyclad at some time, with those that never have definitely in the minority. Most Pagans seem to be very flexible on this issue, feeling that in the end that it is of very little importance and really an individual decision.

14. (Group only) Is your group attached to a wider organization? (Combined group and solo:) Do you attend Festivals or other functions?

Twelve percent of the groups who replied were attached to wider organizations. We received five replies from registered Iseums/Lyceums of the Irish-based Fellowship of Isis and four replies from member covens of the U.S.-based Covenant of the Goddess. Most groups were autonomous, although 68% had members independently belonging to other organizations. Forty-eight percent had members belonging to the British-based Pagan Federation, and this included replies from Germany, the Netherlands and Norway. Other organizations mentioned included Circle Network, the Green Circle, the Ring of Troth, Odinshof, Paganlink, and the Church of All Worlds. Many groups (particularly in Europe) had members belonging to more than one organization:

> Our groups are not attached to any wider organizations, but members do belong to just about everything going—Fellowship of Isis, Pagan Federation, Green Circle, Hoblink and so on.
>
> John Ruse, Canvey Island, Britain.

United States and Canadian group members are more likely to belong to one organization only.

Most groups obviously prefer to remain autonomous from larger organizations, although individual members may belong to these. Even those groups that were attached kept safeguards to maintain their autonomy. This is probably healthy, preventing larger organizations from dictating the actions of smaller groups and therefore the actions of the wider community. The setting-up of organized 'Churches' worries some Pagans, feeling this autonomy may be lost in the future. This worry is probably unfounded; there is little evidence to show that Paganism is becoming centralized or ever will.

Fifty-four percent had attended Festivals, conferences and other Pagan gatherings, whether or not they belonged to any organizations. Interestingly, just as many solo Pagans attended these functions as groups. Such events are important to any growing community—for making contact with local and regional Pagan communities in a relaxed atmosphere—and in many countries (such as the United States) are vitally important for its well-being. Their most important function is in relaying information about politics, news, and the state of the Pagan community as a whole. The number of functions and the number of Pagans attending them has increased; this is a good sign, reflecting the amount of communication that now exists within the community.

15. (Combined group and solo question) Do you find there is harmony, cooperation, and mutual respect between the various Pagan groups and paths in your area? Or is there confrontation, jealousy, and 'bitch-craft'? If the situation is changing, in which direction is it moving? Do you feel it part of your duty to work for its improvement, or do you feel the confrontation is justified, or do you keep yourselves to yourselves?

We could quite easily have brought the besom out of the cupboard and swept this issue under the carpet. But as Pagans we live in a real world, and to ignore the fact that 'bitchcraft' and confrontation exist would have been wrong, and would not have helped to explain or resolve it.

The majority of Pagans, 39%, had experienced both harmony, coop-eration and mutual respect, and confrontation, jealousy and 'bitchcraft.' Thirty-four percent had found only the former, and 12% had experi-enced only the latter. Many gave reasons why they felt that such confrontation existed:

> It varies. I have found 'bitchcraft' and to my shame joined in once. I feel it is based on insecurity and fear. Just because we're witches we ask so much of ourselves and think we'll behave better than the wider society. But we have prejudices, fears, anxieties—just like anyone else. Wherever possible I try to accept the differences in others and try to help people understand why they feel an antagonism. Often I find the ones who are most threatened are the ones who feel they have to 'teach' others or Pagans/Wiccans who aren't trained themselves. It's lack of support which often creates these situations. It's very painful for all of us to feel our beliefs and values challenged.
>
> Deborah, Fleetwood, Britain.

Thirty-two percent kept to themselves and avoided any problems within their local Pagan community. Most felt that to become involved in any way would only increase the problem. The majority who felt this way were practicing solo, whereas the majority who felt compelled to work actively for its resolution (34%) were groups. Very few felt confrontation was justified (only 2%) and those that did considered it a last resort:

> Mostly we keep to ourselves, but do teach tolerance in all things, and that individually, at all times, we may work towards the improvement of the Craft. As a coven there are times when it is not possible for us to avoid confrontation for the betterment and enlightenment of the Craft.
>
> Anon. Coven, Ontario.

Seventeen percent felt that the situation had improved and was continuing to improve. Most put this down to better communication between themselves and other groups in their area:

> The situation has definitely changed in the past few years. Firstly, the Pagan movement has grown tremendously. Secondly, there is far less 'bitchcraft' and 'bicker' between individuals and groups. There is more contact and cooperation. We have more contact with a lot of other Pagans and groups in the area, and have on occasion attended each other's rituals. We also do FOI (Fellowship of Isis) rituals and some of the coven are FOI members and run an FOI Lyceum (Teaching Center).
>
> Ariadne and Lupus, Cardiff, Wales.

Confrontation and 'bitchcraft' are unavoidable in any growing movement. What is important is how that movement deals with it. The Pagan movement as a whole is dealing with it well, and finding ways of resolving problems. It is unlikely that these problems will disappear overnight, but they will certainly lessen and turn into constructive dialogue.

16. (Combined group and solo question) What is the public, non-Pagan reaction to Paganism in your area? Is there, at the good extreme, reasonable tolerance by grass-roots Christian and other neighbors— and at the bad extreme, persecution by Fundamentalist elements? We would appreciate specific details of either.

Most had indifferent reactions from the general public (41%) and their Christian neighbors (49%). Reactions varied considerably from country to country and area to area:

> There is no open hostility against Paganism. Mostly people are curious and ask questions, and they always ask the same questions: 'What is Wicca?' 'What do you believe in?' 'How about the Devil?'—and so on. You can't speak of persecution by Fundamentalists here in Sweden.
>
> Gealach Rincedir, Stockholm, Sweden.

> Generally Australians are pretty laissez-faire re other people's weirdness. The main problems occur when certain plonkers get themselves on naff television programs and systematically bugger up several decades of positive image building. You know the sorts. They like to scare old ladies and bishops.
>
> Bill and Antonia, New South Wales, Australia.

Reaction did not seem affected by whether you worked solo or in a group (although some pointed out that Fundamentalists seemed to prefer lone Pagans to verbally attack.) Twenty-six percent had bad experiences with their local Christian community, and 15% from their local population. One of the worst incidents came from South Africa:

> We are considered for the most part as Satanists and therefore keep a very low profile. As far as persecution goes, yes there have been extremes, e.g. homes being trashed by members of the Occult Related Crime Unit. In a similar instance, a home was trashed by some bat-wielding members of the local Christian Motorcyclists Association (Heaven's Angels?).
>
> Cleve Fletcher, South Africa.

In most places problems were not as extreme as this. In the United States, the country as a whole was quite tolerant of Paganism. The exception seemed to be the Southern States:

> Dear hearts, this is the heartland of rural Alabama. That sums up a great deal of ignorance and bigotry. My wife's church recently 'taught' a month-long series on the 'new age movement' which was an unashamedly one-sided pile of anti-everything-not-Biblical propaganda. The Baptist literature I've seen cites Paganism among the social ills bringing about 'the downfall of American society,' and warns against such things as even glancing at horoscopes or opening 'suspicious' books, lest a 'demon' draw

you into its 'evil influence.' A lady who opened a Wiccan book/supply store downtown is under constant watch as a suspected 'drug front' and receives frequent 'fire inspections' and veiled threats from the police. (Yet, any time local hoodlums vandalize property and leave cryptic symbols on anything, those same police officers go to her to identify them! The stuff is invariably drug-induced gibberish, of course.)

Mark, Deatsville, Alabama.

This example is typical of the negative reactions that many Pagans face, both in the United States and in Europe.

Positive reactions again varied from location to location. Good reactions were more likely to come from the general public than from local churches. Twenty-five percent had positive communication with their local Christian community. This could take the form of Pagans being present at inter-faith councils to doing Tarot readings for the local church fete! One reply was particularly promising:

> I am studying for an M.A. in Religious Pluralism at Derby University, and the majority of my fellow students are Christian clergymen. They have taken a positive interest in my beliefs. The Religious Studies Department at the University, and the Religious Research and Resource Center are now very aware of Paganism, and are including Paganism in their courses. They have also written out negative references to Paganism. We recently had an interesting seminar on Pagan-Christian dialogue (a local Vicar and me), and I have been asked to speak on Paganism to the Inter-faith group at Derby Open Center (representatives of local faith groups will include Muslim, Hindu, Sikh, Ba'hai, Christian and Buddhist).
>
> Anon. Druid, Derbyshire, Britain.

Replies confirmed that a polarization was taking place. Positive communication between Pagans and open-minded Christians, and animosity between Pagans and the Fundamentalist fringe, were both increasing at the same time. We noticed that both do not seem to exist in one locality at the same time. Public reaction is obviously affected by the Christian community, but is probably more influenced by the local press and how the local authorities respond to it. Fundamentalism is very political and encourages its adherents to stand for local authority, certainly in the United States where in some areas they have succeeded. This has resulted in the United States having extremes of reaction. Negative reaction to Paganism in Europe seems less extreme, but more widespread.

17. (Combined group and solo question) Do you have any contact with Pagans or Wiccan at home or overseas? If so, how active?

Most had contact with other Pagans. Only 26% had not. This did not seem to be affected by whether they practiced with a group or by themselves. Most had made initial contact with others through the Pagan press and open events. Pagans living any distance from one another communicated mostly by telephone or mail (52%).

> In active, close contact with Sami Noidies, PF in London, Wiccan Pagan Press Alliance in the U.S. and Wiccan covens in 15 countries. Phone/letter contact in general two to six times a year or more, visits (Scandinavia, Germany, Holland and U.K.) about twice a year.
>
> Silver Wheel, Bergen, Norway.

But the most interesting form of communication was by computer bulletin board networks (BBS). By this medium, 22% were communicating internationally. Most Pagans using these systems were based in the United States (although we also received replies from South Africa, Canada and Germany):

> Electronic mail contacts. I use the UseNet BBS, and it has users from all over the world. I am also on several electronic mailing lists with members from South Africa, Norway, Canada, Mexico, Australia, Austria, Germany, France, and the U.S. Note that this survey reply is international, and I got the source form on the UseNet BBS.
>
> Doug Freyburger, Pasadena, California.

The majority of solo Pagans and groups are in contact with others in their own countries. The use of BBS systems is already increasing international contact, and such systems are spreading to Europe. (It may be added here that computer communication, both national and international, has become a major underground activity in dictatorship countries, and is making such dictatorship far more difficult.)

18. (Combined group and solo question) Is your group, or are you, public or secret? If public, may we quote your name? Your address? If secret, we promise to keep its identity and yours confidential.

The main reason for including this question was to respect the right of privacy of those who were replying. Secondary to this, it gave an indication of the proportion of Pagans who still feel it necessary to remain secret. Eighteen percent remained completely secret and 50% remained moderately secret, willing to divulge their spiritual beliefs if they felt comfortable to do so:

> I would say I was neither totally public, nor totally secret. I do not openly broadcast my religious beliefs, or openly bring them up in conversation, unless asked. But saying this, it is one of my principles never to deny my spiritual beliefs; to do so would be to deny the God and Goddess. As a professional I have to be very careful where I work, so when asked I tend to use language that the average member of the general public understands. I have found that using the terms Witch or Pagan immediately invokes stereotypes, so I tend to use Wiccan. People are less familiar with this, so it normally requires further explanation, which I find to my benefit. Strangely enough I have found that I have sometimes had to do this with members of the non-Wiccan Pagan community. It's amazing how many Pagans have stereotyped images of what a Wiccan is. They seem to think that we all use Cabala, believe in the three-degree system, and fit in to the Gardnerian/Alexandrian mould.
>
> John W, Midwich, Britain.

Only 32% were totally open. Obviously many Pagans still feel they have to be careful in telling others about their beliefs—understandable considering the sensationalist newspaper reports and the activities of the Fundamentalist Christian fringe over the past few years. Viewpoints on being open varied; some felt the only way for Paganism to survive was to remain totally secret until the current period of intolerance passed; others felt it was necessary to be totally open (see next question). The Pagan community can afford to 'hedge its bets.' There is room for both trains of thought; having some members of the Pagan community totally open, while others remain underground, will ensure its survival.

One of the most amusing replies came from someone who classified himself as a 'Queer Saxon-foe Heathen.' He felt the need to be totally open:

> Name me! Name me! Publish my phone number, book me for balls, picnics and other charity events!
>
> Gordon Hunt, Hove, Britain.

19. (Combined group and solo) What is your view of the future of Paganism?

An apt conclusion to this chapter. Many gave not only a view of the future of Paganism, but also suggestions for that future. Seventy percent expressed a positive viewpoint:

> Positive!!! I feel that this is the only way to be 'at one' with the all and stop our self-destructive dash into oblivion. The Pagan way is the most beautiful gift we can pass on to our children. The Pagan Federation and similar groups are needed to sanely and practically put our ways across. Open fairs and festivals, and eco/green projects are the way forward.
>
> Steven Le Geyt, St. Helier, Jersey.

> Paganism is currently expanding, whereas Christianity is shrinking (despite the efforts of the evangelists and the fundamentalist fringe). It would grow faster if more people were open about who and what they are. By that I do not mean walking around the streets with a placard, shouting, 'Look at me, I'm Pagan!', but by becoming more active in the open face of Paganism—organizing and supporting open festivals, writing letters to television and newspapers when Paganism is slighted, organizing sponsored activities for charity in the name of Pagan groups, and so on. It is mainly through raising the profile of Paganism on a national level, that we will ultimately gain greater acceptance.
>
> Graham Lidstone, Westcliff-on-Sea, Britain.

Only 18% had negative views. Some worried that Paganism would suffer as it became larger, more public and organized:

> There is potential for hungry newcomers to be exploited by opportunistic and unethical people. Wicca and Paganism may get a bad name and the arts degraded by commercialism, as well as the need of disenfranchised people to have a label with shock value.
>
> Anon coven, Massachusetts

Forty-eight percent felt that it would grow (they did not always consider this as positive). Only 6% felt the numbers of practicing Pagans would remain static. No one felt that these numbers would decrease substantially. Many expressed both positive and negative attitudes, and believed that the current nature of Paganism would change:

I worry at the white-light syndrome where Paganism becomes a sweet and twee version of Christianity. Nature is red in tooth and claw, so we should acknowledge the dark side, not just a fluffy bunny Disney interpretation. I also find that people are less prepared to study; they want Paganism spoon-feeding in four easy lessons. I've also experienced people asking for initiation, then losing interest if it was not immediately forthcoming. This devalues the teachings into just a badge-wearing club. In my area fortune-telling and spiritualism are many times more popular than Paganism. On the plus side I sense society generally is becoming more ecologically aware, perhaps this will increase as children learn in school about the earth and that we should look after her. Perhaps this will bring more people into Paganism. The hierarchical structure seems to be breaking down, and there appears to be a less selfish approach with more emphasis on getting together to chant, sing and drum rather than work spells or invoke some powerful force which will do wonderful things or give powerful teachings. Because there is now so much information available, and more Networking, it may be less easy for idiots to abuse the Craft for egotistical ends. I'm not sure how to explain this properly, but there is a sense of earth power, as opposed to deities, becoming prominent. Paganism could become slightly less religious as shamanistic techniques teach folk how to connect themselves with the earth, not just get the plastic statues out once a month and wave athames at the furniture in a meaningless fashion.

Amanda, Hessle, Britain.

Attitudes to the future were not necessarily affected by which side of the Atlantic they came from. The overall view was that Paganism was set to grow in a positive fashion, but not without first solving several problems. Whether it should, or should not, become an organized religion seemed to be the most important of these. Some felt it would 'lose its soul' if it did, while others felt organizing and obtaining legal status was the only way to protect themselves, and secure a future for Paganism, while the potential for a Fundamentalist backlash increased.

Before summing up overall, we finish with a positive, thought-provoking reply from the United States:

I believe that we will fill the cultural wasteland in the Western World. People need a belief system to validate themselves and their purpose in existence. The violence and despair today indicate that this need is not being satiated. Monotheism does not supply the individual support system required by the populace. It advocates blind faith in oppressive, bigoted hierarchy based on mandates that are obsolete for the modern era. Paganism is based on soul-searching and experience, not blind faith. This may make it more appealing to those of an artistic or intellectual bent. Those who advocate the easy way of blind faith will probably never be attracted to Paganism. Yet I believe we will probably have more voice in the world. We cry for the salvation of Mama Earth and her children. We offer a system not based on dogma, a system that adjusts to change as a willow bends to blow in the wind. Perhaps we shall always be small, but our voice shall be increasingly heard as the madness destroys our planet. People tend to listen to us now rather than burn us at a stake. I'm not saying that this is always the case, but the world has made a startling improvement in the tolerance of the Craft, an improvement that will continue if we work for it. A case in point is our recent participation in the World Parliament of Religions.

> Morrigan Aa, Woodbridge Township,
> New Jersey.

* * * * * * * * * *

If one deity is presently of most importance to the fate of global Paganism, it is Mercury, the God of Communication. The call for communication and positive interaction appeared throughout the replies we received.

Our hopes of a small, orderly survey were frustrated by the response from you all. Many of you felt a need to communicate to the Pagan community outside your area. Organizations and computer bulletin boards spread the Questionnaires wider. All this resulted in over four times as many replies as we originally expected.

In Questions 1 and 2 we looked at how people defined their method of practice. Your replies made it clear that false labeling (remember Mercury is also a Trickster God!) can result in a breakdown in communication and understanding, and in the danger of excluding members of the community because of their individuality. Discussions were necessary between paths and traditions to allay this and find common ground. We received more replies from Wiccans because of the better communication between them. This is no doubt a controversial point, and we will be sorely disappointed with the Pagan community if no one argues with us on it!

On the merits of dividing a group into an Inner and Outer Circle, the principal motive of those groups which did so seemed, again, to be effective communication—particularly in large groups involved in teaching students.

The replies about how solo Pagans were initiated showed that views on this have been drastically affected by the communication medium of books and magazines. It is certainly not the Sacred Cow it use to be.

The importance of communication to effective leadership, to the uniting of heterosexual and homosexual Pagans, and to the expressing of political concerns, became evident throughout. Sound organizations and festivals encouraged communication, while poor communication resulted in 'bitchcraft,' and provoked intolerance from the Christian community and the general public. The survey confirmed for us that the future of Paganism will be hugely affected by how Pagans continue to communicate.

If Paganism is to survive (and most Pagans believe that it will) the global Pagan community will have to learn to communicate more effectively, both within itself and with the world outside. It is already embracing the new technology of computers to do this. The world is effectively getting smaller, while at the same time the Pagan community continues to grow.

If the word 'communication' seems to have been repeated ad nauseam throughout this summing-up—the message was yours.

22.

To What End?

Paganism is here to stay—and to grow. At this point in human evolution, it is as inevitable as was the discovery that the Earth is round and not flat.

This development is not a takeover, in the way that the Church took over the Western world in the Middle Ages. It is a contribution, an adjustment of the balance in terms of the needs of today's world. Paganism is a healthy and necessary element in the total spectrum of thought and action, respecting the other elements and demanding the same respect in return.

At national, religious, and global levels, imposed uniformity is no longer tolerable—or even workable.

Now that the Cold War is over, and the Global Village is struggling into existence, religion as a whole in the Western world is polarizing into two attitudes. On the positive side, many grass-roots worshippers are more and more losing patience with dictatorial hierarchies, and moving towards running their religions themselves—a tendency which is growing even within Catholicism. On the negative extreme, sectarianism has replaced atom-bomb confrontation as the main danger.

Solutions are not easy, as humanitarian aid workers in dismembered Yugoslavia where 'ethnic (i.e., religious) cleansing' is rampant, conflicting elements in the newly independent ex-Soviet states, and many others are discovering daily.

Paganism has much to offer in this birth-process. Pagans have to understand their own philosophy, and to see that non-Pagans are given an undistorted picture of it.

Which is why this book has been written. And it is of the essential nature of Paganism that everything in it is open to debate.

Glossary

These definitions are for the benefit of non-Pagan readers who although interested in the subject may be unfamiliar with some of its vocabulary.

Akasha The all-pervading spiritual 'ether.'

Akashic Records The 'recordings' left in the Akasha by past events. It is claimed that gifted psychics can access them.

Alexandrian A form of Gardnerian Wiccan practice developed by Alex and Maxine Sanders in Britain in the 1960s. See p. 24.

Amulet An object worn as a protective charm. See also Talisman.

Athame A witch's black-handled knife, his or her personal ritual tool. In most traditions it is never used for actual cutting. In Britain it is generally pronounced 'ath-AY-mee,' and in America 'ATH-a-mee.'

Banishing Three meanings: Banishing the Circle is the formal dismantling of a Magic Circle when the ritual is over. Banishing an individual means expelling him or her from the coven for an unforgivable offense, or from Wicca itself, though some regard the latter as impossible. Banishing an entity means disabling a harmful non-material entity.

Beltane, Bealtaine The May Eve festival. The first spelling is a centuries-old word in England. The second spelling is Gaelic, and is only used in Ireland, where it is pronounced 'b'YOL-tinna.'

Book of Shadows An individual witch's handwritten or typed collection of rituals and similar material (in these days, often enough a Disk of Shadows). Some covens insist on its being copied unaltered from that of the High Priestess and High Priest.

Boomerang Effect The occult principle that a psychic attack which comes up against a stronger defense rebounds on the attacker—traditionally 'threefold,' though this is metaphorical.

Charge, The The traditional Gardnerian/Alexandrian declaration by the High Priestess in the name of the Goddess.

Cone of Power A traditional Wiccan name for the power raised by a coven at work, visualized as an astral cone whose base is the circle of Witches.

Covenstead The place where a particular coven habitually meets.

Craft, The A term used by witches to mean Wicca. Inherited from Freemasonry.

Deosil In a clockwise direction (cf. Widdershins).

Drawing Down the Moon The invocation by the High Priest of the spirit of the Goddess into the High Priestess.

Druidic Of groups which base their practice on the traditions of the Celtic Druids. See p. 27.

Elemental A primitive, non-material and non-human entity of the nature of one of the four Elements of Earth, Air, Fire and Water.

Evoking Summoning a non-material entity of a lower nature than human (cf. Invoking).

Familiar An animal kept by a witch or coven for the psychic support it can give.

Fetch A male witch who acts as messenger and general assistant to a coven's High Priestess and High Priest. Also called the Summoner.

Gardnerian Wiccan practices as laid down by Gerald Gardner in the 1950s, though many covens calling themselves Gardnerian today have expanded and modified these.

Gnome The traditional term for an Earth Elemental.

Great Rite In Wicca, the major ritual of polarity between a man and a woman. It can be either symbolic or 'actual'—i.e., involving intercourse. In most traditions, the actual Great Rite is performed by the couple in private, and only between a married pair or established lovers.

Handfasting A Wiccan marriage ritual.

Hereditary The name used by witches who claim their practices have been continuous in the family. See also Traditional.

Hexagram A six-pointed star of two equilateral triangles. In occultism, it is not a specifically Jewish symbol, but represents the principle of 'As above, so below'—harmony between the Macrocosm and the Microcosm.

Hiving Off The process whereby some members of a coven leave to form a new coven of their own.

Imbolc The February 2 festival. A Gaelic word, pronounced 'immOL'g' and meaning 'in the belly'—the first stirrings of Spring in the womb of Mother Earth.

Invoking Summoning a non-material entity of a higher nature than human (cf. Evoking).

Litha The Summer Solstice festival, June 21.

Lughnasadh, Lunasa ('Festival of Lugh') The Autumn festival on July 31. It is a Gaelic word, the name of the month of August, and is pronounced 'LOO-na-sa.'

Mabon The Fall Equinox festival, September 22.

Macrocosm The Cosmos as a whole, in relation to the Microcosm, its detailed manifestation (human in particular). See also Hexagram.

Magus A male occult adept.

Maiden In a coven, the Assistant High Priestess in ritual practice, who may or may not be her deputy in leadership.

Microcosm—see Macrocosm.

Ostara The Spring Equinox festival, March 21.

Pentacle A disk, usually of metal, representing the element of Earth, placed in the center of a Wiccan altar.

Pentagram The five-pointed star, a familiar symbol of Paganism, occultism, and witchcraft. In America it is always portrayed with a single point upwards, because with two points upwards, it is a symbol used by American Satanists. In Britain, two-points-upwards used to be the symbol of the Wiccan Second Degree; British Satanists have always used the inverted crucifix. But many British Wiccans are abandoning the two-points-upwards Second Degree symbol as com-munication with American Pagans increases.

Prâna The vital force of the Cosmos as it operates on the Etheric level, permeating everything.

Rune A letter of one of the various ancient Nordic or Anglo-Saxon alphabets. Each of them has a specific symbolic significance, and they are used both for magical working and for divination. See p. 71.

Salamander The traditional term for a Fire Elemental.

Samhain The November-Eve ritual better known as Hallowe'en. It is a Gaelic word, the name of the month of November, and is pronounced 'SOW'en' (the first syllable to rhyme with 'now').

Scourge A ritual whip symbolizing firmness, in balance with the Wand which symbolizes mercy. Most ritual scourges are quite harmless, made for example with silk thongs.

Scrying Any form of divination which involves gazing at or into something, such as a crystal ball or black mirror, to observe psychically-perceived images. See p. 66.

Shamanistic Of groups which base their practices on the trance or semi-trance probing of the Unconscious, Collective or Individual. See pp. 28–31.

Sigil A word often encountered in occult terminology to mean a symbol used for a particular concept or aspect. It is pronounced 'SIDGE-il.'

Skyclad Of naked ritual practice.

Smudging Waving a smoldering handful of herbs around a person, as a ritual cleansing gesture. An American practice adopted from Native Americans, though the Native American practice itself is said to have arisen only in the past hundred years.

Summoner—see Fetch.

Sylph The traditional term for an Air Elemental.

Talisman A protective charm, similar to an Amulet, but worn with a specific purpose in mind.

Traditional A name used by British witches and covens who claim that their practices pre-dated Gardnerian ones. In America, it tends to mean adhering consistently to a particular cultural tradition, often from family racial roots. See also Hereditary.

Undine The traditional term for a Water Elemental.

Wiccaning The Wiccan equivalent of a Christening.

Widdershins In an anti-clockwise direction (cf. Deosil).

Yule The Winter Solstice festival, December 22.

Useful Addresses

The following list can never be complete, because with the steady expansion of the Pagan movement worldwide, useful organizations and networks are constantly taking shape. We have tried to include at least one organization from each of the countries dealt with in this book, and a selection of informative magazines and newsletters (each of which we have defined as 'magazine,' since the borderline is uncertain). More detailed information on some of these organizations will be found in Chapter 19, *Around the World*.

If you want an address in a country not listed here, it may well be worth writing to the Church of All Worlds (see U.S.A. below) and/or the Pagan Federation (see England), as both have contacts in many lands.

Australia

Rubicon, P.O. Box 362, Wentworth Building, University of Sydney, NSW 2006. Ecumenical Pagan magazine launched Summer 1993. Editor Brendan French.

Austria

FSS Österreich, Neuwaldeggerstrasse 38/4/6, A-1170 Vienna. Foundation for Shamanic Studies. Run seminars in Austria, Germany and Switzerland.

Baltic States (see also Estonia)

Romuva Association, Lietuvos Ramuvos Sajunga, 232009 Vilnius, Vivulskio 27-4, Lithuania. A Lithuanian Pagan organization. Write to Jonas Trinkūnas, an Elder and one of the organizers.

Kaunas Folklore Center, Kaunas 233005, K. Petrausko 31, Lithuania.

Algis Jucevicius, Didzioji 11, 2000 Vilnius, Lithuania. Lithuanian Baltic Religion Elder.

Jonas Trinkūnas, Vivulskio 27-4, 2009 Vilnius, Lithuania.

Romuva. English-language quarterly for indigenous Baltic religion and spirituality. Editor Audrius Dundzila, Ph.D., 6443 Clarendon Hills Rd., #210-J, Willowbrook, IL 80514, U.S.A.

Romuva/Canada, P.O. Box 232, Station 'D', Ontario M9A 4X2, Canada. Lana Vyte, c/o this address, is expert on Lithuanian Pagan mythology and folklore.

Dans Bertulis, Paganian Europe, Riga 2267168, 2 Republic Square, Riga, Latvia. They are working to recover Latvian folklore and Pagan material.

Janis Tupesis & Karlis Grencionis, Rt.1, Box 114a, Warrens, WI 54666, U.S.A. Latvians, expert on Latvian Pagan traditions.

Dievturi, Latvian Pagan Church, Elder Olgerts Auns, Kr. Barona iela 37-7, Riga, Latvia.

Brazil

Alceu Dias de Oliviera, Caixa Postal 448, Porto Alegre - RS, 90001-970. Very well informed on Brazilian deities and on Pagan situation there.

Canada

Hecate's Loom, P.O. Box 5206, Station B, Victoria, B.C. V8R 6N4. Canada's national Pagan magazine.

Temple of the Lady, P.O. Box 8575, Victoria, B.C. V8W 3S2. An inter-traditional Pagan church.

Pagan Affirmation Network, Box 521, 918 16th Ave. N.W., Calgary, Alberta T2M 0K3.

Denmark

Write to Stein Jarving (see Norway) for contacts.

Egypt

The Ammonite Foundation—see Nancy J. McEwen & Arville G. Lester, under U.S.A.

England

The Pagan Federation, BM Box 7097, London WC1N 3XX. Magazine *The Wiccan*.

Paganlink. No central headquarters, but John Male, 25 East Hill, Dartford, Kent is in touch with various local coordinators.

The Pagan Way (magazine), David Stasin, 51 Loates Lane, Watford.

The Order of Bards, Ovates & Druids, P.O. Box 1333, Lewes, E. Sussex BN7 3ZG.

Estonia

Art Leete, Raudtee 4, NJO, Tartu Maakond, EE-2440.

Finland

Iseum of Mielikki and Tapio, P.O. Box 452, 00101 Helsinki. Pagan group, including Wiccan. Very well-informed on Finnish mythology and deities.

France

Wicca-Française, 8 rue Danton, 94270 Kremlin-Bicêtre. Groups in France, some other European countries, and French-speaking Canada. Magazine *L'Étoile.*

Germany

Arbeitsgruppe Hexen, Heidi Staschen, Erikastrasse 97, 2000 Hamburg.

Wicca-Brief (magazine), Henning Duve & Brigit Alpert, Georgstrasse 4, 2000 Hamburg 70.

Greece

Diiepetes Quarterly, P.O.B. 20037, GR-11810, Athens.

Holland—see Netherlands

Hungary

Gabriella & Istevan Koloniks, 1092 Budapest, Kvgyes E11.

Iceland

Huginn & Muninn, Raudalek 14, 105 Reykjavik. English-language magazine, 'introduces old and new wisdom of the North; promotes the cause of the Aesir on Planet Earth.' Editor Thorsteinn Gudjónsson.

Ireland

Fellowship of Isis, Clonegal Castle, Enniscorthy, Co. Wexford. Open to Goddess-worshippers of any path or religion. Claims 12,000 members round the world, but local Fellowship of Isis organizations are basically self-supporting.

Peter Doyle & Barbara Lee, 123 O'Rourke Park, Sallynoggin, Co. Dublin. Helpful Wiccan couple.

Francis De'Venney & Alison Kelly, 31 Moneymoor, Drogheda, Co. Louth. Helpful Wiccan couple.

Italy

Sylvia Gilbertson, Via Casale Garabuso 33, 22040 Casere di Cremono (CO).

Japan

The Pagan Project, c/o Tamainu Kikaku, 4360 Niida, Kochi City, Kochi Ken 781-01.

Ikari Segawa, 7-22-4 Minamisyowa-Cho, Tokushima City 770.

Latvia—see Baltic States

Lithuania—see Baltic States

Netherlands

Silver Circle, Centrum voor de Oude Religion, Denis & Lesley ten Siethoff, Postbox 473, NL-3700 Al Zeist. Bilingual (Dutch and English) magazine *Wiccan Rede*.

Norway

Stein Jarving, Loftsvollen, Langan, Tvedestrand, Norway 4900. Active festival organizer, and editor of magazine *Gaia*.

Portugal

Maria Joao e Mario, Ap. 2049, Belas, 2746 Queluz Codex. Wiccan couple.

Russia

Serguey Matveyev, The Vedic Culture Society, League of Spiritual Unity, P.O. Box 182, St. Petersburg 195426. He appealed urgently in *The Wiccan*, Imbolc '92, for 'books, magazines, audio and visual cassettes on spiritual topics,' since these are virtually unobtainable in Russia.

Yaroslav Koryakov, Gottwald St.11-33, Ekaterinburg 620034. He has appealed through us for the same kind of material. Neither, of course, can obtain the currency to pay for it, but we feel that gifts would enhance global Pagan understanding.

Scotland

Charis & Jim, The Pagan Federation Scotland, P.O. Box 932, Edinburgh EH17 7PW. Wiccan and Pagan Federation contacts.

Keltic Research Society, Caer Aldean, 8 Annadale Street, Edinburgh. President John A. Johnston.

Sweden

Write to Stein Jarving (see Norway) for contacts.

Ukraine

Sergei B. Kapzanov, 100, 270020 Odessa 20.

Yaroslav Koryakov, Gottwald 11-33, Ekaterinburg 620034.

U.S.A.

Free Spirit Alliance, P.O. Box 25242, Baltimore, MD 21229. Primary sponsors of our 1991 lecture tour of U.S.A. and Canada, with many contacts.

Church of all Worlds and *Green Egg* (magazine), P.O. Box 1542, Ukiah, CA 95482. About three dozen 'Nests' worldwide, including seven in Australia.

Heartland Spiritual Alliance, 3808 Virginia Avenue, Kansas City, MO 64108. Run Gaia Center. Our primary sponsors on 1993 tour. Many contacts.

Universal Federation of Pagans (Headquarters), P.O. Box d674884, Marietta, GA 30067.

Circle, P.O. Box 219, Mt. Horeb, WI 53572. Run large-area Circle Sanctuary, magazine *Circle Network News*, and much networking.

PAN—To avoid confusion, there are four organizations using these initials:

Pagan Alliance Network, 2505 Main, Suite 114A, Stratford, CT 06497.

Pagan Allied Network, P.O. Box 86616, Madeira Beach, FL 33738.

Pagan Arizona Network, P.O. Box 17933, Phoenix, AZ 85011.

Pagan Affirmation Network—see under Canada.

Nancy J. McEwen & Arville G. Lester, Western Branch Office, Ammonite Foundation, LB 155, P.O. Box 140279, Irving, TX 75014-0279. Important relationship with an organization in Egypt which is wary of publicity in that country, but this Western Branch Office will handle communication.

Wales

The Cauldron (magazine), Mike Howard, Caemorgan Cottage, Caemorgan Road, Cardigan, Dyfed SA43 1QU. A long-established and respected journal.

Bibliography

The literature relevant to Paganism is immense, and is growing faster than ever. It should be appreciated that the following is merely a selection of titles which readers may find useful to give them an overall picture, both of Paganism's ancient roots and of its contemporary nature. It also includes every book referred to in the text.

Adler, Margot. *Drawing Down the Moon.* Revised and Expanded Edition, Beacon Press, Boston, 1986.

Andersen, Jorgen. *The Witch On the Wall.* George Allen & Unwin, London, 1977.

Apuleius, Lucius. *The Golden Ass.* Robert Graves translation, Penguin Books, Harmondsworth, Middlesex, 1950.

Ashe, Geoffrey. *The Virgin.* Routledge & Kegan Paul, London, 1976.

Aswynn, Freya. *Leaves of Yggdrasil.* Llewellyn Publications, St. Paul, MN, 1990.

Barnstone, Willis. *The Other Bible.* Harper & Row, San Francisco and London, 1984.

Bates, Brian. *The Way of Wyrd.* Arrow Books, London, 1987.

Battersby, William. *The Three Sisters At the Well.* William Battersby, Kells, Co. Meath, 1991.

Beauvoir, Simone de. *The Second Sex.* (Le Deuxiéme Sexe) 1949; English translation Jonathan Cape, London, 1953; paperback Penguin Books, Harmondsworth, Middlesex, 1973.

Beltz, Walter. *God and The Gods.* English translation by Peter Heinegg, Penguin Books, Harmondsworth, Middlesex, 1983.

Blavatsky, H. P. *The Secret Doctrine.* Vols. I & II Theosophical Publishing Co., London, 1974. Reprint of 1888 original.

Bonewits, Philip Emmons Isaac. *Real Magic.* Creative Arts Book Co., Berkeley, CA., 1971 & 1979; Macmillan, London, 1972; paperback Sphere Books, London, 1974.

Bord, Janet & Colin. *Earth Rites.* Granada Publishing, St. Albans, Herts, 1982.

Bradford, Ernle. *Ulysses Found.* Hodder & Stoughton, London, 1963; paperback Sphere Books, London, 1967.

Branston, Brian. *The Lost Gods of England.* Thames & Hudson, London, 1957.

British Museum. *A General Introductory Guide to the Egyptian Collection.* Trustees of the British Museum, London, 1969.

Buckland, Raymond. *The Tree: The Complete Book of Saxon Witchcraft.* Samuel Weiser, New York, 1974.

Buckley, Fr. Pat *A Thorn In the Side.* O'Brien Press, Dublin, 1994.

Budge, Sir E. A. Wallis. *The Book of the Dead.* Second edition, Routledge & Kegan Paul, London, 1969.

———— *Egyptian Magic.* Routledge & Kegan Paul, reprint 1972.

———— *Egyptian Religion.* Routledge & Kegan Paul, reprint 1972.

———— *Osiris and the Egyptian Resurrection.* Two volumes, Dover Publications, New York, reprint 1973.

Burland, C. A. *The Magical Arts: A History.* Arthur Baker, London, 1966.

Campbell, Joseph. *The Masks of God: Primitive Mythology.* Viking Press, New York, 1959; Souvenir Press, London, 1971.

Capra, Fritjof. *The Tao of Physics.* Wildwood House, London, 1976; paperback Fontana, London, 1976.

Carmichael, Alexander. *Carmina Gadelica–Hymns and Incantations, With Illustrated Notes of Words, Rites and Customs Dying and Obsolete.* Oliver & Boyd, Edinburgh, Vols. I & II, 1900; 2nd edition, vols. I-VI, 1928 onwards.

———— *The Sun Dances.* Floris Books, Edinburgh, 1977 Paperback selection from *Carmina Gadelica.*

Chetwynd, Tom. *A Dictionary of Symbols.* Granada, St. Albans, Herts., 1982.

Coghlan, Ronan. *Dictionary of Irish Myth and Legend.* Donard Publishing Co., Bangor, Co. Down, 1979.

Crossley-Holland, Kevin (translator). *Beowulf.* Folio Society, London, 1973.

———— *The Norse Myths: Gods of the Vikings.* Penguin Books, London, 1982.

Crow, W. B. *The Arcana of Symbolism.* Aquarian Press, London, 1970.

Crowley, Aleister. *777 Revised.* Neptune Press, London, 1952.

Crowther, Patricia. *Lid Off The Cauldron.* Frederick Muller, London, 1973.

Culpeper, N. *Culpeper's Complete Herbal.* Foulsham, London.

Deren, Maya. *Divine Horsemen.* Thames & Hudson, London, 1953; paperback under title *The Voodoo Gods*, Granada, St. Albans, Herts., 1975.

Dillon, Myles & Chadwick, Nora. *The Celtic Realms.* Weidenfeld & Nicolson, London, 1967; paperback Cardinal, London, 1973.

Drury, Nevill. *The Elements of Shamanism.* Element Books Ltd., Shaftesbury, Dorset, 1989.

Durdin-Robertson, Lawrence. *The Goddesses of Chaldaea, Syria and Egypt.* Cesara Publications, Enniscorthy, Co. Wexford, 1975.

———— *The Goddesses of India, Tibet, China and Japan.* Cesara, 1976.

———— *The Symbolism of Temple Architecture.* Cesara, 1978.

———— *God The Mother.* Cesara, 1982.

Eliade, Mircea. *Shamanism: Archaic Techniques of Ecstasy.* Pantheon, New York, 1951; revised and enlarged from original French edition.

Ellis, Peter Berresford. Dictionary of Celtic Mythology. Constable, London, 1992.

Evans-Wentz, W. Y. *The Fairy Faith In Celtic Countries*. Oxford University Press, 1911; Colin Smythe Ltd., Gerrards Cross, Bucks., 1977).

Farmer, David Hugh. *The Oxford Dictionary of Saints*. Clarendon Press, Oxford, 1978.

Farrar, Frank A. *Old Greek Nature Stories*. Harrap, London, 1910.

Farrar, Stewart. *What Witches Do*. Reissue, with Foreword to Second Edition, Phoenix Publishing, Custer, WA, 1983; Robert Hale, London, 1992.

Farrar, Janet & Stewart. *Eight Sabbats for Witches*. Robert Hale, London, 1981; Phoenix Publishing, Custer, WA, 1988. Paperback Hale, 1992.

—— *The Witches' Way*. Hale, 1984; Phoenix, 1988.

(These two also published in American paperback under the title *A Witches Bible* vols. 1 & 2, Magickal Childe, New York, 1984, and as *A Witches Bible Compleat*.)

—— *The Witches' Goddess: The Feminine Principle of Divinity*. Hale, 1987; Phoenix, 1988.

—— *The Witches' God: Lord of the Dance*. Hale, 1989; Phoenix, 1989. Published in Portuguese by Agencia Siciliano de Livros, Brazil, 1993.

—— *Life and Times of a Modern Witch*. Piatkus Books, London, 1987; paperback Headline Books, London, 1988; Phoenix, 1988.

—— *Spells and How They Work*. Hale, hardback 1990, paperback 1992; Phoenix, 1990.

Farrar, Janet & Virginia Russell. *The Magical History of the Horse*. Robert Hale, London, 1992.

Reader's Digest. *Folklore, Myths and Legends of Britain*. Readers Digest Association, London, 1973.

Fortune, Dion. *The Mystical Qabalah*. Ernest Benn, London, 1935.

—— *The Sea Priestess*. Aquarian Press, London, 1957; paperback Wyndham Publications, London, 1976.

—— *Moon Magic*. Aquarian Press, 1956; paperback Wyndham, 1976.

Frazer, Sir J. G. *The Golden Bough*. Macmillan, London, 1922. Abridged edition paperback 1957.

Ganz, Jeffrey (translator). *The Mabinogion*. Penguin Books, London, 1974.

Gardner, Gerald B. *Witchcraft Today*. Rider, London, 1954.

—— *The Meaning of Witchcraft*. Aquarian Press, London, 1959.

Garner, Alan. *The Owl Service*. Collins, London, 1967.

Gettings, Fred. *Dictionary of Demons*. Guild Publishing, London, 1988.

Gooch, Stan. *The Secret Life of Humans*. J. M. Dent, London, 1981.

Graves, Robert. *The White Goddess*. Third edition, Faber & Faber, London, 1952.

—— *The Greek Myths*, vols. I & II Penguin Books, London, 1960.

Gray, John. *Near Eastern Mythology*. Hamlyn, London, 1969.

Green, Roger Lancelyn. *Myths of the Norsemen*. Puffin Books, Harmondsworth, Middlesex, 1970 reissue; original title *The Saga of Asgard*.

Gray, Eden. *A Complete Guide to the Tarot.* Studio Vista, London, 1970.

Grigson, Geoffrey. *The Goddess of Love: The Birth, Triumph, Death and Rebirth of Aphrodite.* Constable, London, 1976; paperback Quartet Books, London, 1978.

Guiley, Rosemary. *The Encyclopedia of Witches and Witchcraft.* Facts on File Ltd., Oxford and New York, 1989.

Gundarsson, Kveldulf. *Teutonic Magic.* Llewellyn Publications, St. Paul, MN, 1990.

Hadingham, Evan. *Ancient Carvings in Britain: A Mystery.* Garnstone Press, London, 1974.

Hampden-Turner, Charles. *Maps of the Mind.* Mitchell Beazely, London, 1981.

Harding, M. Esther. *Women's Mysteries.* Rider, London, 1971.

Harner, Michael. *The Way of the Shaman.* Harper & Row, New York, 1980; paperback Bantam Books, New York, 1982.

Harrison, Michael. *The Roots of Witchcraft.* Frederick Muller, London, 1973; paperback Tandem Publishing, London, 1975.

Hart, George. *A Dictionary of Egyptian Gods and Goddesses.* Routledge & Kegan Paul, London, 1986.

Hawkes, Jacquetta. *Dawn of the Gods.* Chatto & Windus, London, 1968; paperback Sphere Books, London, 1972.

Herm, Gerhard. *The Celts.* Weidenfeld & Nicolson, London, 1975.

Hollander, Lee M. (translator). *The Poetic Edda.* University of Texas Press, 1990.

Hooke, S. M. *Middle Eastern Mythology.* Penguin Books, London, 1963.

Hope, Murry. *Practical Celtic Magic.* Aquarian Press, Wellingborough, 1987.

Howe, Ellic. *The Magicians of the Golden Dawn.* Routledge & Kegan Paul, London, 1972; amended paperback Aquarian Press, Wellingborough, 1985.

Ions, Veronica. *Egyptian Mythology.* Hamlyn, London, 1968.

Jenkins, David, Bishop of Durham, & Rebecca Jenkins. *Free To Believe.* BBC Books, London, 1991.

Jones, Evan John, with Valiente, Doreen. *Witchcraft: A Tradition Renewed.* Robert Hale, London, 1990; Phoenix, 1990.

Jordan, Michael. *Encyclopaedia of Gods.* Kyle Cathie, London, 1992.

Joyce, Donovan. *The Jesus Scroll.* Angus & Robertson, London, 1973; paperback Sphere Books, London, 1975.

Kaufman, Friedrich, translated by M. Steel Smith. *Northern Mythology.* J. M. Dent, London, 1903.

King, Francis. *Ritual Magic in England, 1887 to the Present Day.* Neville Spearman Ltd., London, 1970.

Kinsella, Thomas (translator). *The Tain.* Oxford University Press, London, 1970.

Larousse World Mythology. Chartwell Books Inc., Secaucus, NJ, 1973.

Leadbeater, C. W. *The Chakras, A Monograph.* The Theosophical Publishing House, London, 1969.

Leland, Charles G. *Aradia: The Gospel of the Witches.* C. W. Daniel, London, 1974, reissue of late 19th-century original, with Foreword by Stewart Farrar; Phoenix, 1990.

Lethbridge, T. C. *Witches: Investigating An Ancient Religion.* Routledge & Kegan Paul, London, 1972.

Lovelock, J. E. *Gaia: A New Look At Life On Earth.* Oxford University Press, London, 1979; paperback 1982.

MacAlister, Stewart (editor and translator). *Lebor Gabala Erenn, The Book of the Taking of Ireland*, Parts I-V Irish Texts Society, Dublin, 1938-56; commonly known as *The Book of Invasions.*

McLeish, Kenneth. *Children of the Gods.* Longman, Harlow, Essex, 1983.

MacNeil, Maire. *The Festival of Lughnasa.* Oxford University Press, London, 1962; paperback, two volumes, Comhairle Bheadolais Iireann, University College, Dublin, 1982.

MacQuitty, William. *Buddha.* Thomas Nelson, London, 1969.

Malaclypse the Younger. *Principia Discordia.* Second edition, IllumiNet Press, Avondale Estates, GA, 1991.

Markale, Jean. *Women of the Celts.* translated by A. Mygind, C. Hauch & P. Henry Cremonesi, London, 1975.

Mascaro, Juan (translator). *The Bhagavad Gita.* Penguin Books, Harmondsworth, Middlesex, 1962.

Mathers, S. Lidell Macgregor. *The Key of Solomon the King (Clavicula Solomonis).* Routledge & Kegan Paul, London, 1972; originally published 1888.

Matthews, Caitlin. *The Celtic Tradition.* Element Books, Shaftesbury, 1989.

Monaghan, Patricia. *The Book of Goddesses and Heroines.* Llewellyn Publications, St. Paul, MN, 1990.

Montet, Pierre. *Eternal Egypt.* Translated by Doreen Weightman. Weidenfeld & Nicolson, London, 1965.

Morganweg, Iolo (compiler). *The Triads of Britain.* Wildwood House, London, 1977.

Murray, Keith. *Ancient Rites and Ceremonies.* Tutor Press, Toronto, 1980.

Neumann, Erich. *The Great Mother.* Second edition, Routledge & Kegan Paul, London, 1963.

Patai, Dr. Raphael. *Man and Temple in Ancient Jewish Myth and Ritual.* Nelson, London, 1947.

—————— *The Hebrew Goddess.* Ktav Publishing House, New York, 1968.

Patrick, Richard. *All Colour Book of Greek Mythology.* Octopus Books, London, 1972.

—————— *All Colour Book of Egyptian Mythology.* Octopus, 1972.

Peake, Arthur S. *Commentary on the Bible.* Nelson, London, 1919.

Pennick, Nigel. *Practical Magic in the Northern Tradition.* Aquarian Press, Wellingborough, Northants, 1989.

Perowne, Stewart. *Roman Mythology.* Hamlyn, London, 1969.

Perry, Canon Michael. *Gods Within.* SPCK, London, 1992.

Phillips, Guy Ragland. *Brigantia: A Mysteriography*. Routledge & Kegan Paul, London, 1976.

Phipps, W. E. *Was Jesus Married?* Harper & Row, New York, 1970.

Pinsent, John. *Greek Mythology*. Hamlyn, London, 1969.

Pirani, Alix (editor). *The Absent Mother: Restoring the Goddess to Judaism and Christianity*. Mandala, London, 1991.

Poignant, Roslyn. *Myths and Legends of the South Seas*. Hamlyn, London, 1970.

Powell, A. E. *The Astral Body*. The Theosophical Publishing House, London, 1965.

—— *The Mental Body*. The Theosophical Publishing House, London, 1967.

Pukui, Mary Kawena & Elber, Samuel H. *Hawaiian Dictionary*. Third edition, University Press of Hawaii, Honolulu, 1965.

Rawson, Philip. *Tantra: The Indian Cult of Ecstasy*. Thames & Hudson, London, 1973.

Reader's Digest. *Magic and Medicine of Plants*. The Readers Digest Association, New York, 1989.

Reed, A. W. *Aboriginal Myths: Tales of the Dreamtime*. Reed Books, French's Forest, N.S.W., 1978.

—— *Aboriginal Legends: Animal Tales*. Reed Books, 1978.

Rees, Alwyn & Brinley Rees. *Celtic Heritage*. Thames & Hudson, London, 1961.

Regardie, Israel. *The Golden Dawn*. Third Revised and Enlarged two-volume edition, Hazel Hilla Corp., River Falls, WI, 1970; first published in four volumes 1937-40.

—— *My Rosicrucian Adventure*. Llewellyn Publications, St. Paul, MN, 1971.

Richmond, L. A. *The Pelican History of England, I: Roman Britain*. Penguin Books, London, 1955.

Ross, Anne. *Pagan Celtic Britain*. Routledge & Kegan Paul, London, 1967.

Rowan, John. *The Horned God: Feminism and Men as Wounding and Healing*. Routledge & Kegan Paul, London, 1987.

Schonfield, Hugo J. *The Passover Plot*. Hutchinson, London, 1965; paperback Corgi, London, 1967.

St. Clair, David. *Drum and Candle*. Macdonald, London, 1971.

Sety, Omm & Hanny Elzeini. *Abydos: Holy City of Ancient Egypt*. LL Company, Los Angeles, 1981.

Shapiro, Max S. & Rhoda A. Hendricks. *Mythologies of the World: A Concise Encyclopedia*. Doubleday, New York, 1977. U.K. edition entitled *A Dictionary of Mythologies* Paladin, London, 1981.

Shorter, Alan W. *The Egyptian Gods: A Handbook*. Routledge & Kegan Paul, London, 1937; reprint 1983.

Shuttle, Penelope & Redgrove, Peter. *The Wise Wound: Menstruation and Everywoman*. Revised edition, Paladin, London, 1986.

Skelton, Robin & Margaret Blackwood. *Earth, Air, Fire, Water*. Penguin Group, London and abroad, 1990.

Smith, Peter Alderson. *W. B. Yeats and the Tribes of Danu*. Colin Smythe, Gerrards Cross, Bucks, 1987; Barnes & Noble Books, Totowa, NJ, 1987.

Soustelle, Jacques. *The Daily Life of the Aztecs.* French original Librairie Hachette, Paris 1955; English translation Weidenfeld & Nicolson, 1961; paperback Pelican Books, Harmondsworth, Middlesex, 1964.

Stone, Merlin. *The Paradise Papers.* Virago, London, 1976; paperback 1977.

Sun Bear & Wabun. *The Medicine Wheel: Earth Astrology.* Prentice Hall Press, New York, 1980.

Sykes, Egerton. *Everyman's Dictionary of Non-classical Mythology.* J. M. Dent, London, 1968.

Thorson, Edred. *A Book of Troth.* Llewellyn Publications, St. Paul, MN, 1989.

Valiente, Doreen. *Where Witchcraft Lives.* Aquarian Press, London, 1962.

——— *An ABC of Witchcraft Past and Present.* Robert Hale, London, 1973; Phoenix, 1985.

——— *Natural Magic.* Hale, 1975; Phoenix, 1991.

——— *Witchcraft For Tomorrow.* Hale, 1978; Phoenix, 1986.

Valliant, George. *The Aztecs of Mexico.* Doubleday, Doran Inc., New York, 1944; Pelican Books, Harmondsworth, Middlesex, 1950.

Warner, Maria. *Alone of All Her Sex: The Myth and the Cult of the Virgin Mary.* Weidenfeld & Nicolson, London, 1976.

Wilhelm, Richard. *The I Ching, Or Book of Changes.* Translator Cary F. Baynes, third edition, Routledge & Kegan Paul, London, 1968.

Wilson, David. *Anglo-Saxon Paganism.* Routledge, London and New York, 1992.

Witt, R. E. *Isis In the Graeco-Roman World.* Thames & Hudson, London, 1971.

Wood, David. *Genesis: The First Book of Revelations.* Baton Press, Tunbridge Wells, 1985.

Wood, Frederick H. *The Egyptian Miracle.* John M. Watkins, London, 1955.

Index